Niki de Saint Phalle

Kunst- und Ausstellungshalle
der Bundesrepublik Deutschland

Pontus Hulten

Niki de Saint Phalle

Verlag Gerd Hatje

This Catalogue was published upon the occasion of the exhibition *Niki de Saint Phalle* from June 19 to November 1, 1992 at the Kunst- und Ausstellungshalle der Bundesrepublik Deutschland in Bonn

Publisher
Kunst- und Ausstellungshalle der Bundesrepublik Deutschland GmbH

Artistic Director
Pontus Hulten

Managing Director
Wenzel Jacob

Exhibition and Catalogue Conception
Pontus Hulten

Project Management and Sculpture Garden Installation
Uta Grosenick

Assistance
Hubert Ringwald

Catalogue Coordination
Annette Kulenkampff

Graphic Design
Pierluigi Cerri
with Marion Hauff
and Sara Ricciardi

Editorial Coordination
Ute Harre

Editional Staff
Cornelia Plaas

Reproductions
C+S Repro, Filderstadt

Printing and Production
Dr. Cantz'sche Druckerei
Ostfildern/Stuttgart

Photographs
see photo credits

Printed in Germany

2nd Edition, 1995
ISBN 3 7757 0582 1

Jacket photograph
Hans Hammarskiöld

Contents

Wenzel Jacob
9 Preface

Marie-Louise von Plessen
11 Niki in California

Pontus Hulten
13 Working with fury and with pleasure

19 Niki de Saint Phalle – a pictorial documentation

Uta Grosenick
144 Niki de Saint Phalle's letters – an introduction

Niki de Saint Phalle
146 Letters

187 Artworks 1953–1992

283 List of illustrations

287 Biography and Appendix

311 Photo credits

Preface

Wenzel Jacob

This volume comprises the most comprehensive single study to date on Niki de Saint Phalle, providing a multi-facetted retrospective of the artist's life and work. The catalogue was first published in June 1992 for the comprehensive exhibition on Niki de Saint Phalle inaugurating the Federal Republic of Germany's Art and Exhibition Center in Bonn. The great success of both exhibition and book constitute renewed testimony to the artist's extraordinary popularity, as indeed does this new edition.
The catalogue is conceived as a companion to the exhibition which embraced works from four decades of creativity: oil paintings from the early 1950's, the legendary "shooting" pictures from the 1960's, right through to the *Nanas* and polished and painted bronzes of fantastic deities from the early 1990's. Numerous collages, assemblages, drawings, prints, books on artists and photographs of architectonic works also bear witness to Niki de Saint Phalle's apparently inexhaustible inventiveness.
The exhibition is divided into two sections, breathing life into both the upper floor of the atrium and our roof garden. The vibrantly colored sculptures, some of which are open-access, were all but made for the Art and Exhibition Center's roofscape with its trinity of striking, cone-shaped towers of light and their sky-blue tiled mosaics designed by architect Gustav Peichl. The sculptures rendered the roof a garden of the imagination, an architectural invitation to stroll or linger, transforming it into a public square that welcomes visitors.
The colorful, sensuously shaped sculptures possess a magnetism that seems almost predestined to make of public places popular forums. It is, for instance, all but impossible to resist the enchantment of the fountain – designed by the artist in conjunction with Jean Tinguely – in the Place Igor Stravinsky near the Centre Pompidou in Paris.
With the aim of unleashing her audiences' imaginations, she constantly stretches her own, setting herself targets which often require years of arduous effort. Niki de Saint Phalle embarked on her most extensive work to date in 1979: the *Tarot Garden* in Garavicchio, an Italian village in the Tuscan hills. It consists of several sculptures, some of them habitable and all of them as tall as houses; despite their scale, the structures appear incongruously airy and capricious. And although the *Tarot Garden* placed extreme demands on the artist, she simultaneously succeeded in finishing a number of totally different projects. In 1986, for example, she produced the book *AIDS: You Can't Catch It Holding Hands* – making her one of the first well-known artists to call for AIDS education and to campaign for solidarity with people who were HIV-positive or already suffering from the disease.
The artist played an active and extremely enthusiastic part in putting together this exhibition and book. We would like to express our heartfelt gratitude for her energy and commitment. We would also like to thank her associates Phyllis Stigliano and Janice Parente whose contribution included compiling the information for the documentary appendix, and Yvonne Robinson whose research laid the foundations for the detailed biography.
We are also grateful to the photographers who supplied pictures of the works and historical photographs, particularly Leonardo Bezzola, Laurent Condominas and Harry Shunk.

Translated from the German by Mary Fran Gilbert & Keith Bartlett

Niki in California

Marie-Louise von Plessen

Three years have passed since Niki's comprehensive retrospective (June 19 to November 1, 1992) during the year marking the opening of the German Federal Art and Exhibition Hall in Bonn. The exhibit then moved to the McLellan Galleries in Glasgow (January 22 to April 4, 1993) and on to the Musée d'Art Moderne de la Ville de Paris from June to September 1993, where it was shown together with other works. From October 3 that year to January 9, 1994, another major show was held at the Musée d'art et d'histoire in the Swiss city of Fribourg with the provocative title "Aventure Suisse". In her introductory essay for the catalog, Niki took the opportunity of venting what are at best ambivalent sentiments about Switzerland and the Swiss. "Switzerland stands for order, money, reason, balance sheets, equilibrium, self-satisfaction, a chauvinism that nearly rivals that of the French. What is more, Switzerland was the last country in Europe to grant women the right to vote."

This most recent exhibition also represents the artist's stocktaking of her own work and life in Europe following the death of her husband Jean Tinguely in 1991. She made a decision ostensibly for health reasons, yet one which was also certainly motivated in part by a curiosity about her American identity, a yearning to unearth early roots – childhood and youth, life as the young spouse of Harry Matthews – from a time in the U.S. that ended in 1952. She cautiously began to uncover those origins and gradually prepare for a return to America. It was not an easy step; everything had to be reorganized and reclaimed: people and houses, projects and plans. As a place to live and work she chose the Southern Californian city of La Jolla near San Diego, located close to the Mexican border, a town with magnificent beaches and brilliant light contrasts located at the edge of the great, mysterious Pacific Ocean teeming with marine life. Since then Niki has become attuned to Nature, launching a voyage of discovery through the world of flora and fauna. On her daily walks along the beach she watches the seals engage in their underwater gyrations, playing hide-and-seek among the coastal cliffs. She talks to the seagulls, she marvels at the elegant grace of the dolphins and killer whales performing their acrobatics at the nearby "Sea World" adventure park. The light-flooded "tableaux éclatés", first begun in 1993 and shown in Maxwell Davidson's and James Goodman's New York galleries in 1994, are electronically controlled transformational pictures. They exemplify an acute awareness of and involvement with the big, expansive sky, glaring sunlight and sparse vegetation of the vast desertlands to the north; with budding cactus plants, strange biblical Joshua trees and rocks that line the path to the legendary Death Valley like huge loaves of bread, sliced open. Niki can no longer imagine a life without animals, wind and water. Perched in her Californian cockpit, she adapts to spectacular sunrises and sunsets with perfect pitch and timing, via telecommunications links she monitors her current projects in distant Europe: the increasingly popular *Tarot Garden* in the Tuscan village of Garavicchio, the people pouring through Tinguely's monumental, openaccess iron sculpture *Cyclope* near Fontainebleau, a donation from the French government which was unveiled by President Mitterrand on May 24, 1994. Her new Californian love affair with the animal kingdom, expressed in a wealth of drawings, sculptures and sketches in letters, has given rise to the idea of a huge walk-through sculpture, *Noah's Ark*, due to be erected in Jerusalem in cooperation with Swiss architect Mario Botta. Tessin-born Botta is also the architect of the Tinguely Museum under construction for Hoffmann-La Roche on the banks of the Rhine in Basle and scheduled to open in the autumn of 1996. Niki herself has been heavily involved in the planning and realization of this project.

Niki's geographical sphere is widening, and her family is keeping pace. In 1993 she became a great grandmother; in summer 1995 her second grandchild was born. This branching out of her international genealogical tree is a cause for celebration, as she devotes much love and affection to her new offspring. The fact that her family is growing – and growing younger – provided the impetus for a "dramatic documentary with two very creative leading actors" by Peter Schamoni (93 minutes, 35 mm, color, Dolby stereo) on the artist's life, her work and her collaboration with Jean Tinguely until his death in August 1991: *Niki de Saint Phalle – Who is the Monster – You or Me?* The highly acclaimed film, dedicated by its director to Pontus Hulten, will premiere at various film festivals in Europe and the U.S. in the summer and fall of 1995. Its recurring references to the Italian *Tarot Garden* make the work a vibrant and vivid tribute to Niki de Saint Phalle's extremely eventful artistic and intellctual life. Taking as its starting point the "shooting" happenings of the early sixties, it depicts the many monumental *Nanas,* the groups of *Devouring Mothers* (1970), the *HON* sculpture in Stockholm (1966), the *Golem* in Jerusalem (1971), the *Dragon* in Knokke le Zoute (1973), and the *Stravinsky Fountain* in Paris (1982). It traces the roots and evolution of Tinguely's *Cyclope* in the Fontainebleau forest (since 1969) and finally documents the planning and realization of the *Tarot Garden* from 1978 to its opening in 1994. This documentation on "work-in-progress" is punctuated by clips from Niki's own film œuvre, taken from *Daddy* (1972/73) and *Un rêve plus long que la nuit* (1975). Schamoni has succeeded in making this film a graphic portrait of Niki's manifold and many-sided creations. The film, a work of art in itself, contains comments by the artist and statements from Jean Tinguely designed to promote an understanding of her work that is liberated from the constraints of feminism.

In the few years since the comprehensive retrospective in Bonn, Niki de Saint Phalle has become more focussed, more independent and even more intense. She has looked and listened inside herself, harnessing memories of early childhood due to her father's influence in a book entitled *Mon secret* which was published (only in French) by Editions La Différence in 1993. She lives and works free of pressure, in tune and in time with her own inner rhythms, the pulse of her spirit and health, the mood of the weather and the play of light; with a minimum of management and organizational effort, almost without full-time support. Niki is now discovering the myths of the world's religions. She has become the great grandmother, grandmother, mother and child of her own myriad and colorful creations, skinny ones or fat ones, which allow her to engage people of every age and every color in a direct dialog – and give them a gift as simple and precious as joy.

Translation: Mary Fran Gilbert & Keith Bartlett

Working with fury and with pleasure

Pontus Hulten

Niki de Saint Phalle is an artist of the century. She has made good use of the accomplishments in the world of art of the first half of the century and she has made the second half more beautiful. Through a knowledge that is of a rather intuitive kind, she looks at what the great artists of modern art preceding her have produced. With innocence, like a blithe spirit, she borrows from them, as if she were picking flowers in a beautiful garden. As everything she does is very closely related to herself, what she touches becomes hers as if struck with a magic wand. The originality of her work comes directly from her personality. This simplicity, this lack of sophistication which is implied by her work, is in reality a true sophistication, not at all superficial and conventional, but profoundly original.

A certain lack of pretensions, something like an "aristocratic" touch, permits Niki de Saint Phalle to listen to and to question people around her with a curiosity that is attractive and stimulating by its intelligence. As she has no extensive academic or other kind of formal education, she adds to her world what she hears, what she finds interesting, without using the critical methods learned in schools. She replaces them with plain common sense.

Sketch for a portrait

Niki de Saint Phalle loves myths. She invents them without preoccupying herself with art history or popular traditions, without having studied the civilizations which invented the symbols to try and understand their enigmas. She doesn't depend on knowledge, but relies on her independence. Niki de Saint Phalle has been vigilant her whole life to preserve what is her strength: her freedom.

In this context she has known how to leave relationships that were holding her back and separated herself from people whose influence was contrary to this violent need, yet. She was never aggressive in her ways of finding freedom. Even the shooting-paintings were not invented in order to attain this goal. They came into existence so that she could show to others possibilities for discovery that one could call almost childlike, in any case innocent, like a first approach towards the superior beings that form and define the universe. In spite of many difficult experiences, a strain of bad health, pain and anguish, she has stayed innocent and complete in her self-feminine sense of giving to others the desire to live and work. She invites us to penetrate, in her company, the universe of colours, images, monsters, phantoms and myths; to enter inside the myth, as into the *Empress*, the *Sphinx* at the Tarot Garden in Garavicchio; and in this way to live and breed in the empty space that she knows so well how to fill with the spirit of eros, love and passion, but also with mystery, with the inexplicable.

Niki de Saint Phalle is a priestess that can handle the contradictions of life in the form of death, who knows how to dominate despair and fear by making them emotionally acceptable, and gentle, even joyful and pleasurable, who knows how to attract the eye to make us discover poetry, fairy tales and children's stories while adding magic inspiration, constantly opposing and comparing it to the realities and brutality of society. She has taken great care in creating her own power of imagination and commands of visual strength, capable of destroying evil but also to deal with it because of its fascination.

Niki de Saint Phalle is a seductress who knows how to put together elements that attract us, that oblige us to become part of unexpected, violent, even destructive experiences, so that we then can appreciate the positive forces that she puts into play, makes visible, makes reign and rule. Her universe of signs, forms, colours and structures, whether they are made out of plaster and chicken wire, polyester and fiberglass or drawn with coloured crayons, has affinities with the bestiaries of Hindu temples when they are invaded by wild animals and human beauties of an undomesticated nature.

Niki de Saint Phalle is sometimes a wild being who knows how to survive when others give up, because her desire, her ambition is not to become master of the negative forces around her and in her, but rather to confront them again and again and become friends with the powers of darkness. She does not put them outside of her universe nor is she separating the masculine and the feminine. For her, it is a joy and delight to bring them together, defining each side and giving them the space and importance that they need. Regarding the masculine and the feminine she has been neither led by the will of male society nor the determination of the women's movement, but has followed her own uniquely personal revolutionary spirit.
Through her spontaneous force she can create beauty, like a goddess of nature, with a totally convincing strength. The best portraits of Niki de Saint Phalle are found in her sculptures, her drawings and her writings. She is an expressionist artist in the sense that there is little distance between herself and her work. Relations are intuitive rather than meditative or reflective; more emotional than critical or analytical. One can say, without irony, she realizes herself in her work. This being said, her œuvre is particularly diverse. This catalogue contains reproductions of works made during almost forty years, in the different studios or in environments that she has chosen. Reproduced here are three or four works from each year of her artist's life. It is sufficient to contemplate this fact for a moment, to realize the extent of Niki de Saint Phalle's production, an œuvre immense. We have tried to choose what is most significant and most impressive. In this selection one can observe that she has acquired full control of the means of expression, an expansion of confidence and a great faithfulness towards herself.

Themes and different periods
There are themes and subjects that recur over the decades: the birth of a child, the house, the monster and, especially, man and woman. They all are present in the oil paintings from the 1950's, which, like an unconscious pre-inventory of future works, give the promise of works to come. The oil paintings, the beginnings of her œuvre, are surprising in their freedom and their violence. What might seem awkward and clumsy is already the expression of this independence from conventions and accepted ideas.

The assemblages
The aggression that is contained in the act of fixing an object from everyday life, a kitchen tool or an article of toilette, in order to transform it into a work of art by capturing it with other objects in a bed of plaster was not without pleasing aspects for the rebellious person that used art as a form of revolution against a comfortable and well-established social milieu in which she had been raised and in which, despite everything else, she was still living. In this way, Niki de Saint Phalle transformed her bourgeois interior; the handrail of the staircase and the fireside of the living room become sets in a horror scene where one could hurt oneself everywhere on knives, scissors and nails, with all the sharp ends pointing up and out of the plaster. Axes, all sorts of sharp kitchen irons, revolvers and nails then went into the paintings, and into the panels, where they formed sinister landscapes. But as often happens, when all possible means are employed in order to frighten, the hysteric giggle comes along. There is too much horror, the pleasure of being alive takes over through the force of contradiction. These reliefs are at times so beautiful that the horror is forgotten. The very lyrical rhythms that little by little are created between the objects, that are now nicely put to bed in the plaster that has become as gentle as whipped cream.
Portrait of my Lover, where the head is made out of a target at which one is invited to throw little darts (the man's shirt that constitutes the body comes from "Sak's", New

York) is suspended over an emptiness where hell and horror border on what is desperately comic.

The Shooting paintings
In this sequence, the shooting paintings open up another area where the new and the beautiful coexist in a climate of outrage and violence. It is necessary to mention that at the time, the beginning of the 1960's, the world was going through a very difficult moment of violent political convolutions and that in Paris the wars in the Congo and Algeria had an immediate reality.
In this catalogue, Niki de Saint Phalle describes the birth of the shooting paintings, the discovery of this territory of adventure in which she would live during several years and which more than any other invention liberated her creative forces. After the shooting paintings everything was possible.

The altars of brides and monsters
A religious education inevitably leaves traces. At the time she made these works Niki de Saint Phalle decided to attack these memories from her past that she wanted to destroy at all costs. She made altars that were shot at including the O.A.S. altar (O.A.S. was a terrorist organization of the extreme right, that defended the French occupation of Algeria). On this altar, crucifixes, stuffed bats, pistols, revolvers, rats, knives, Madonnas and odalisks are mixed.
The forces that had brought about the shooting pictures and the altars remained powerful for many years. At the same time, other elements and beings of a gentler kind began to arrive: the brides and the Nanas. The brides sometimes sit on the ground, sometimes on horses, sometimes they are accompanied by monsters. They are built up from toys or other small size articles made of plastic that had started to appear on the market at that time (1962–1963) and which possessed a vulgarity composed of what is stupid, useless, seductive and charming at the same time. Niki de Saint Phalle transformed them by grouping them together in order to make beautiful brides and great monsters, affixing them in her fashion on structures of textile and chicken wire.

The Nanas
The Nanas make their first appearance very discreetly, they take their time. But once they are there they will reign for a rather long time in Niki de Saint Phalle's œuvre. In reality, they are a large tribe and they take forms and shapes of many different kinds. Niki de Saint Phalle is known in the art world especially for her Nanas, sometimes only for her Nanas. It is certain that she found a way to create an apotheosis of woman in all her aspects that gave her great freedom, joy and the power of conviction. The word "Nana" had nothing respectful when it was used in French vernacular, but Niki de Saint Phalle somehow ennobled it. In this catalogue, she speaks about the largest of all the Nanas, the "Hon" of Stockholm.

The Hon and the monumental sculptures
The *Hon* brought about the creation of an entire family of other monumental sculptures like *The Fantastic Paradise, The Golem* in Jerusalem, *The Cyclop* in Milly-la-Forêt in France or *The Dragon* in Knokke-le-Zoute in Belgium. This experience with very large sculptures is not finished, but for the moment its climax is the Tarot Garden in Garavicchio, Italy. Close to the seashore near Grosseto in Tuscany is a small former quarry, facing South, where Niki de Saint Phalle has labored for more than ten years, building a garden where the twenty-two symbols of the Major Arcana are present. Some cards

have become buildings, with interiors to live in or meditate, while others are huge sculptures dispersed in this garden. "Il giardino dei Tarocchi" is a *tour de force* of an architectural and technical kind, but first and above all a great monument to the joy of life and the world's positive forces.
This monument, which is now a French foundation, will be open to visitors quite soon, since many essential parts of the work are finished.
The difficulties in building such huge structures without plans, without specialized technicians, and evidently without an architect, are easy to imagine. As frequently, Niki de Saint Phalle has turned the difficulties into advantages, like those who work on the basis of plans and ideas that are secret, and exist only in their heads; who are not obliged to render account to anybody, now or later; and who profit from a working process where there are no administrative meetings and no fixed budget. The importance and the strength of art produced by this method lies in the fact that it is traditionally made by single individuals, as a work that constantly develops in somebody's head, in a process that never stops. It is no surprise then that this kind of work has attracted and inspired the best of each generation.

Theatre
It is not a surprise that people in the performing arts have been attracted by Niki de Saint Phalle's work and she has contributed to some very beautiful collaborations in theatre and dance. Ballets have been realized in collaboration with Jean Tinguely that must be counted amongst the really great moments of ballet after the war including Roland Petit's *Eloge de la folie* in 1966.
The sets and costumes that Niki de Saint Phalle could design for the opera would give it a new and greatly needed visual aspect. But the responsible people, lacking confidence and knowledge of contemporary art, have not understood the opportunities that such a collaboration would provide. Obviously missed occasions affect the entire generation to which Niki de Saint Phalle belongs.

The films
Niki de Saint Phalle has made a number of films of an intimate and personal kind. The making of sculptures is an entirely different process than that of film-making, where the image is captured in the dark inner chamber of the camera. Probably her most beautiful film is the one that Niki de Saint Phalle is now putting together, that combines parts of her old films with images of her sculptures and other documents, uniting these images in the large collage-fresque manner that she knows so well and which she can use at ease.

Skinnies and Lamps
The major commitments and responsibilities involved in large groups of sculptures in a landscape or in a city are challenges that have to be lived *in situ*, for the time it takes. In that way, the landscape becomes a loved body. After many years of working with volumes, small, big and very, very big, the Skinnies appear. They are very thin in volume, like drawings in the air, carrying electric bulbs that light up, or they are simply lines in space that throw their shadows where they want.

The Bronzes
The taboos are destroyed. The studio is no longer a quiet haven and not at all a museum, but rather a laboratory where the results, even if they seem magnificent and impressive, have to be questioned constantly.

There are still taboos. The taboos of materials such as bronze. If one looks at all the vacuity that has been cast in bronze, it is evident that this material has been coloured by the ridiculous. When treated with liberty and a certain lack of respect, bronze is a beautiful material that permits the artist to realize works on a grand scale that can transcend the test of time. Niki de Saint Phalle has used bronze for a series of Egyptian Gods with a strong physical presence. The oil paint and the polished bronze produce effects of beauty which justify the choice of the material.

There are always stormy waves recurring in one's life. The generosity that radiates from Niki de Saint Phalle's work, which is so unorthodox, calms our anxieties, real or imaginary.

Why has Niki de Saint Phalle's work been considered marginal by some? For several reasons, most of them without interest: anti-feminism, indifference, prejudice, lack of curiosity. There are, nevertheless, more profound reasons: science and rationalism have dominated our century, in spite of the marvelous clairvoyance of Dada; in spite of the inroads of the surrealists in areas usually inaccessible to the conscious mind; in spite of Cubism and in spite of our fundamental individualism, the exaltation of the joy of life of which Matisse was the master is no longer fashionable. Whereas it is this joy that nourishes all the work of Niki de Saint Phalle, even if here and there certain anxieties appear. This joy diffuses a light which chases away the flattering shadows which are not to everyone's taste.

A pictorial documentation

Niki de Saint Phalle's parents

3 Jacqueline Harper with one of her nephews on her wedding day, 6 June 1927

1 Jeanne Jacqueline de Saint Phalle *née* Harper

2 André Marie Fal de Saint Phalle

4

5

4 The cover of *Vogue*, November 1952

5 Modelling for Cartier in *Vogue*

6 Cover of *Life* magazine, showing Niki de Saint Phalle as a popular New York débutante. Photo by Arnold Newman

Earliest works: gouaches and oil paintings dating from the mid-1950s, when she was married to the American writer, Harry Mathews

1 *Untitled*, 1954
Oil on canvas
Collection Harry Mathews

2 *Jeanne d'Arc*, 1959
Oil on wooden door
Collection Harry Mathews

3 *Nightscape*, 1958
Oil on canvas

4 *Untitled*, 1958
Oil on canvas

4

6

5

5 *Untitled*, 1958
Oil on canvas

6 *Le château du monstre et la mariée*, 1955/56
Oil on canvas
Collection Eva Aeppli

First assemblages
Collages from objets trouvés
Plaster and paint on wood

2 *Hors d'oeuvre*, 1960
First work by Niki de Saint Phalle to be shown at the group exhibition, *Comparaisons: Peinture Sculpture*, held at the Musée d'Art Moderne de la Ville de Paris, 6 February – 6 March 1961. Niki de Saint Phalle uses darts for the first time, inviting visitors to throw them at the target.

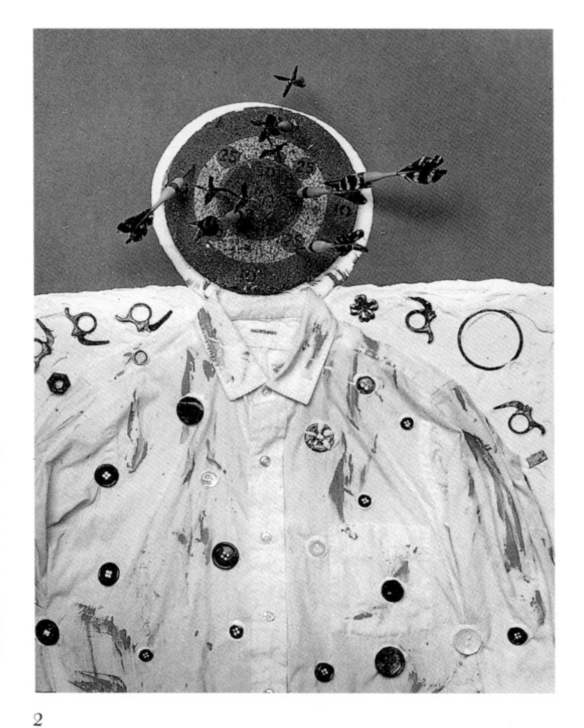

2

1 *Untitled*, 1958/59

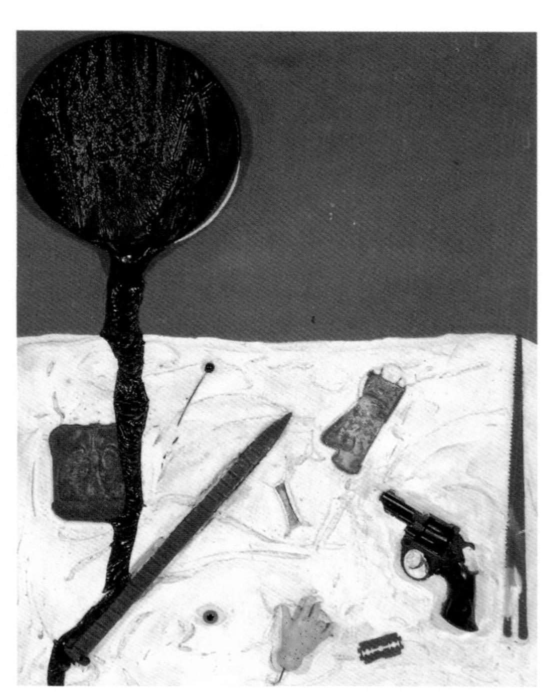

3 *Paysage de la mort*, 1960

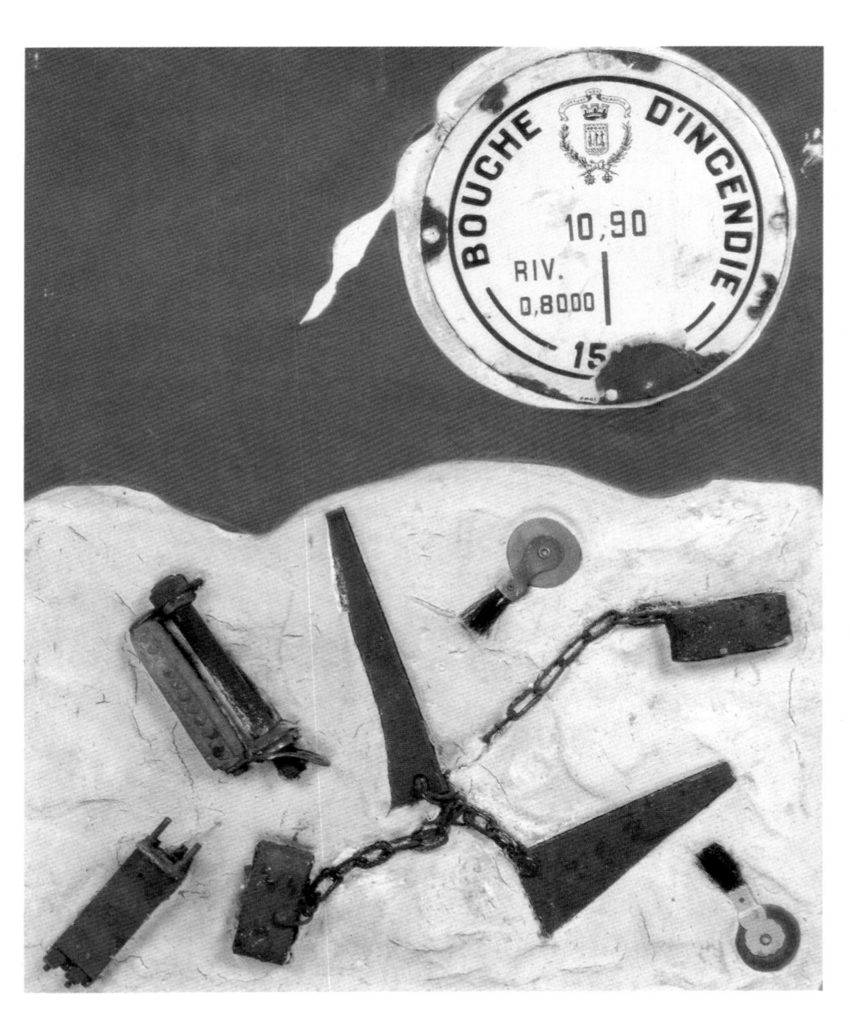

4 *Bouche d'incendie*, 1959

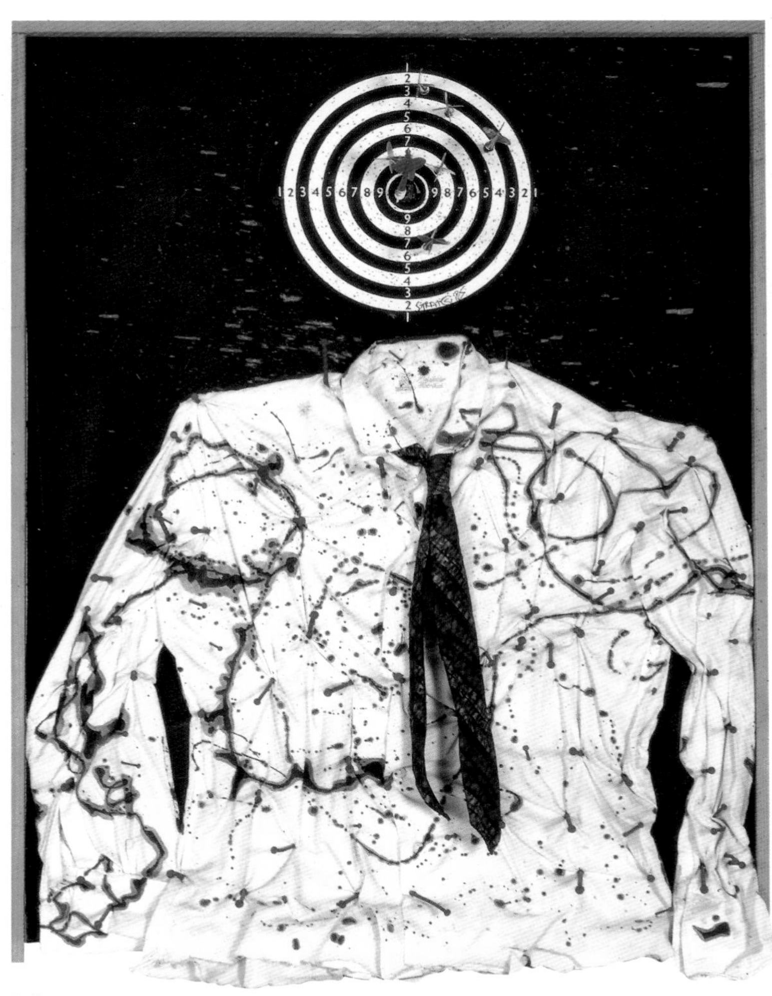

5 *Saint-Sébastien or Portrait of My Lover*, 1961
Also shown at the *Bewogen Beweging* exhibition held at the Stedelijk Museum, Amsterdam, from 10 March to 17 April 1961

2 + 3 Niki de Saint Phalle making assemblages in her studio in the Rue Alfred Durand-Claye in Paris

2

3

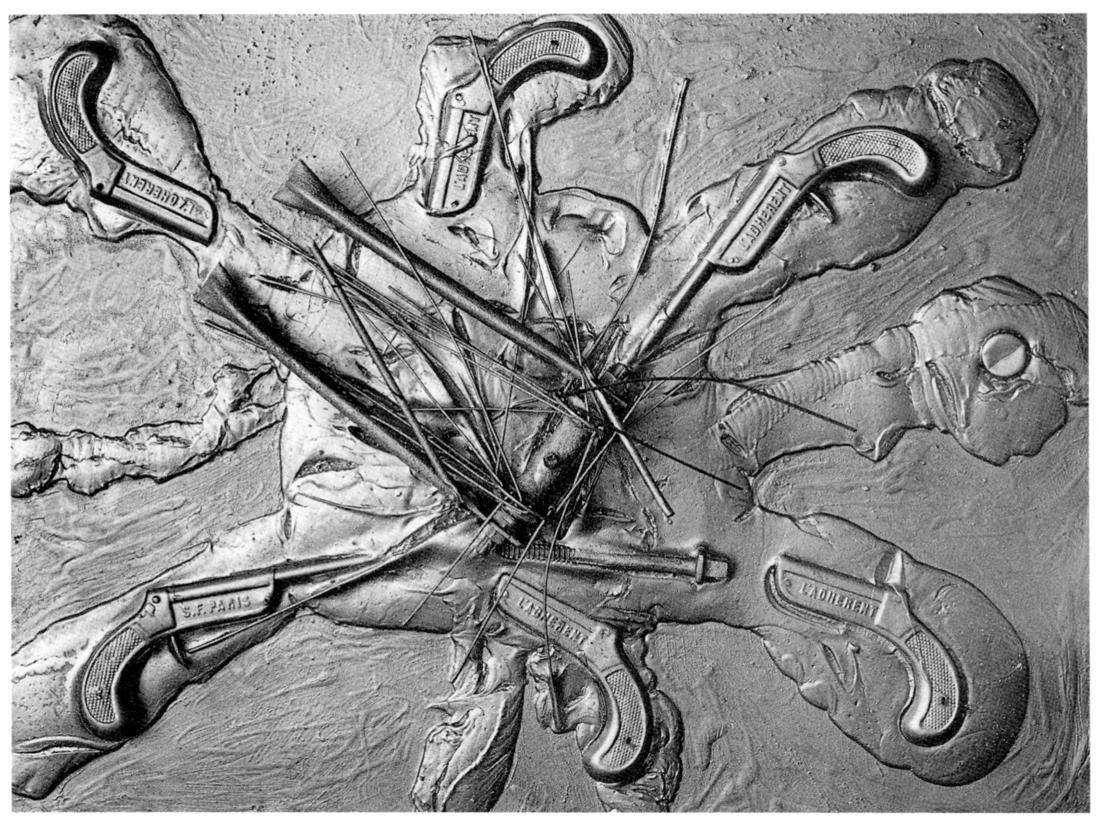

1 *Assemblage aux pistolets*, 1960

4–6 *Untitled Assemblages*, 1960

4

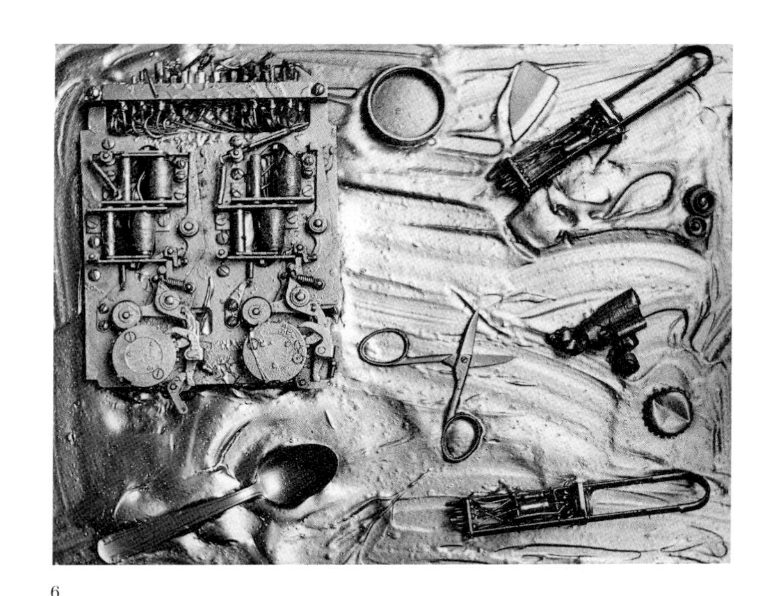

6

5

1961: Niki de Saint Phalle produces her first 'shooting paintings'. Using a technique which she herself developed and which involves a destructive process to create an artwork, she would embed small containers of liquid paint or cans of spray paint in plaster on wood; when fired at either by herself or by an invited audience, the paint would be released

1 The first 'shooting painting' was created on 12 February 1961 on a vacant lot behind Niki de Saint Phalle's studio at 11 Impasse Ronsin in Paris. Four works were created on this occasion. Pierre Restany is seen shooting at the painting, surrounded by Jeannine de Goldschmidt, Daniel Spoerri and the owner of the gun

2 Jeannine de Goldschmidt is seen shooting, watched by Vera and Daniel Spoerri, Niki de Saint Phalle, the owner of the gun, Jean Tinguely, Pierre Restany, Hugh Weiss and others

3 Niki de Saint Phalle shooting with a .22 rifle

4 Niki de Saint Phalle

5 Jean Tinguely, Niki de Saint Phalle and Pierre Restany looking at the results of a finished 'shooting painting'. After the session, Niki de Saint Phalle was invited to become a member of the Nouveaux Réalistes by the group's founder, Pierre Restany

4

3

5

25 February 1961: Niki de Saint Phalle is seen in her studio, preparing a further series of 'shooting paintings'

The second 'shooting painting' session was held in the Impasse Ronsin on 26 February. Six works were produced

1

2

3

4

1–4 She is sticking spaghetti, tomatoes, eggs, objets trouvés and paint-filled plastic bags to a wooden base, which is then covered with plaster

5 Hugh Weiss is seen shooting, with Sabine Weiss at his side

6

7

10

8

9

6 Gérard Deschamps shooting

7 An unidentified person shooting, watched by Niki de Saint Phalle, Gérard Deschamps, Sabine Weiss, Shirley Goldfarb, Hugh Weiss, Jimmy Metcalf and the owner of the gun

8 Niki de Saint Phalle, Mr Goldfarb, Shirley Goldfarb, John Ashbery and Hugh Weiss

9 Also present were Raymond Hains and others

10 Sam Mercer, Eva Aeppli and Niki de Saint Phalle

10 March – 17 April 1961:
Bewogen Beweging exhibition at the Stedelijk Museum, Amsterdam

1

3

2

1 A visitor is seen throwing darts at *Hors d'œuvre* (now retitled *Portrait of Myself*). The darts were left on a table beside the painting and members of the public invited to help themselves

2 Schoolchildren joining in the action

3 Heinz Mack, Louisa Calder, Niki de Saint Phalle, Jean Tinguely and Alexander Calder at the opening reception

12 March 1961: outdoor shooting session as part of the Amsterdam exhibition, *Bewogen Beweging*

5

6

5 'Shooting paintings' hanging from a tree

6 Pontus Hulten with the 'shooting paintings'

7 Pontus Hulten shooting, watched by Elizabeth de Saint Phalle, William Seitz, Niki de Saint Phalle and Anna Lena Wibom

8 Jean Tinguely, Niki de Saint Phalle and William Seitz approaching the finished 'shooting paintings'

9 Five reliefs hanging in a tree

4 Jean Tinguely shooting, with Anna Lena Wibom and Elizabeth de Saint Phalle behind him

7

8

9

17 May – 13 September 1961: the *Bewogen Beweging* exhibition is taken over, in an expanded form, by the Moderna Museet in Stockholm, where it is shown under the title *Rörelse i konsten*. On 23 May Niki de Saint Phalle organises a shooting session in a sandpit near Wik on Värmdö. Two works are created on this occasion

2

2 Katrin Wibom, Ulf Linde and Gösta Wibom watching the event

1 Jean Tinguely and Niki de Saint Phalle preparing a 'shooting painting'

3

4

3 Robert Rauschenberg shooting

4 Gösta Wibom shooting at the smaller relief, while Jean Tinguely and Niki de Saint Phalle shoot at the larger one with a .22 rifle

5

6

5 Gösta Wibom shooting

6 Jean Tinguely and Niki de Saint Phalle in front of the completed 'shooting painting', which is now in the Moderna Museet

Niki de Saint Phalle creating a 'shooting painting', which is exhibited with other 'shooting paintings' at her first solo exhibition in Paris, *Feu à volonté*, held at the Galerie J between 30 June and 12 July 1961

2 The different stages of the 'shooting painting' as seen in the exhibition booklet

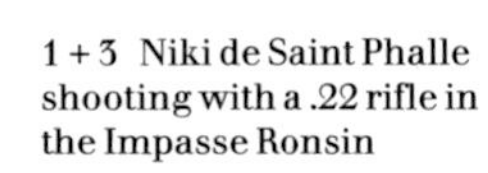

1 + 3 Niki de Saint Phalle shooting with a .22 rifle in the Impasse Ronsin

4 Niki de Saint Phalle in front of the finished work

20 June 1961: Niki de Saint Phalle, Jean Tinguely, Robert Rauschenberg and Jasper Johns take part in a concert performance of John Cage's *Variations II*, performed by David Tudor at the theatre of the American Embassy in Paris. Works by the artists serve as a constantly changing backdrop

1

2

1 Jean Tinguely's striptease machine, which lost all its feathers during the performance. Niki de Saint Phalle is seen sitting in the background, with David Tudor at the piano

2 Niki de Saint Phalle's 'shooting painting', with a target made by Jasper Johns out of real flowers. Jean Tinguely is seen watching Robert Rauschenberg, who worked on a painting on stage which the audience was never allowed to see

3 Niki de Saint Phalle and Robert Rauschenberg on stage

4 Since Niki de Saint Phalle's 'shooting paintings' were regarded as a high-risk activity, the American Embassy hired a professional marksman. He is seen here shooting the relief while Robert Rauschenberg paints

5 A general view of the stage, showing the works by Jasper Johns and Niki de Saint Phalle, with Robert Rauschenberg still painting. Jean Tinguely and the marksman are seen standing on the far right

6 The finished 'shooting painting', *Tir de l'Ambassade Américaine* or *Tir au siège*

26 June 1961: a shooting session in the Impasse Ronsin

3

1 Niki de Saint Phalle preparing the 'shooting painting' on 15 June

2 Niki de Saint Phalle installing the work on 26 June

4

5

3 Niki de Saint Phalle shooting

4 Niki de Saint Phalle loading her rifle

5 Jean Tinguely, Niki de Saint Phalle and a third person shooting simultaneously

6 Niki de Saint Phalle adding a further element to her work

7 Niki de Saint Phalle in front of the finished 'shooting painting'

30 June – 12 July 1961: Niki de Saint Phalle's first one-woman exhibition, organised by Pierre Restany at Paris's Galerie J. Visitors were invited to fire at the works on show

1 Niki de Saint Phalle, Jasper Johns, Kichka and Daniel Spoerri at the entrance to the gallery

2

3

4

5

6

2 Niki de Saint Phalle shooting

3 A visitor shooting, watched by Frank Stella

4 Robert Rauschenberg and Leo Castelli

5 Jasper Johns shooting, watched by Frank Stella

6 A visitor shooting, with Jean Fautrier (second from left) beside her

7 Harry Mathews, Niki de Saint Phalle, Eva Aeppli and Lawrence Rubin at the official opening

8 Dinner at La Coupole following the official opening: (l. to r.) Jasper Johns, Niki de Saint Phalle, Jean Tinguely, Gérard Deschamps and Jean Fautrier; (r. to l.) Leo Castelli, Elizabeth Rubin and Robert Rauschenberg

7

8

4 March 1962: the first shooting event in the USA, sponsored by the Everett Ellin Gallery and held in a parking lot on Sunset Strip in Los Angeles

3

1

2

4

5

6

1 + 2 Niki de Saint Phalle wearing her white suit, which she wore only at shooting events

3 John Cage, Jean Tinguely and Niki de Saint Phalle

4 Niki de Saint Phalle shooting

5 The finished 'shooting painting'

6 The audience viewing the finished work

7 Drawing by Walter Molino published in *Domenica del Corriere* on 1 April 1962

1 APRILE 1962 DOMENICA DEL CORRIERE ANNO 64 - N. 13 - L. 50 LA COPIA

Sparando dipinge. La giovane artista francese Niki de Saint-Phalle ha escogitato un curioso sistema per fare dei quadri a suon di fucilate e rivoltellate: il colore è racchiuso in sacchetti di plastica, sotto una superficie di gesso e, quando i proiettili rompono le vescichette, la tinta cola a rivoli. Servizio di Dino Buzzati alle pagg. 18-19 *(Disegno di Walter Molino)*

L'AUTOSTRADA MANGIA TROPPO

Servizio di Renato Albanese alle pagine 28 - 29

1

2

3

4

5

6

A shooting event is held in the hills overlooking Malibu one Sunday afternoon in late March or early April 1962. Among the audience are personalities from the worlds of cinema and art. At the end of the session Jean Tinguely sets off a small cannon, releasing yellow smoke

1 Jane Fonda (right) and others watching the 'shooting painting' being installed

2 Peggy Moffit and other photographer's models

3 Before the shooting starts, Jane Fonda lays on a picnic lunch for the film director, John Houseman

4 While the audience – which includes Henry Geldzahler, a representative from The Metropolitan Museum of Art in New York – tucks into a picnic lunch, Niki de Saint Phalle, assisted by Ed Kienholz, puts the finishing touches to her preparations for the shooting session

5 Niki de Saint Phalle shooting

6 Niki de Saint Phalle and Ed Kienholz in front of the finished work, which is later purchased by the art dealer, Virginia Dwan

Niki de Saint Phalle takes part in Kenneth Koch's *The Construction of Boston*, which is performed under the direction of Merce Cunningham at New York's Maidman Playhouse. Her part in the play is to bring art to Boston, for which she creates her only 'shooting sculpture' on stage, titled *Vénus de Milo*

Official opening of the *DYLABY* exhibition, which is held at the Stedelijk Museum, Amsterdam, between 30 August and 30 September 1962. *DYLABY* stands for Dynamic Labyrinth and is a joint project by Robert Rauschenberg, Martial Raysse, Niki de Saint Phalle, Daniel Spoerri, Jean Tinguely and Per Olof Ultvedt

15 October – 3 November: first one-woman exhibition at the Alexander Iolas Gallery, New York

1

3

2

4

1 Among the performers are Henry Geldzahler, Jean Tinguely, Maxine Groffsky, Robert Rauschenberg, Frank Stella, Billy Klüver and Kenneth Koch

2 The finished 'shooting sculpture', *Vénus de Milo*, with Jean Tinguely and Niki de Saint Phalle

3 At the shooting gallery: Niki de Saint Phalle is seen shooting, watched by a security guard dressed as a safari hunter. Beside her is the exhibition curator, Ad Petersen

4 Niki de Saint Phalle between Jean Tinguely and security guard

5 Willem Sandberg, the director of the Stedelijk Museum, with Niki de Saint Phalle

6 Leo Castelli and other visitors waiting their turn at the shooting gallery. Niki de Saint Phalle is standing between them and the 'shooting painting', offering advice

7 Niki de Saint Phalle in front of the finished 'shooting painting', *Homage to Le Facteur Cheval*

5

6

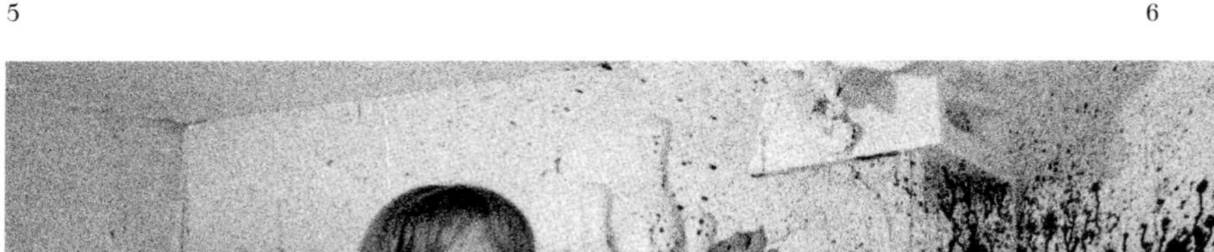

7

During her 'white period' between 1963 and 1964, Niki de Saint Phalle creates a series of works devoted to brides, mothers giving birth, heads and hearts

1

2

3

1 Niki de Saint Phalle in the living room of her home, 'Auberge du cheval blanc', at Soisy-sur-Ecole. On the wall is her head relief, *Napoléon*

2 + 3 Niki de Saint Phalle working on her 'bride', *Cécile*, at Jean Tinguely's house at Outry, Switzerland

4 Niki de Saint Phalle completing *Cécile* on the terrace. The head, *La tête aux roues*, is already finished

4

In 1963 Niki de Saint Phalle and Jean Tinguely bought the former auberge 'Auberge du cheval blanc', at Soisy-sur-Ecole and made it into their home

1 Niki de Saint Phalle working on *Le cheval et la mariée* in the garden

2

3

2 Niki de Saint Phalle shooting *The Red Witch* in her yard at Soisy

3 A further 'shooting painting' is created

4 Niki de Saint Phalle in her studio at Soisy, with *The Red Witch*, *La femme brune*, *Pink Heart* and other works

5 Niki de Saint Phalle surrounded by *Le mangeur d'enfants*, *La mariée sous l'arbre* and *Le cheval et la mariée*

4

5

Summer 1963: the monumental outdoor 'shooting painting', *King Kong*, was sponsored by the Dwan Gallery and created in Los Angeles, California

1 *Tir des hommes politiques*, 1963, a study for *King Kong*

2 *King Kong*, a gift of the artist, in the Moderna Museet, Stockholm

The inspiration for the 'Nanas' came from a drawing by Larry Rivers, showing his pregnant wife, Clarice Rivers, prior to the birth of their daughter, Gwynne, in 1964

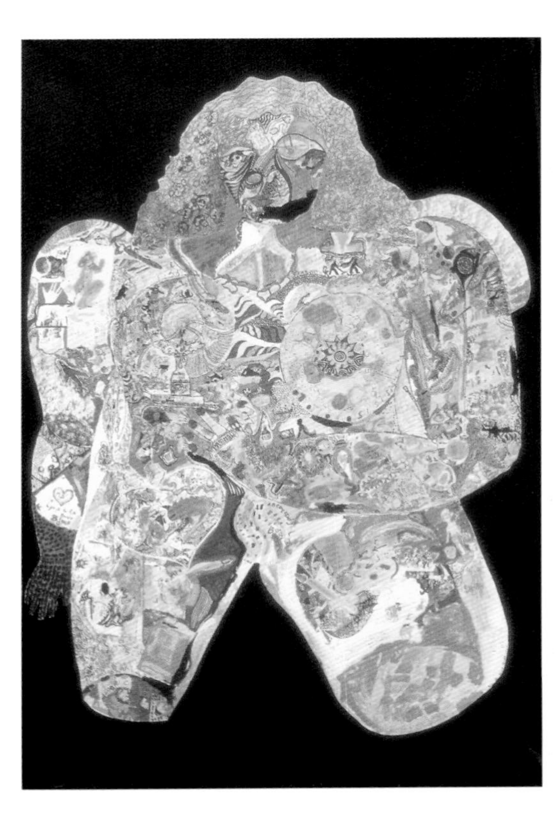

3 *Pink Lady*, 1964
Oil on canvas and collage
Collection Hirshhorn Museum and Sculpture Garden, Smithsonian Institution, Washington, D.C.

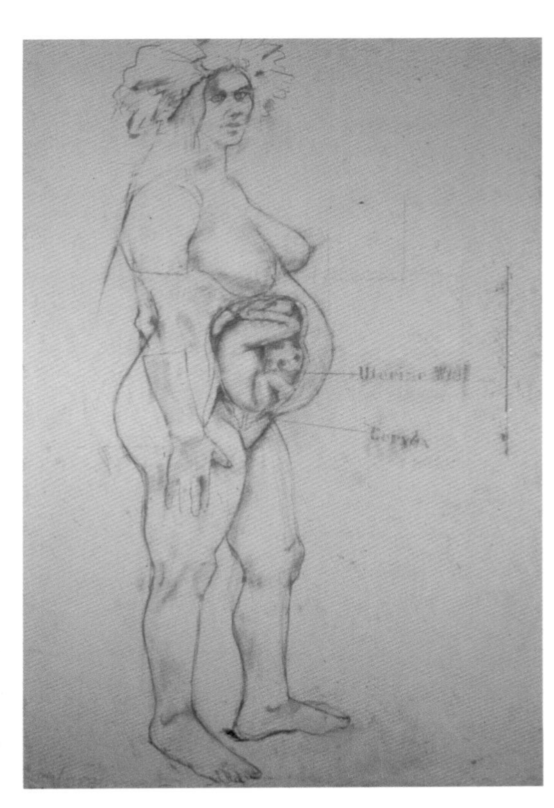

4 Larry Rivers' drawing

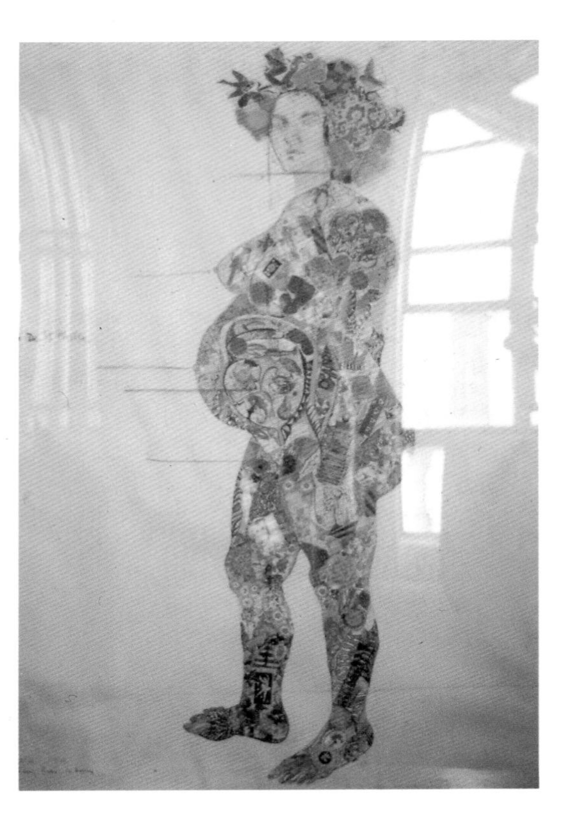

5 Collaboration between Niki de Saint Phalle and Larry Rivers, who drew the face for her collage

3 Exhibition poster with a drawing of the Nana, *Elizabeth*

4 Niki de Saint Phalle and her daughter, Laura Mathews, standing in front of *Elizabeth* at the Galerie Alexandre Iolas

1

2

1 Jean Tinguely, Niki de Saint Phalle and Larry Rivers in Rivers' New York studio, 1965

2 Clarice Rivers and Niki de Saint Phalle working on the wire frame for a Nana at Southampton, Long Island, summer 1965

3

4

First showing of Nanas made from cloth, yarn and papier mâché at the Galerie Alexandre Iolas in Paris, 30 September – 30 October 1965

5 Niki de Saint Phalle among her Nanas at the Galerie Alexandre Iolas

Auberge du cheval blanc in Soisy-sur-Ecole

2

1 *La baigneuse*, 1965
Repainted in 1967 as *Black Venus*

3

2 A series of painted cats outside the 'Auberge du cheval blanc'

3 Jean Tinguely and Niki de Saint Phalle in the courtyard of their home at Soisy-sur-Ecole. The courtyard serves as Jean Tinguely's studio, while Niki de Saint Phalle has her own studio indoors

4 The interior of Niki de Saint Phalle's studio, with Nanas in progress and *La Waldaff* on the far right

9 June – 4 September 1966: exhibition of a collaborative project by Niki de Saint Phalle, Jean Tinguely and Per Olof Ultvedt, animated by the director of the Moderna Museet Pontus Hulten. The artists install a monumental Nana, lying on its back with its legs apart. The sculpture measures 6.10 x 28.70 x 9.15 metres and is called *Hon* (the Swedish for 'she')

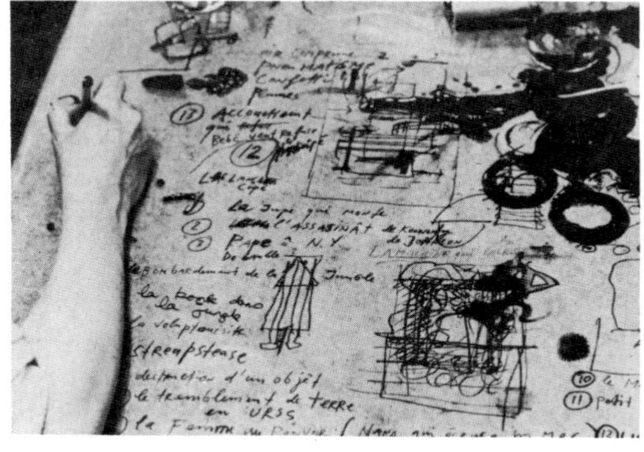

1

2

1 Working drawing
Construction begins

2 Per Olof Ultvedt, Niki de Saint Phalle, Jean Tinguely and Pontus Hulten beginning work on the project

3 Niki de Saint Phalle and Jean Tinguely

4 Niki de Saint Phalle lying on the floor, demonstrating the position of *Hon*

5 Jean Tinguely and Per Olof Ultvedt

3

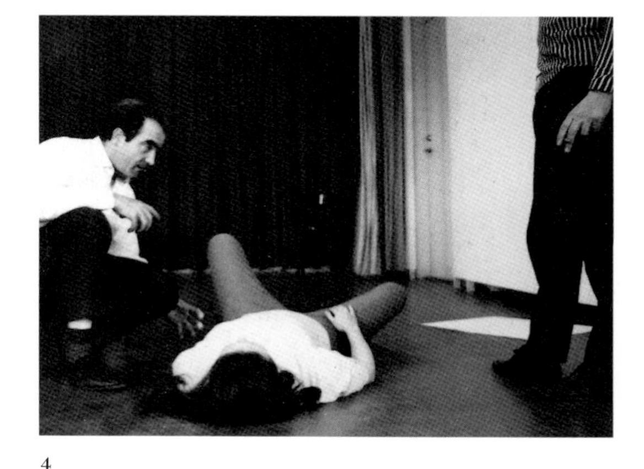

4

5

6

6 Jean Tinguely, Niki de Saint Phalle, Per Olof Ultvedt and Pontus Hulten discussing the project at the Moderna Museet on 27 May 1966

7

7 Niki de Saint Phalle, Pontus Hulten, Jean Tinguely and Per Olof Ultvedt working on the hand of *Hon*

8 Per Olof Ultvedt, Niki de Saint Phalle and Jean Tinguely working on a sketch

9 Building the scaffolding for *Hon*

10 The skeleton of the head

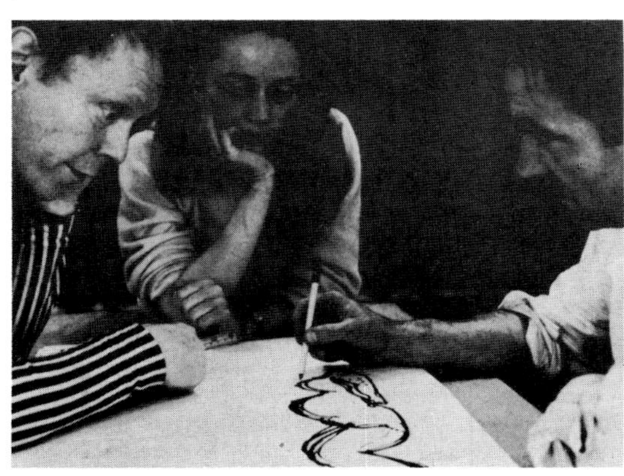

8

9

10

1 Niki de Saint Phalle preparing between 20 and 30 litres of animal glue a day

2 Niki de Saint Phalle with fabric soaked in glue before it is stretched over the wire frame

3 The legs of *Hon*

4 Niki de Saint Phalle painting the right leg of *Hon*

6 A wheel for one of Jean Tinguely's machines in the interior of *Hon*

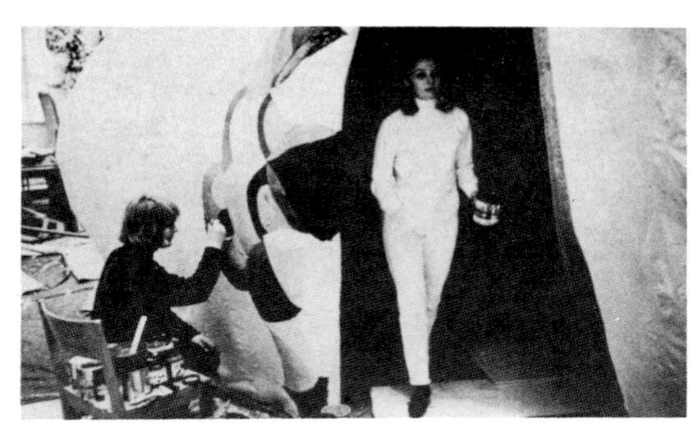

7 Niki de Saint Phalle painting the interior, while her assistant, Maja-Lena Engström, works on the exterior

5 Niki de Saint Phalle, Jean Tinguely, Sidsel Wibom, Rico Weber, Anna Lena Wibom, Klara Hulten, Katrin Wibom and Axel Wibom

8

9

8 Per Olof Ultvedt working on the interior

9 Per Olof Ultvedt

1

2

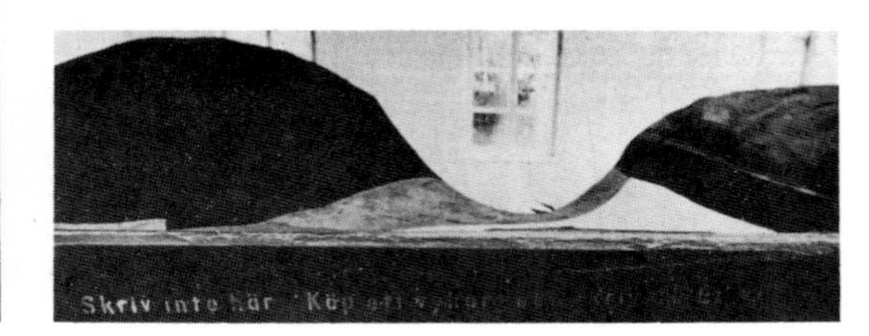

3

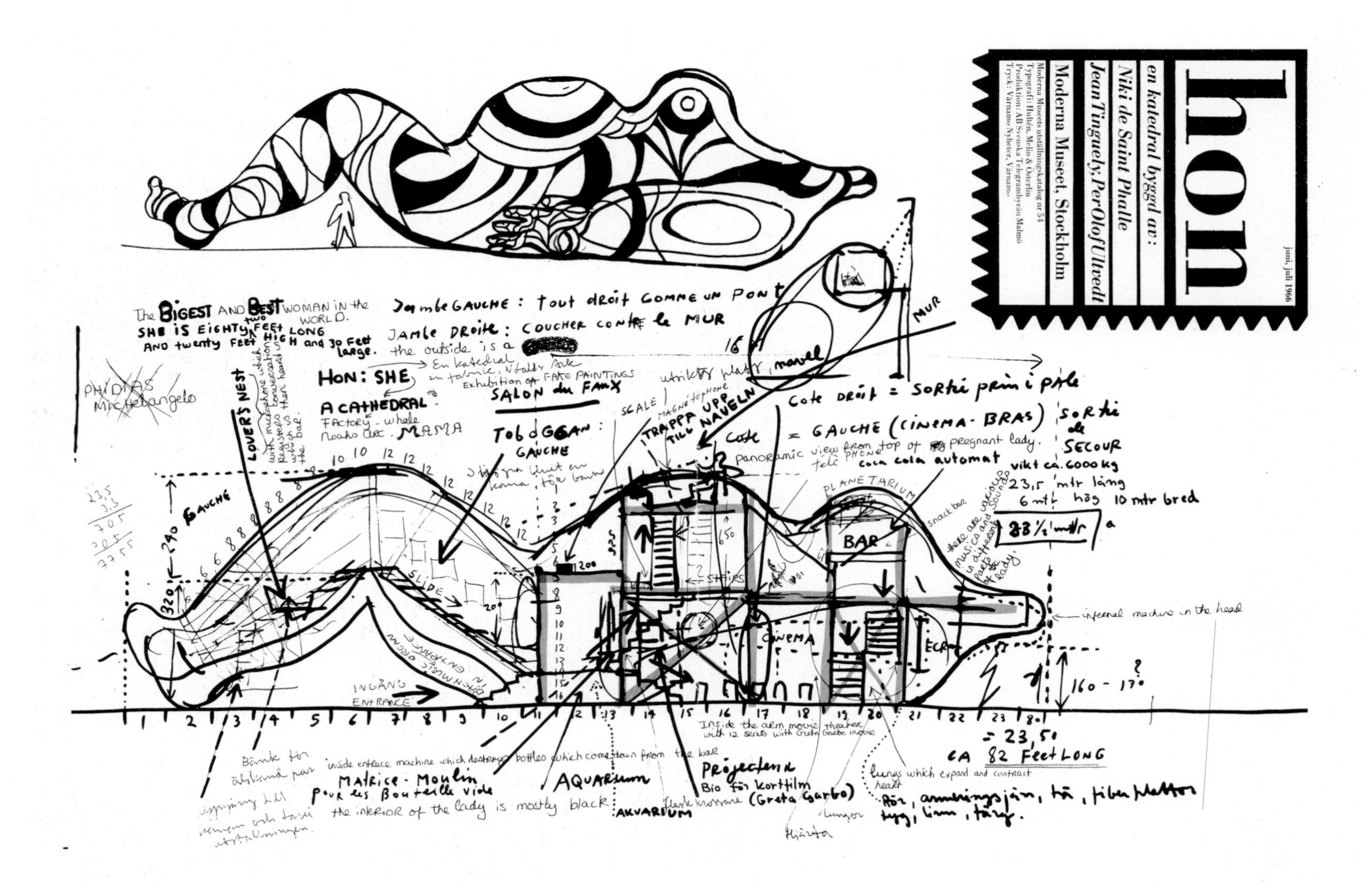
hon
en katedral byggd av:
Niki de Saint Phalle
Jean Tinguely, Per Olof Ultvedt
Moderna Museet, Stockholm
juni, juli 1966
The BIGEST AND BEST WOMAN in the WORLD.
SHE IS EIGHTY two FEET LONG
AND twenty FEET HIGH and 30 Feet large.
Jambe GAUCHE : tout droit comme un Pont
JAMBE DROITE : COUCHER CONTRE le MUR
HON: SHE
A CATHEDRAL
SALON du FAUX
LOVERS NEST
MUR
Cote droit = SORTIE prin i pale
= GAUCHE (CINEMA - BRAS)
SORTIE de SECOUR
TOBOGGAN : GAUCHE
TRAPPA UPP TILL NAVELN
Panoramic view from top of pregnant lady.
coca cola automat
vikt ca. 6000 kg
23,5 mtr lång
6 mtr hög 10 mtr bred
PLANETARIUM
BAR
CINEMA
SLIDE
INGÅNG
ENTRANCE
infernal machine in the head
= 23,51
CA 82 Feet LONG
MATRICE - Moulin
Pour les Bouteille vide
AQUARIUM
AKVARIUM
Projection
Bio för kortfilm
(Greta Garbo)
the interior of the lady is mostly black

4

5

6

5 The production of the folder

6 Per Olof Ultvedt, Niki de Saint Phalle and Jean Tinguely following the completion of *Hon*

7 The upper portion of the body of *Hon*

8 The lower portion of the body of *Hon*

1 Standing: Gösta Wibom, Björn Eneroth, Jean Tinguely, Pontus Hulten, Rico Weber, Jörgen Hammarberg and Per Olof Ultvedt; sitting: Anna Lena Wibom, Mette Prawitz, Klara Hulten and Niki de Saint Phalle

2 Niki de Saint Phalle painting the head

3 The outer skin of *Hon*

4 The cover of the folder that accompanied the Moderna Museet exhibition, showing a working drawing itemising the interior of *Hon* playrooms: in the left arm is a twelve-seat cinema, showing Greta Garbo's first film, *Luffarpetter*; in the head a moving wooden brain; in the left breast a planetarium; in the left thigh a radio sculpture, *Radio Stockholm*; in the knee a microphoned 'Lovers' Seat' in red velvet lit by a spotlight and visible only in a rear-view mirror by those who use the seat; in the right breast a milk bar and bottle-crusher; in one leg a 'Gallery of Fakes' in which each painting has its own bronze lamp; also a payphone, automatic food vendor, postcard 'Piennale' of paintings from the Moderna Museet, a roof terrace on top of the belly and an aquarium. Music by Johann Sebastian Bach is piped through to various parts of *Hon*

7

8

1 Niki de Saint Phalle and Jean Tinguely at the opening reception

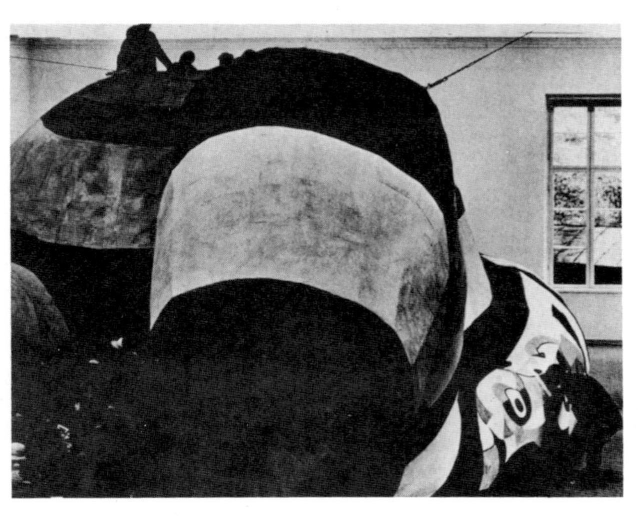

2 Visitors on the roof terrace of *Hon*

3 One of the various exhibition posters

4 A gentleman entering *Hon* through the sexual orifice

5 Side view of the entrance

1

2

3

4

1 Interior view of visitors entering *Hon*

2 Jean Tinguely's *Big Mill* inside *Hon*

3 Two visitors under the head

4 + 5 Visitors to *Hon*

5

Since *Hon* was a temporary exhibition, the sculpture had to be dismantled to make room for another exhibition, this time of works by Claes Oldenburg

2

3

1

4

5

1 Pontus Hulten removing the head, which is the only part of *Hon* to remain in the Moderna Museet

2–5 Work begins on dismantling *Hon*

6

6 Sections of the demolished sculpture

7 Part of *Hon* being taken away

8 The scaffolding after the sculpture has been dismantled

7

8

In 1966 Niki de Saint Phalle collaborated with Martial Raysse and Jean Tinguely on designs for the sets and costumes for John Cau's ballet *Eloge de la folie*. Choreographed by Roland Petit, the work takes as its starting point the decay of modern society

2

3

1

4

5

1 Martial Raysse, Jean Tinguely, the composer Marius Constant, Roland Petit and Niki de Saint Phalle taking a curtain call

2 The première at the Théâtre des Champs-Elysées in Paris on 2 March 1966

3 Set design with Nanas

4 Scene from Act VI: *La guerre*

5 Scene from Act IV: *Les femmes au pouvoir*

Also in 1966 Niki de Saint Phalle designed the sets and costumes for Rainer von Diez's production of Aristophanes's *Lysistrata*, which opened at the Kassel Staatstheater in the autumn of that year. The sets were a variant of *Hon*, 10 metres long and 3.60 metres high. The actors could enter or exit through the torso's vagina

6 Two of the actors on the set

7 The company on the first night, 2 October 1966

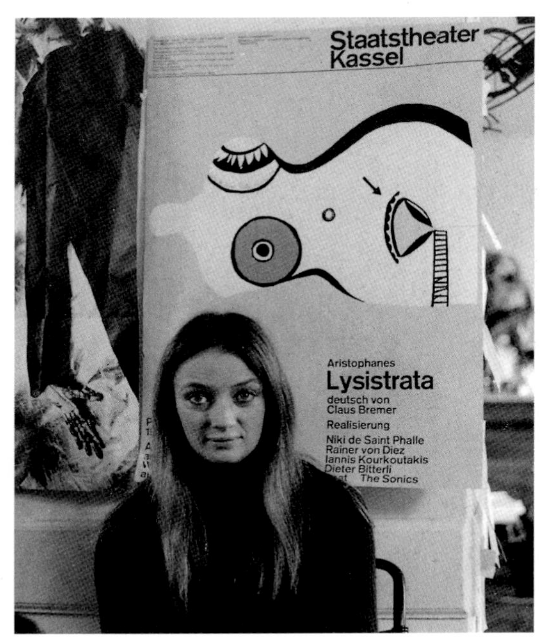

8 Niki de Saint Phalle in front of her own poster for the production

In 1966 Niki de Saint Phalle and Jean Tinguely were awarded a commission by the French government to create an outdoor sculpture for Expo '67, held in Montreal from 28 April to 27 October 1967. *Le paradis fantastique* comprised nine large polystyrene figures painted in neon colours by Niki de Saint Phalle and combined with six kinetic machines by Jean Tinguely.

1

3

2

1 Maquette for *Le paradis fantastique*

2 Maquette for *Nana-arbre*

3 The sculptures are made at the Atelier Simonini, which belongs to a Parisian set designer

4 Niki de Saint Phalle sitting beside *La grosse Nana*

5 View of *La bête gentille*, *Le rotozaza* and *La Nana sur la tête*

5

6 *La baigneuse*

7 *La grosse Nana*

8 The sculptures are taken from their warehouse in order to be shipped to Montreal. *La fleur* is seen being loaded on a lorry

Installation of *Le paradis fantastique* on the roof garden of the French Pavilion in Montreal

1 *Le bébé-monstre et le char Raspoutine, La grosse Nana et la perceuse* and *La Nana embrochée et la machine*

2 *Le bébé-monstre et le char Raspoutine, La grosse Nana et la perceuse, La Nana embrochée et la machine*

At the end of Expo '67, *Le paradis fantastique* travels to Buffalo in late 1967 and is also shown in New York the following spring

2

3

2–5 Children with inflatable Nanas by Niki de Saint Phalle are seen enjoying *Le paradis fantastique* in New York's Central Park

1 Installation in the courtyard of Albright-Knox Art Gallery, Buffalo, 21 November 1967 – 7 January 1968

4

5

6 Niki de Saint Phalle and Jean Tinguely at the official opening on 1 May 1968

6

7 General view of the installation in the Conservatory Garden in Central Park, not far from Harlem

1 *Nana sur la tête, La fleur* and *Nana-arbre et la folle*

Niki de Saint Phalle and Jean Tinguely donate *Le paradis fantastique* to the Moderna Museet in Stockholm. Jean and Dominique de Menil provide financial assistance enabling the sculpture to be transported from the USA to Sweden. After a year's restoration the sculpture is placed on permanent exhibition near the Moderna Museet

2 *Nana sur la tête, La fleur* and *La baigneuse.* A newly constructed fountain by Jean Tinguely spews water over the two Nanas

3 *La Nana embrochée et la machine, La grosse Nana* and *Nana- arbre et la folle*

4 Niki de Saint Phalle and Jean Tinguely in their garden at Soisy

For her first retrospective, *Les Nanas au pouvoir* at the Stedelijk Museum, Amsterdam, from 26 August to 15 October 1967, Niki de Saint Phalle creates her first *Nana Dream House* and her first *Nana Fountain*

1 Nana Fountain, *Teresita*

2 Niki de Saint Phalle working on the exhibition poster for *Nanas au pouvoir*. It shows a maquette for her *Nana Dream House*

3

4

3 A visitor peering inside the *Nana Dream House*

4 Niki de Saint Phalle with her art dealer, Alexandre Iolas, Bénédicte Pesle of the Galerie Alexandre Iolas, and Jean Tinguely with the artist's children, Philip and Laura Mathews

5 The official opening of *Les Nanas au pouvoir* at the Stedelijk Museum

5

6 View of *Black Venus* and *Nana Dream House*

The exhibition, *Les Nanas au pouvoir*, travels to the Dusseldorf Kunstverein, where it is shown from 19 November 1968 to 1 January 1969

1

2

1 Niki de Saint Phalle at her home in Soisy

2 Jean Tinguely, the director of the Stedelijk Museum, Willem Sandberg, and Niki de Saint Phalle in her living room at Soisy

3 Niki de Saint Phalle posing in front of a Nana

4 Back view of *Black Venus*

5 The Kunstverein cash desk, with a Nana on the table

6 View of a dancing Nana and *Anna Lena in Greece*

5

4

6

Niki de Saint Phalle writes *MOI*, a story of a little girl in revolt. Together with Rainer von Diez, she turns it into a stage play, *ICH (All About ME)*, for which she also designs the sets and costumes. The play is premièred on 28 June 1968 at the Kassel Staatstheater as part of *documenta 4*

1

2

3

4

1–4 Scenes from *ICH*

Between 24 October and 6 November 1968 Niki de Saint Phalle presents her eighteen-piece relief, *Last Night I Had a Dream*, at the Galerie Alexandre Iolas in Paris

5

6

7

5 The installation at the Galerie Alexandre Iolas

6 Invitation to the exhibition, designed by Niki de Saint Phalle

7 Detail of installation

1 + 2 Niki de Saint Phalle painting *Le rêve de l'oiseau*

3 Niki de Saint Phalle and Rico Weber painting the door of *Le rêve de l'oiseau*

1

2

3

Between 1969 and 1971 Niki de Saint Phalle creates her first full-scale architectural project, three houses for Rainer von Diez in the mountains in the South of France, each of which functions as a separate room: *Le rêve de l'oiseau* as kitchen, *Big Clarice* as living accommodation and *La sorcière* as bathroom

4 *La sorcière*

5 View of *Big Clarice*, with *Le rêve de l'oiseau* in the background

6 Rainer von Diez and Niki de Saint Phalle painting *Le rêve de l'oiseau*

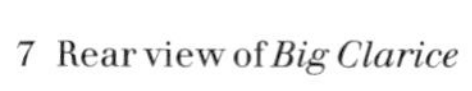

7 Rear view of *Big Clarice*

6

7

1 Installing the one-woman exhibition, *Le rêve de Diane*, at the Galerie Alexandre Iolas in Paris. The exhibition lasts from 5 to 28 February 1970 and includes a huge multi-sectional sculpture. The artist is seen here talking to Lulu Bleibtreu outside the gallery

2 Nana Fountain

3 Niki de Saint Phalle painting *La machine à rêver*

4 Installation of *Le rêve de Diane*

4

5 *La machine à rêver*

6 Niki de Saint Phalle's poster for performances by Merce Cunningham and the Paul Taylor Dance Company at the Théâtre de France in Paris

A festival organised by Pierre Restany and Guido Le Noci to mark the tenth anniversary of the founding of the Nouveaux Réalistes is held at the Galleria Vittorio Emmanuele in Milan on 29 November 1970. One of the opening events is a shooting session by Niki de Saint Phalle

4

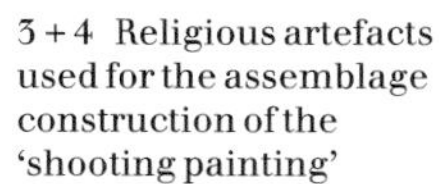

3 + 4 Religious artefacts used for the assemblage construction of the 'shooting painting'

1

2

1 Members of the general public in front of Niki de Saint Phalle's altar inside the gallery; the altar would shortly be the object of a shooting session

2 Niki de Saint Phalle and Fausta Squatritti at Biffi's, where Daniel Spoerri had laid on an elaborate meal. For this 'Last Supper' he offered culinary specialities appropriate to the work of each member of the Nouveaux Réalistes: Niki de Saint Phalle received a Nana icecream and a cake in the shape of a target

5 Niki de Saint Phalle shooting

6 Niki de Saint Phalle preparing the 'shooting painting' on 25 November 1970

7 Jean Tinguely and spectators in front of the altar

8 The altar before the shooting

9 Niki de Saint Phalle and the altar after the shooting

In 1970 Jean Tinguely begins work on a 22.50-metre high sculpture, *La tête (Le cyclope)*, in the forest at Milly-la-Forêt. Among the artists involved in the project are Eva Aeppli, Bernhard Luginbühl, Giovanni Podesta, Jean-Pierre Raynaud, Jesus Rafael Soto, Daniel Spoerri and Niki de Saint Phalle. The sculpture, which has already been declared a French monument, will be unveiled in September 1992

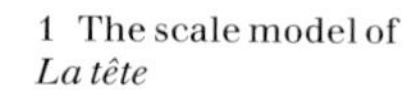

1 The scale model of *La tête*

2 Pontus Hulten and Jean Tinguely in front of the still incomplete *La tête*, 1971

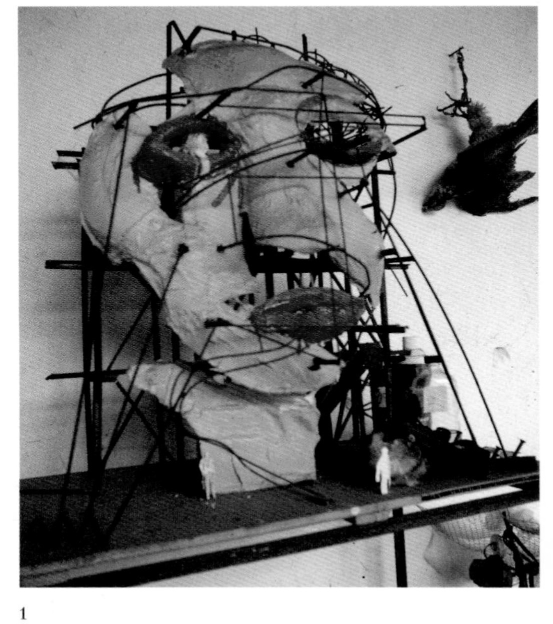

1

2

3 Niki de Saint Phalle works on the façade, using mirror mosaics

Niki de Saint Phalle writes her first filmscript, *Nana Island*, in 1971. The film was not completed

5

6

4

7

4 Rico Weber with one of Jean Tinguely's constructions

5 Mimi Johnson and a child in front of *La Waldaff*

6 Some of the cast of *Nana Island*: Niki de Saint Phalle, Patty Oldenburg, Mme Gérard, Clarice Rivers and Mimi Johnson

7 Niki de Saint Phalle, Patty Oldenburg and Clarice Rivers

8 Mimi Johnson and Niki de Saint Phalle

9 Jean Tinguely

10 Jean Tinguely, Niki de Saint Phalle and Clarice Rivers in front of *La Waldaff*

8

9

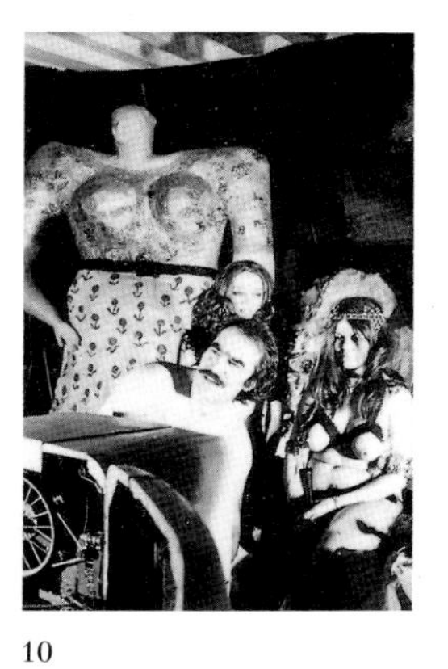

10

In 1972 Niki de Saint Phalle is commissioned by the Rabinovitch family to make *Golem*, her first architectural project for children, for Rabinovitch Park in Kiryat Hayovel, Jerusalem. The mayor of Jerusalem is Teddy Kollek, an enthusiastic supporter of the project

1 2 3

4

1 Niki de Saint Phalle, Jean Tinguely, Rico Weber and Paul Wiedemer in front of the iron subframe

2 Jean Tinguely, who designed the iron subframe, working on *Golem* with his assistants, Rico Weber and Paul Wiedemer

3 Jean Tinguely standing by a model of *Golem*

4 The iron subframe

5

9

6

7

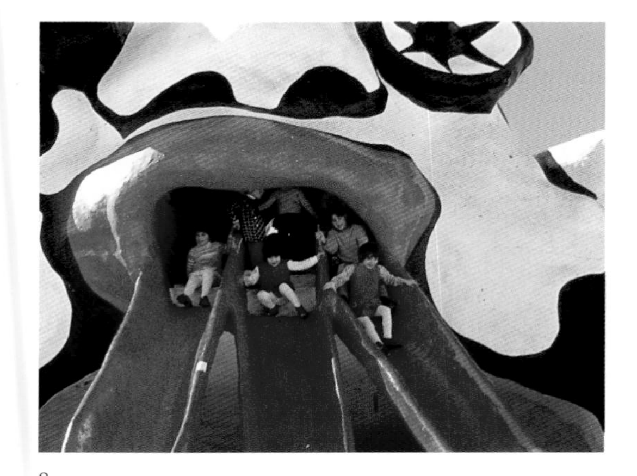

8

10

5 + 6 Applying cement to the subframe

7 + 8 Children playing on *Golem*: three tongues serve as slides

9 Jean Tinguely and Niki de Saint Phalle looking at *Golem*

10 *Golem*

In 1973 Niki de Saint Phalle builds a *Dragon* in the garden of Roger and Fabienne Nellens in the Belgian town of Knokke-le-Zoute. Intended for the use of their children, it is described by the artist as a fully equipped 'house for children', with playroom, kitchen, bathroom and upstairs sleeping accommodation

1

2

3

4

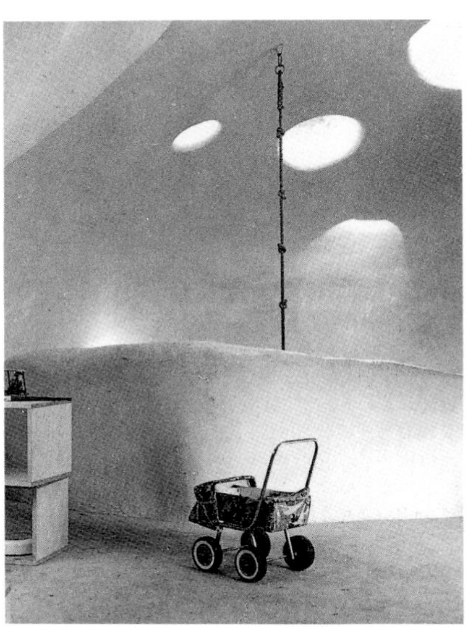

5

1 Maquette of *Dragon*

2 Inauguration of the finished but as yet unpainted *Dragon*

3 The eye of the monster

4 The mouth, with the tongue as a slide

5 The interior of the sculpture

6 The completed *Dragon*, 1973

6

2

3

1 *Tears necklace* from Niki de Saint Phalle's limited edition of jewelry

4

2 A family photo from 1973 showing Rico Weber, Niki de Saint Phalle, Laura Condominas, Jean Tinguely, Niki's granddaughter, Bloum Condominas, and Jacqueline de Saint Phalle

3 Niki de Saint Phalle's son, Philip Mathews

4 Niki de Saint Phalle with her mother, Jacqueline, and her daughter, Laura Condominas with her daughter Bloum

In 1972 Niki de Saint Phalle made her second film, *Daddy*, in collaboration with Peter Whitehead. It was shot on location at the Commandery in Dannemois and at the Château de Mons near Grasse. The cast included Rainer von Diez, Mia Martin and Clarice Rivers. A revised version of the film was premièred in New York in April 1973

5 Niki de Saint Phalle's poster for the film *Daddy*

9

6

7

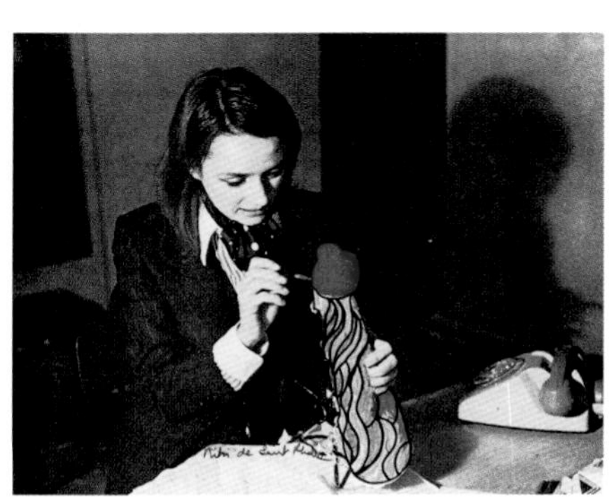

8

6 Jean-Pierre Raynaud and Niki de Saint Phalle

7 Niki de Saint Phalle posing for a film photo

8 Niki de Saint Phalle

9 Niki de Saint Phalle, Clarice Rivers and Rainer von Diez

10 Niki de Saint Phalle in a scene from the film

10

1

2

1+2 Nana brooch and necklace

4

3

5

3 Niki de Saint Phalle working on the maquette of *Le poète et sa muse* in 1974. The 5.50-metre high sculpture was later installed on the campus at Ulm University

4–6 Three giant Nanas, *Caroline*, *Charlotte* and *Sophie*, are installed in Hanover in 1974

Niki de Saint Phalle writes and directs the film, *Un rêve plus long que la nuit*. It tells the story of a young girl whose life unfolds in a dream which takes the form of a single night's journey. The sets (sculptures by Niki de Saint Phalle) and machines (Jean Tinguely) were designed for the film, which lasted 1½ hours and which was made in 1975 in the vicinity of Paris. Many of the artist's friends and family were involved in the production, including Laura Condominas, Marina Karella, Jacqueline Monnier, Bernhard Luginbühl, Jean-Yves Mock, Andrée Putman, Daniel Spoerri, Christian Ledoux and many others

2

3

4

1 Laura Condominas and Bernhard Luginbühl

2 Niki de Saint Phalle's poster for *Un rêve plus long que la nuit*, premièred in Paris on 16 November 1976

3 Laurence Bourqui and Marina Karella

4 – 7 Scenes from the film

8 + 9 Bernhard Luginbühl

10 Laurent Condominas

5

6

In 1977 Niki de Saint Phalle collaborated with Constantin Mulgrave on the film *The Travelling Companion*, an adaptation of a short story by Hans Christian Andersen

7

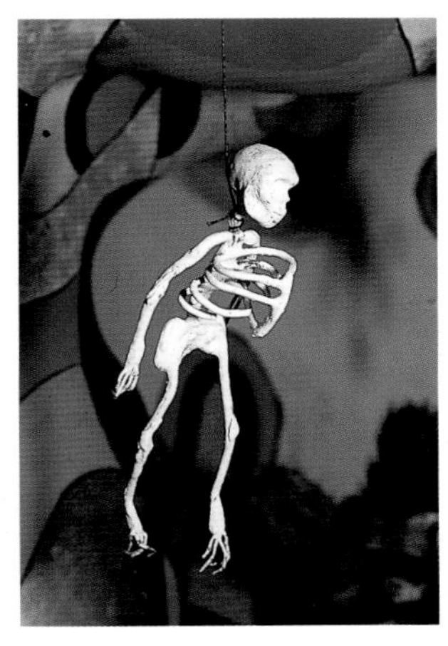

11

8

12

11 + 12 Models of the film set

9

10

1

1 *L'aveugle dans la prairie*, 1978/79
Painted polyester
Collection Musée National d'Art Moderne, Centre Georges Pompidou, Paris

2 Subframe for the man on the bench in *L'aveugle dans la prairie*

2

3

3 Niki de Saint Phalle on her chair, *Charly*, painting a smaller version of *Le monde*. Her first edition of furniture appeared in 1979

4 *Tears* relief, 1979
Painted polyester

4

5 Niki de Saint Phalle and her assistant of many years' standing, Ricardo Menon, working on architectural models on the beach at Malibu, California

In 1979 Niki de Saint Phalle began work on a fantasy garden at Garavicchio in Tuscany. It is based on motifs from the twenty-two cards in the Major Arcana of Tarot. With this project she realises her life's dream of a sculpture park. Through the intermediary of her friend Marella Agnelli, Niki de Saint Phalle is granted the right to use a plot of land belonging to Marella Agnelli's brothers, Carlo and Nicola Caracciolo. All aspects of the project are financed by the artist. Influenced by Italian art, she uses mirrors, glass and ceramic mosaics for the first time in her work. It is hoped to open the garden to visitors in 1993

1

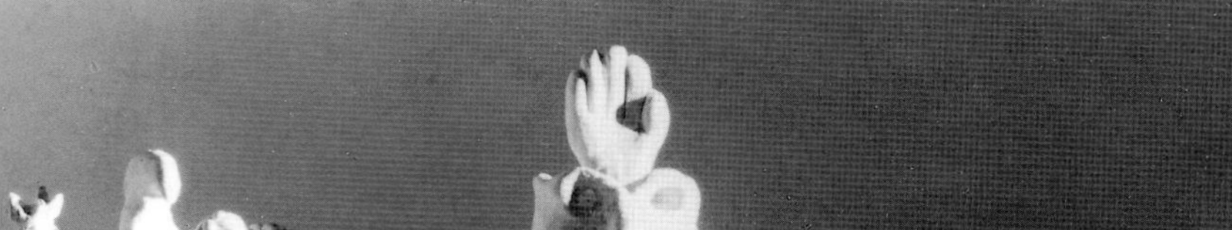

2

3

1 Maquette for *The Magician* and *The High Priestess* (cards I + II)

2 + 3 Maquettes for the Tarot Garden

4

4 Jean Tinguely and Niki de Saint Phalle in the grounds at Garavicchio

5 Sketch by Jean Tinguely and Niki de Saint Phalle on a photograph showing the start of building work on the Tarot Garden

5

1 Sepp Imhof, Jean Tinguely, Ricardo Menon and Niki de Saint Phalle working on an iron subframe

2 The subframe of *The Magician* and *The High Priestess*

3 The subframe of *The Magician*

4 An internal view of the subframe of *The High Priestess*

3

1

2

4

5 The subframe of *The Empress* (card III)

1

1 The subframe of *L'arbre de la vie*, which symbolises lovers (card VI)

3

2 *The Magician, The High Priestess, L'Arbre de la vie* and *L'oiseau de feu*, which represents the sun (card XVII), in the course of construction

4 The subframe of *The Castle of the Emperor* (card IV)

3 + 5 *L'oiseau de feu* being sprayed with cement

4

5

6 *The Magician*, *The High Priestess* and *L'arbre de la vie* covered with cement

7 *The Tower* (card XVI), called 'The Falling Tower' or 'The Tower of Babel' by Niki de Saint Phalle, and *The Castle of the Emperor*

8 Rico Weber, Doc Winsen and others at work on the Tarot Garden

6

7

8

1 Mosaic is applied to *The Empress*

2 *The Tower* with one of Jean Tinguely's machines on top of it, and *The Castle of the Emperor*

1

2

3

4

3 *The Tower*, *The Chariot*, *The Castle of the Emperor*, *The Magician* and *The High Priestess*, which the artist herself calls 'Papesse' ('The Female Pope')

4 The top of *The Tower*, with Jean Tinguely's machine

5 View of *The Tower* from the roof terrace of *The Castle of the Emperor*

5

1

2

3

4

5

6

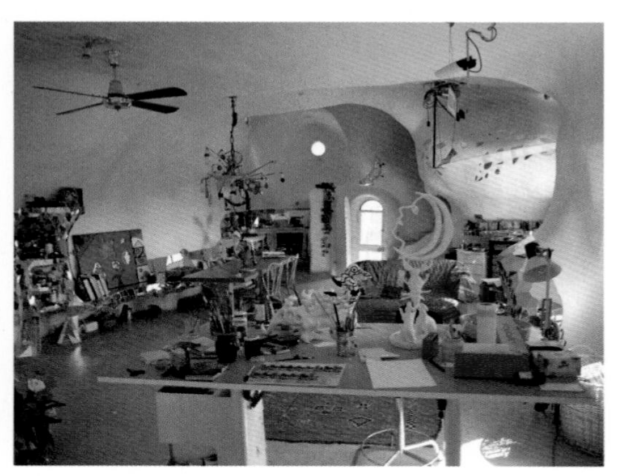
7

1–4 Ceramics for *The Empress*

5 *The Empress*

6 + 7 The interior of *The Empress* is used as a studio by Niki de Saint Phalle

8 Walkway between *The Empress* and *The Castle of the Emperor*

1 The bathroom inside *The Empress*

2 A view of *The Empress* from inside *The Tower*

3 Altar with Black Madonna inside the *Temperance* Chapel (card XIV)

1

2

3

4 The inner courtyard of
The Castle of the Emperor

5 + 6 Details of the
columns in the inner
courtyard of *The Castle of
the Emperor*

4

5

6

1 The *Temperance* Chapel

2 *The Castle of the Emperor*, *The Fool* (card 0), *The Magician*, *The High Priestess*, Jean Tinguely's *Wheel of Fortune* (card X), *Justice* (card VIII) and *L'arbre de la vie*

1

2

3 + 4 Details of *L'arbre de la vie*

3

4

5 *The Hierophant* (card V)

5

From 3 July to 1 September 1980 Niki de Saint Phalle has a major retrospective of her work at the Musée National d'Art Moderne at the Centre Georges Pompidou in Paris

1

2

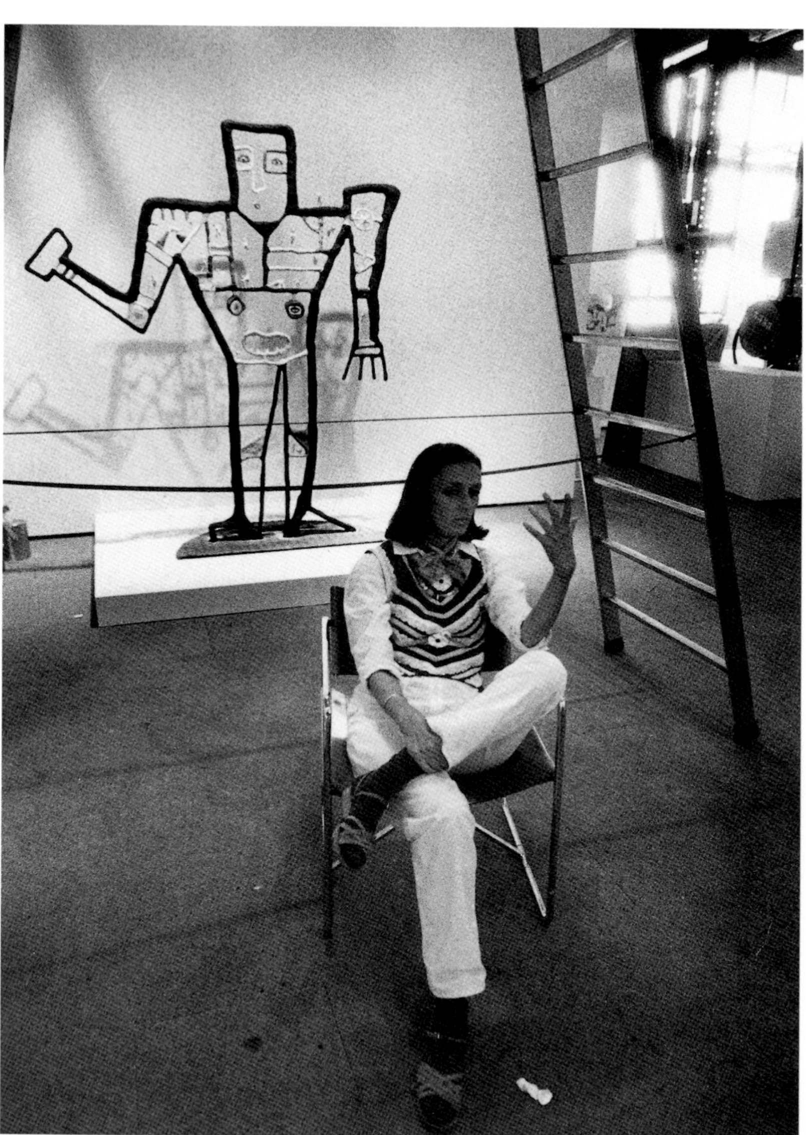

1 *La Waldaff, La promenade du Dimanche* and *Black Rosy*

2 Watched by Jean Tinguely, Niki de Saint Phalle is seen with one of her sculptures in the series, *Devouring Mothers*, during the installation of the exhibition. In the background is *L'oiseau amoureux*

3 Niki de Saint Phalle in front of *New Man is Coming*

4 Niki de Saint Phalle designs the exterior of a new twin- engine aeroplane, *Piper aérostar 602 P*, for the Peter Stuyvesant Foundation in Amsterdam. It takes part in the first transatlantic air race from Paris to New York and back, held on the night of 8/9 June 1981, and finishes in second place

In 1983 the Stuart Foundation of California awards Niki de Saint Phalle a commission for an outdoor sculpture, *Sun God*, for the campus at the University of California at San Diego

1–3 *Sun God* being installed

4 *Sun God*, height 10.50 metres

1

2

3

4

In 1982 the City of Paris commissions a fountain from Jean Tinguely and Niki de Saint Phalle for the Place Igor Stravinsky next to the Centre Georges Pompidou. The fountain is sited directly above IRCAM, the centre's subterranean music department, and consists of sixteen combined sculptural elements. Inspired by works by Igor Stravinsky, it is inaugurated on 16 March 1983

6

6 *Le cœur*

7 *La clef de sol*, *Ragtime* and *La spirale*

8 *L'amour*

5 Invitation by Niki de Saint Phalle and Jean Tinguely to an exhibition of works related to the fountain project

7

8

1

2

3

1 *L'éléphant*

2 *La mort*

3 View of the fountain, showing *Ragtime*, *La clef de sol*, *L'amour*, *Le rossignol*, *Le serpent*, *L'oiseau de feu* and *La spirale*

4 The fountain by night, with *Ragtime*, *Le cœur*, *Le serpent*, *La vie* and *L'oiseau de feu*

In 1982 Niki de Saint Phalle creates the perfume named after her for the New York firm of Jacqueline Cochran. The perfume is launched in Paris in 1984

1 Scent bottle with stopper in the shape of entwined serpents

2

Niki de Saint Phalle's first retrospective in Germany is held at the Kunsthalle der Hypo-Kulturstiftung, Munich, from 26 March to 21 June 1987

3

2 General view of the Kunsthalle showing *Les funérailles du père*, *Les baigneuses* and *Le témoin*

3 Keith Haring at the official opening of the exhibition, at which visitors were asked by the artist to wear hats

4 Niki de Saint Phalle at the opening

François Mitterrand invites Niki de Saint Phalle and Jean Tinguely to create a sculpture fountain for the Town Hall at Château-Chinon in Nièvre, where he was mayor for many years. The fountain, *Château-Chinon*, is unveiled on 10 March 1988

2

2 The installation of *Château-Chinon*

3 The installation of *Château-Chinon*; Niki de Saint Phalle's assistant, Marcelo Zitelli, can be seen on the extreme left, with Jean Tinguely's assistant, Sepp Imhof, second from right

4 Jean Tinguely and Niki de Saint Phalle during the installation

1 François Mitterrand, Niki de Saint Phalle and Jean Tinguely with the maquette of *Château-Chinon* as a cake

3

4

5

5 Jean Tinguely and Niki de Saint Phalle at the inauguration

6 Niki de Saint Phalle and François Mitterrand

7 A detail of *Château-Chinon*

6

7

1 Robert Haligon standing between his assistants at the installation of *Château-Chinon*

2 General view of *Château-Chinon*

1

2

3

3 Niki de Saint Phalle with Bernhard Luginbühl and his wife, Ursi, in the garden at Soisy

4 Jean Tinguely and Bernhard Luginbühl unloading *La tête de mort*

5 Niki de Saint Phalle and her Paris art dealer, Jean Gabriel Mitterrand

6 *La tête de mort* and *Obélisque*

7 *La tête de mort* in Niki de Saint Phalle's studio

4

5

6

7

Niki de Saint Phalle's first American retrospective was held at the Nassau County Museum of Fine Art at Roslyn, Long Island, between 27 September 1987 and 3 January 1988

3

1 General view of the exhibition, with *Black Venus*

2 *Gorgo in New York* and *Vénus de Milo*

3 Work on *La mort* in 1989

4 *La mort*

2

4

The two Paris art dealers, Catherine Thieck and Jean-Gabriel Mitterrand, organise a joint exhibition of works by Niki de Saint Phalle, *Œuvres des années 80*, which is held at their two galleries simultaneously: from 12 May to 17 June 1989 at the Galerie de France and from 12 May to 24 June at the JGM. Galerie

5

6

7

8

5 + 6 Niki de Saint Phalle at the installation

7 Niki de Saint Phalle with her sculpture, *Le champignon magique*

8 The Galerie de France, with *La main* and *Le diable*

2

2–4 Niki de Saint Phalle writing in the wet cement of the walkways

1 Marina Karella, Marcelo Zitelli, Sepp Imhof, Niki de Saint Phalle, Dorothée Bouveret, Philippe Bouveret and Jean Tinguely behind *Le monde* (card XXI) at the Commandery in Dannemois. One sculpture of the edition is now in the foyer at the Opéra-Bastille in Paris

3

4

5 Niki de Saint Phalle's new studio in the Tarot Garden, built in 1989

6 + 8 Niki de Saint Phalle and her assistants outside her studio, working on clay models of Egyptian gods

7 Tonio Urtis, Marco Iacotonio, Pierre-Marie Lejeune, Gigi Pecoraro and Gérard Haligon installing *Le monde*

9 Niki de Saint Phalle and Venera Finocchiaro in the artist's studio, while Marco Iacotonio works outside on *Anubis*

5

8

6

9

7

10 Ugo Celletti applying mirror mosaics to *The Empress*

Together with Professor Silvio Barandun, Niki de Saint Phalle writes and illustrates *AIDS: You Can't Catch It Holding Hands*. The first edition (of 500 copies) was published in English in 1986 by C.J. Bucher, Munich and Lucerne. In 1987 a second edition, in a larger print run, was published by Lapis Press, San Francisco and Santa Monica, California, while French, German, Italian and Japanese editions followed within the space of a year. In 1990 Niki de Saint Phalle collaborates with Philip Mathews on a revised edition and on a cartoon film, both of which are financed by the Agence française de lutte contre le sida, Paris

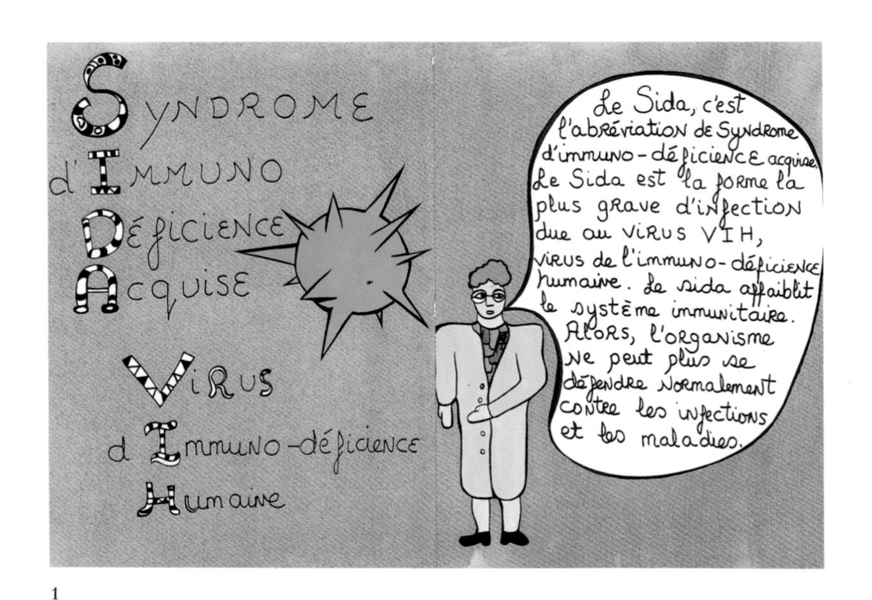

1

2

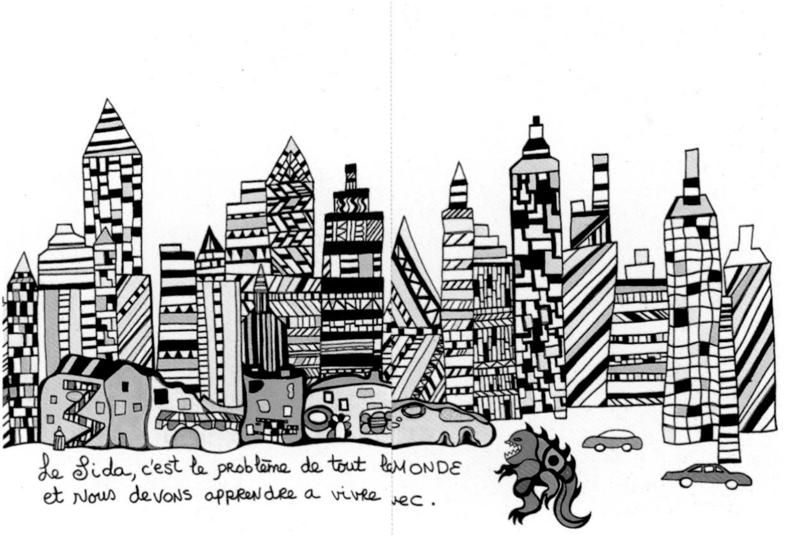

3

4

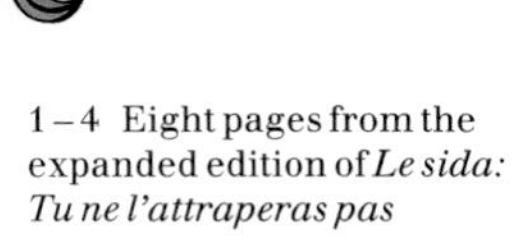
1–4 Eight pages from the expanded edition of *Le sida: Tu ne l'attraperas pas*

1 Large-scale model for *Le temple idéal*, an interdenominational church 16 metres high which will be built in Nîmes at the invitation of the local mayor, Jean Bousquet. It is planned to inaugurate the building in 1993

Letters

Niki de Saint Phalle's letters – an introduction

Uta Grosenick

'What do you like the most about me?', Niki de Saint Phalle asks in a volume of her illustrations, *My Love.*

What is it that constitutes the fascination of this artist's living works – a fascination that we can escape from only with difficulty?

The following autobiographical texts by Niki de Saint Phalle help to throw light on this question. At first sight they are letters, but they are letters which were never sent. In them Niki de Saint Phalle addresses herself to an imaginary correspondent. The letters are stories in which the artist takes friends into her confidence and tells them a chapter of her life story, a story in which they themselves have played a part.

Essentially, however, she is relating the episode to all who read it, to all who seek to understand her art and life. In this way people who appear not to be part of that life become participants in it.

With virtually no other artist of her generation are life and works so inextricably linked as is the case with Niki de Saint Phalle. Born in France, she received an upper-class American upbringing and even as a child rebelled against the woman's role that was marked out for her. Initially, however, she had no means of breaking out of such a role and, for a time, followed the course expected of her: she was barely nineteen when she married the young, good-looking and affluent Harry Mathews and within a matter of years was the mother of two young children. She grew so painfully conscious of the contradiction between her claims to independence and her day-to-day existence that she suffered a nervous breakdown and had to spend a period in hospital.

It was during her time in hospital that she returned to the oil painting which had previously been a spare-time activity, and her desire to become an artist helped her to overcome this emotional crisis in her life. At a later date she was to ask herself whether it was in these early oil paintings that all her future directions were already mapped out.

Niki de Saint Phalle's letters make it clear that every new period in her life is marked by a change of style in her work as an artist – which also means that every change in her work brings with it a previously unknown feeling of being alive.

Her personal liberation began long before there was any such thing as the 'women's movement', long before the term 'emancipation' was on everyone's lips.

Her first step was to acknowledge her own aggressions. To begin with, it was a passive form of acceptance in which she collected guns, knives and meat cleavers in order to create assemblages from them. In her imagination she used these murderous weapons to threaten all the men who were in a position to inhibit her emotionally or physically.

During the second stage she threw darts at pictorial representations of these men or shot at them with a rifle.

For Niki de Saint Phalle the process of shooting gained increasingly in importance, so that the male attributes of the symbols soon receded into relative insignificance. She shot all manner of objects, which she first turned into reliefs by means of plaster and paint bombs.

Her acceptance by the Nouveaux Réalistes and, not least, the international press's interest in her shooting sessions made it clear to Niki de Saint Phalle that she had already achieved her aim of becoming a 'professional artist'.

From now on she listened to her inner voices and considered the various roles of women in society, which she represented in reliefs and sculptures – brides, women giving birth, mothers, whores and witches.

For Niki de Saint Phalle, many different images of women merge in a single woman, whom she affectionately calls 'Nana' and of which she has produced innumerable examples. All female characteristics are combined in this one figure, which is a hymn to all women (and also to the artist herself).

As a child Niki de Saint Phalle had told herself that she would make 'the greatest sculptures' of her generation. They would be 'bigger and stronger than those of men'. With *Hon* this wish was realised.
In a letter to her friend Clarice Rivers she describes the way in which this monumental environment came into being.
Just as it was more or less by chance that *Hon* became the work of which Niki de Saint Phalle had been dreaming for many years, so her other works were created intuitively, on the basis of feeling, but always with the instinctive certainty that the time had come to create the sculpture in such and such a way rather than in any other.
Niki de Saint Phalle tries to describe this intuitive process in her stories, seeking to explain it not only to others but also to herself.
And then there is the long story of the creation of her Tarot Garden in Tuscany. Ever since she had first visited Gaudí's Güell Park in Barcelona and wandered through the fantastic Giardino di Bomarzo in central Italy, she had toyed with the idea of creating a similar park for herself. She would be the first woman to risk such a project, for which she would be her own patron. 'It's no accident that I'm creating this garden. There's a reason. My hand is being led. I'm following a course that was chosen for me, following a pressing need to show that a woman can work on a monumental scale.'
Niki de Saint Phalle is attracted by the idea of competing with men and of emerging as victor from this imaginary contest. To this end she deploys her own means, using soft, organic and curving forms. Her aesthetic outlook, however, is not feminist: it was only recently that she declined to take part in an exhibition at which only women artists were to be represented. She needs her work to be compared and contrasted with that of male artists: nothing else is acceptable to her.
It is her individual view of things which finds expression in Niki de Saint Phalle's letters: even a close friend would give a completely different version of the same event. Like her art, what she writes is wholly individual.
The reader senses that Niki de Saint Phalle's account of many events and emotions is straightforward and fluent, whereas other passages make for harder reading. Sometimes the reader will stop short involuntarily, just as Niki de Saint Phalle must have done when writing the passage.
Such passages deal with events from which she has not yet distanced herself. She was in the process of writing to Jean Tinguely when he died suddenly. For weeks she was incapable of continuing with her work or of going on with her writing. She was sufficiently strong-willed to complete the letter, but what were the thoughts that prompted her to do so?
'As always, I solved my problems through metamorphosis.' As so often before in Niki de Saint Phalle's life, the new situation coincided with a new phase in her work. For the first time she incorporated the moving hands and mechanism of a clock into a portrait of Jean Tinguely. Only a few months earlier it would never have entered her head to produce kinetic art, but now it gave her enormous pleasure to observe the moving parts. 'My new way of communicating with Jean is my "Méta-Tinguelys".'
'What do you like the most about me?' – Just the way you are, Niki!

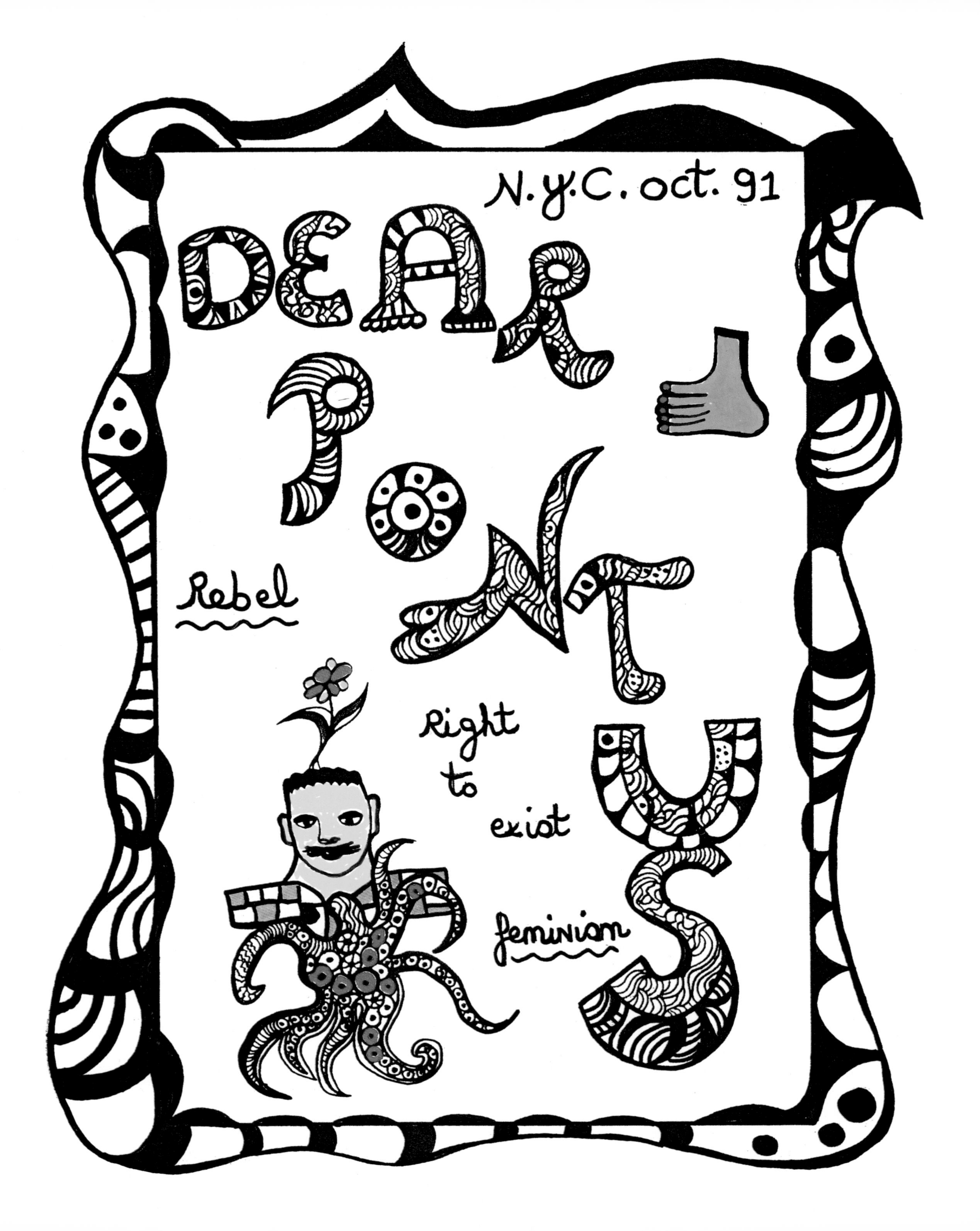
N.Y.C. oct. 91
DEAR
PONTUS
Rebel
Right
to
exist
feminism

Dear Pontus,

When does one start being a rebel? In the womb? At five? At ten?

I was born in 1930. A DEPRESSION BABY. While my mother was expecting me my father lost all their money. At the same time she discovered my father's INFIDELITY. She cried all through her pregnancy. I felt those TEARS.

Later she would tell me EVERYTHING WAS MY FAULT; I brought trouble.

Certain Tarot cards were dealt to me the day I was born. The Magician (card of creativity and energy) and the hanged man (card of permeability and sensitivity to everything and everyone). I was also handed the card of the moon (imagination and its counterpoint negative imagination).

These cards would become the material, the canvas, on which I would paint my life.

I would have to prove my mother WRONG! I would spend my life proving I had the RIGHT TO EXIST. I would one day make her proud of me by becoming famous and rich. It was my capacity to achieve that was important for me to prove. One day I would make the biggest sculpture garden since Gaudi's park in Barcelona.

O.K., perhaps I had brought down the fall of the Saint Phalle bank, but I would become much more famous than my father's bank.

Yes, I would prove my mother WRONG. I would also prove my mother RIGHT.

One day I would do something unpardonable. The very worst thing a woman can do. I would abandon my children for my work. I would give myself a good reason to feel guilty.

As a child I could not identify with my mother or my grandmother, my aunts or my mother's friends. They seemed a pretty unhappy lot. Our home was confining. A narrow space with little liberty or privacy. I didn't want to become like them, guardians of the hearth, I wanted the world and the world then belonged to MEN. A women could be queen bee in the home but that was it. The roles men and women were allotted were subjected to very strict rules on either side.

When my father left the apartment after breakfast at 8:30 every morning he was free (so I thought). He had the right to two lives, one outside, the other inside the home.

I wanted the outside world to be mine also. Very early I got the message that MEN HAD POWER AND I WANTED IT.

YES, I WOULD STEAL THEIR FIRE FROM THEM. I would not accept the boundaries that my mother tried to impose on my life because I was a woman.

No, I would trespass into the world of men which seemed to me adventurous, mysterious, exciting. My optimistic nature helped me then as it still does today.

To an optimist nothing seems impossible. I wanted heroines to identify with. In school, history class was a long recital of the superiority of the male species and this annoyed me tremendously. We did learn about a few women – Catherine the Great, Joan of Arc, Elizabeth of England. But there weren't enough heroines. I wanted more. SO I STARTED DREAMING ABOUT BEING A HEROINE.

I had already identified with the hero in the innumerable fairy tales my grandmother read me. The hero was ALWAYS a boy and always a fool.

The hero, by listening to his inner voice and never losing sight of the final goal, would eventually, after many difficulties, find the treasure he was seeking.

I did not want to reject my mother entirely. I retained things from her that have given me a lot of pleasure – my love of clothes, fashion, hats, dressing up, mirrors. My mother had lots of mirrors in her house. Years later, mirrors would become one of the main materials I would use in the "Tarot Garden" in Italy and "The Cyclops" in the Forest of Fontainebleau outside of Paris. My mother was a great lover of music, art, good food and had a certain style and charm. These things I took from her and they helped me to stay in touch with a certain part of my femininity.

I liked my mother's looks, I liked the power it gave her, I liked her Chanel No. 5 perfume, her 1930 glass dressing table covered with creams and powders and lipsticks. I loved her auburn curls and her flawless white skin. She looked like Merle Oberon, a well-known actress.

I saw this beautiful creature, my mother, whom I was a bit in love with (when I didn't feel like killing her) as a prisoner of an imposed role. A role handed down generation after generation by a long tradition she never questioned.

Men's roles seem to give them a great deal more freedom, and I WAS RESOLVED THAT FREEDOM WOULD BE MINE.

My brother, John, was encouraged to develop his brain. Achievement as a possible choice for me was denied. I felt jealous and resentful that the only power allotted to me was the power of attracting men. It didn't really matter whether I studied or not as long as I passed my exams. It became clear that my virginity, looks, charm, and a certain social veneer were more important. My mother's desire was that I should marry a rich and socially acceptable man.

As a young girl I not only refused my mother and father as models for future behavior, I also refused their social position. The only room in the house I found comfort and warmth was in the kitchen with our black cook.

At the age of eight all my pocket money went to buying Wonderwoman or Batman comics. (I was forbidden to read them so they were hidden under my mattress.) Quite a bit of the money I stole from my father and my grandmother went to beggars. I liked beggars. They seemed somehow more real than a lot of people that walked the streets of New York City. This was 1940 and I was ten years old.

I went to the convent of the Sacred Heart School for Girls on 91st Street.

Each week (or was it each month?) a beautiful red ribbon was given for excellence in work. I never got it (not surprising as I never worked). One day I decided to go out and buy myself a red ribbon which I put on my uniform as though I had won the prize. This was not appreciated.

The uniform at school was green, a dark ugly green with a beige blouse and green tie. No wonder I was longing for the red sash.

Christmas time 1940 the nuns took us to HARLEM to bring gifts for poor black families.

How embarrassed I felt for them. The nun made some ridiculous speech; we stood around (there must have been ten of us) while two black ladies thanked us. I remember thinking if I were them. I would hate us. I felt ashamed.

The streets of New York with its misery and its excitement was a real school of life.

In the street we spoke English while at home French was spoken. French educational values for children at that time said that children should be seen and not heard. No nonsense. Everything must be finished on one's plate. If I answered back (and I often did) I would get slapped across the face (a common practice at that time).

I was exposed to diverse and sometimes CONFLICTING cultural influences which pushed me very early to make up my own mind about things. I chose what I wanted to believe.

My Aunt Joy (from Georgia) on the American side of the family was a sweet old lady who used to spoil me – read fairy tales to me and take me to a lot of soda fountains. I was a fanatical fan of chocolate butterscotch sundaes. These outings sometimes ended in drama. If there was anyone BLACK there, my Aunt Joy would beat a hasty retreat. For me they were people. BLACK white and yellow didn't exist.

Why wasn't I allowed to sit next to a black lady when at home we had a black cook whom I considered a great FRIEND?

After rejecting my parents and their social class, I would be FACED WITH THE ENORMOUS PROBLEM OF REINVENTING AND RECREATING MYSELF. To add to the problem, I had no clear national feelings. I felt half French, half American.

Also half man and half woman.

What saved me during those difficult adolescent years was an IMAGINARY SECRET MAGIC BOX I kept under the bed. It was made of fine carved wood inlaid with enamel of the brightest colors.

NO ONE BUT ME COULD SEE THIS BOX.

When I was alone I would open it up and all kinds of extraordinary colored fish, genies, and wild sweet smelling flowers would come tumbling out.

In this box which was my very own I kept my first poems, my first dreams of grandeur.

THE BOX WAS MY SPIRITUAL HOME. The beginning of a life of my own where they, my parents, could not intrude. In the box I put my soul. I started having conversations with it. As I could not relate in a profound way with my family, I started communicating with myself. From this came a lifelong need for SOLITUDE. It is there in that solitude, alone, that my ideas for my work come. It is as necessary for my creation as air for my lungs.

Still today, Pontus, my magic box is under my bed. I open it up everyday. My structure, my backbone, my skeleton are in the box.

Sometimes it is filled with sand and I become five years old again and make castles and dream palaces.

My box makes up for the adult world, which I have learned with difficulty to deal with, but which I am not too crazy about.

The box has kept me from becoming a cynic and disillusioned.

It is Pandora's box. What remains in it is Hope.

Printemps 90
Cher JEAN
qui est le monstre toi ou moi ?

Dear Jean,

I remember very well meeting you and Eva for the first time in 1955. I was 25 years old. I immediately fell in love with your work. Your studio looked like a huge pile of iron garbage hiding wonderful treasures.

A long, black and white moving relief was hanging on the back wall of your studio. It had a little hammer hitting a bottle and numerous little wheels with wires which were trembling and turning. I had never seen anything like it and I was crazy about it.

Harry and I didn't have much money but we decided to buy it. You were very pleased: you and Eva had just enough to eat and work. You used to steal the coal to heat your studio in winter from the piles behind the hospital adjacent to l'Impasse Ronsin where you lived.

Your dealer at the time, used to buy your entire production. For this she gave you less than $ 100 a month, starvation wages.

In your studio there was a ladder which one climbed up and there received a fantastic surprise. Eva had installed in her space perched near the skylight a wonderful world of her own. She had made her first big sculpture in cloth with extraordinary embroidery. She would soon make my portrait.

You liked my paintings, which you took seriously, and also my badly drawn projects on little bits of paper. I drew projects of my future architecture which I showed you. One of them was a chapel, and you said you would put in motion all the sculptures of the Stations of the Cross.

I talked to you about Gaudi and about the Facteur Cheval whom I had just discovered and who were my heroes, and the beauty of man alone in his folly without any intermediaries, without museums, without galleries. You were against this idea, you thought art ought to be in society, not outside of it. Then I provoked you by saying that the Facteur Cheval was a much greater sculptor than you.

"I never heard of that idiot," you said. "Let's go and see him right away," you persisted.

We did and you felt a tremendous satisfaction with this creative outsider and you told me: "You're right. He's a greater sculptor than me."

You were seduced by the poetry and fanaticism of this little postman who realized his insane, immense dream.

Jean, you were very good looking. You walked like a panther and you had those magnetic eyes which you knew very well how to use. A very handsome, dark, dangerous looking man.

I was in love with my husband, Harry Mathews, and I was amused to see you with other women. For me, you were a great seducer. You told me all your techniques about how to seduce women. If you didn't have money often you'd go to one in a cafe and say,

"Please buy me a cup of coffee." Women enjoyed helping a starving artist.
We had formed a real friendship based on our mutual passion for art.

Eva and you formed a unique couple. Each one as original as the other. Eva had a young lover who lived with you, and your favorite girlfriend liked Eva very much. There was a great complicity between you and Eva and a great love which you lived in your own way.

In 1955 I wanted to make my first sculpture. It was natural that I asked you to weld a structure in iron on which I would put plaster. You borrowed some oxygen bottles – you weren't welding yet.

The sculpture looked like a tree gone crazy. In its branches were stuck all kinds of objects including multicolored, feathered bait for fish, colored papers, and paint. I had used the fireplace in the bedroom of my two small children, Laura and Philip, as a base. My first sculpture would be for them. Unfortunately, a sculptor friend who later rented the apartment saw fit to destroy it.

It was around 1959 that you spoke to me about Yves Klein, Marcel Duchamp and Daniel Spoerri. Until then Hugh Weiss had been my mentor. He encouraged me not to go to art school. I trusted him; the many museums and cathedrals I visited became my art school.

At the same time there was a great huge show of American art in Paris. For the first time I saw Jackson Pollock, de Kooning etc...
I was completely bowled over. My paintings suddenly seemed very little in comparison. This was to be my first big artistic crisis. I'd resolve this in the same way I always would in the future: metamorphosis.

I started making reliefs of imaginary landscapes with objects, and had stopped painting in oils and used gouache and lacquer paints, bought toys in stores, and found objects at the flea market. These were mainly objects of violence like a hatchet, knives, and guns. Sometimes I would put in other things such as a shoe. It was fun, exciting. I liked this new, immediate way of expressing myself instead of the months of slow, patient work on my oil paints.

I showed you my new works, Jean; you liked them very much. You took me to see Daniel Spoerri's work which fascinated me. He captured life by gluing tables that had been eaten on. This attitude towards art, which was new to me, was stimulating. You then introduced me to Arman and Yves Klein.

One day I got into a fight with Daniel Spoerri. When he saw one of my reliefs on which I put nails to represent a rocket he said, "Why didn't you use a real rocket?"
It was part of the New Realists philosophy to use only found objects. This annoyed me. Why make rules? I slapped him. Obviously it hit home.

It was also at this time I met the painters Joan Mitchell and Jean Paul Riopelle. I was mortified because Joan didn't take me seriously as an artist. For her I was a married woman who was painting. I didn't have a gallery so I wasn't a professional. Joan fired my ambition and my desire to prove myself to the world by treating me like the wife of a writer. I thought my paintings were just as good as hers and her painter friends, and I also wanted to prove to them that I existed.

Meeting this group of artists fueled my desire to live the artistic adventure to the hilt without the marvelous equilibrium which I'd found between my work, Harry and my children. I owe a lot to Joan Mitchell because she was the person who pushed me to live my art to the hilt.

I was never bored with Harry for one moment in the 11 years we lived together. I loved my children and my work, my life was filled. A refrain, however, kept coming through my head from time to time: Paradise... How I'd like to descend into HELL and you know HELL! Maybe intense painful reminiscences from the past were creeping up. I didn't want to stay in HELL but I wanted to go down into the DEPTHS.

There were times when I used to dream about leaving this almost perfect life that I had made such an effort to build with Harry.

I started to talk to Harry about separating and living alone for a year or two, to go to the end of my potential as an artist. I felt I needed solitude.

Harry wasn't happy, but he never did anything to hold me back. He had many weapons he could have used, like the children. Perhaps he had too much respect for me and my art to use them.

I had a brief love affair with a well known artist at the time who was running after me. He was married or at any rate he was living with someone and his specialty was to break up couples and seduce the wives of friends. I wasn't in love with him but he held me in a certain way. I didn't like this dependence so I bought a gun to kill him symbolically. There were no bullets in the gun. The revolver was in my handbag and it made me feel better.

One day I had the idea to do his portrait. I bought a target in a toy shop, a target to throw darts at, and I asked him if he would give me one of his shirts. Then I put a tie on it. All of this was glued on wood. I called it "Portrait of my Lover". I started to have fun by throwing darts at his head. It was successful therapy because I began to detach myself from him.

You came to my studio one day with Daniel Spoerri. You both saw this relief and were crazy about it and decided immediately to use it in a new exhibition where the New Realists were shown. I was delighted.

There was a lot of aggression in me that was starting to come out at this time; one night at "La Coupôle", which was still only a cafe-brasserie where artists used to hang out in Paris, I was with Jean Paul Riopelle and Joan Mitchell. Giacometti was at the table; later Saul Steinberg arrived. It was quite late at night. He started coming on too obviously. I didn't like it and I felt humiliated by his exaggerated attention. But I liked his great mustache.

He was carefully and extravagantly dressed. He had on a beautiful grey cape. A great uncontrolled violence suddenly surged up in me. So I took a glass of beer that was on the table and threw it at his head. Giacometti was so thrilled by my doing this that he kissed me on the mouth and spent four or five hours talking to me.

Giacometti talked about art and about his hatred for Picasso. I've always been a great admirer of Picasso and was amazed by the hatred he aroused in many important artists. Picasso was very important to me. I liked his immense freedom with materials and his continual research. His changing of styles stimulated me. For everyone else, at the time, it was Duchamp YES, Picasso NO. I always liked both, and Matisse too.

I started putting my violence into my work. I made reliefs of death and desolation. One of them had the revolver which I had bought to symbolically kill my lover. The moon in these reliefs was always black, with images of violence. Yes, I was starting to descend into HELL.

I started living alone. Harry generously bought my paintings which permitted me to live very modestly. I was able to work on my art all day long without getting a job. It seemed logical for the children to stay with Harry as I didn't have enough money to look after them. I went to see the three of them often.

Daniel Spoerri started to court me. I wasn't indifferent to his charm. He looked like Louis Jouvet, whom I found attractive. You were Daniel's best friend and I noticed that you didn't like this very much.

You and Eva had separated. Eva was going to New York City to join a brilliant and rather crazy scientist, Billy Klüver. Two days before she was to leave I presented her to a great friend of mine, Sam Mercer, who was a lawyer and painter, full of charm, originality and surprises. It was love at first sight for them. She decided to remain in France and live with Sam. She moved into Sam's apartment a week later. I was very happy because I didn't like the idea of Eva being so far away. I was also proud of my match-making.

Jean, I used to see you often at this time. You would come by and I would accompany you to the iron yard and choose pieces that excited you. We continued our interminable discussions on art. You talked to me a lot about the Dadaists. You and Yves Klein saw the Abstract Expressionists as the enemy to be defeated. You wanted your vision of the universe to replace theirs.

The day of my 30th birthday, October 29th, 1960, Harry bought me a gorgeous white curly lamb wool jacket. I looked very spectacular and Jean and Daniel were enthusiastic. I was very proud of my new jacket. Daniel invited me to have dinner with him. I accepted with pleasure and I asked myself: would he be my next lover? When Daniel turned his back, Jean, you came to me and said, "I forbid you to go out with him."

I was very surprised and replied, "Why?"

"I want you to have dinner with me," you said.

I didn't want to break the friendship between you and Daniel nor mine with you. I responded,

"OK, but what do I tell him?"

"Just lie, invent anything."

I saw in your eyes that something had changed. You looked at me differently. I asked you,

"What is it? What's going on?"

You continued, "I can't bear the idea of his going out with you in that beautiful coat. I like it even less than the idea of his touching you."

Two days later I didn't resist your eyes anymore. You were looking at me in this new way I found very disturbing. We didn't leave each other anymore. (It's sometimes dangerous to buy too beautiful clothes for your wife.)

I wanted to be independent, FREE. I had no intentions of becoming a couple. I saw myself rather as a Mata Hari of art having plenty of adventures and eventually returning to Harry a year or two later.

Life, however, is never the way one imagines it. It surprises you, it amazes you and it makes you laugh or cry when you don't expect it.

REMEMBER 1960-61-62?
Dear
Cher
Pontus
PERFORMANCE
PARTICIPATION
BANG
darts
target
cible
ACTION
RAGE
VIOLENCE
MANS SHIRt
mis a mort
PORTRAIT OF MY LOVER
ROUGE
smoke
DEATH
REBIRTH
GUN
tABLEAUX tir
SURPRISE
SHOOTING PAINTINGS

Dear Pontus,

You asked me about the Shooting Paintings.

One Spring day in 1961 I was visiting the Salon de Comparisons exhibition in Paris. A relief of mine was hanging in the show. It was called "Portrait of my Lover".

There were darts on the table for spectators to throw at the man's head. I was thrilled to see people throw the darts and become part of my sculpture. Near my work, there hung a completely white plaster relief by an artist named Bram Bogart. Looking at it – FLASH! I imagined the painting bleeding – wounded; the way people can be wounded. For me, the painting became a person with feelings and sensations.

What if there were paint behind the plaster? I told Jean Tinguely about my vision and my desire to make a painting bleed by shooting at it. Jean was crazy about the idea; he suggested I start right away.

There was some plaster at l'Impasse Ronsin. We found an old board then bought some paint at the nearest store. We hammered nails into the wood to give the plaster something to hold on to, then I went wild and not only put in paint but anything else that was lying around, including spaghetti and eggs.

When 5 or 6 reliefs had been finished, Jean thought it was time to find a gun. We didn't have enough money to buy one so we went to a fairground in the Boulevard Pasteur and convinced the man at the shooting stand to rent us his gun. It was a .22 long rifle with real bullets which would pierce the plaster, hit the paint in little plastic bags embedded inside the relief, causing the paint to trickle down through the hole made by the bullet, and color the outside surface. The man from the shooting stand insisted on coming along. Maybe he was afraid we wouldn't return his gun.

We had to wait a couple of days before he came which, of course, added to the excitement and gave us time to invite a few friends including Shunk and Kender, photographer friends who documented the first shoot-out. Jean also invited Pierre Restany who then and there decided, while watching red, blue, green, rice, spaghetti, and eggs (where was the yellow?), to include me among the New Realists. I was getting a great kick out of provoking society through ART. No victims.

We took turns shooting. It was an amazing feeling shooting at a painting and watching it transform itself into a new being. It was not only EXCITING and SEXY, but TRAGIC – as though one were witnessing a birth and a death at the same moment. It was a MYSTERIOUS event that completely captivated anyone who shot.

We nailed the reliefs to a back wall of l'Impasse Ronsin. There was a long, grassy field in front of the wall which gave us plenty of room to shoot.

L'Impasse Ronsin was situated near the Hôpital des Enfants Malades in the middle of Paris, just off the rue Vaugirard. Brancusi still lived there and Max Ernst had previously lived in these little ramshackle studios. They were a poetic group of little shacks with no water or bathrooms.

Today it seems quite incredible that one was able to shoot freely in the middle of Paris. A retired cop who lived nearby came and watched the shoot-outs as soon as he heard the shooting begin! He liked these events and never asked about a gun permit – this was in the middle of the Algerian war!

For the next six months I experimented by mixing rubbish and objects with colors. I forgot about the spaghetti and rice and started concentrating on making the shooting paintings more spectacular. I started to use cans of spray paint, which, when hit by a bullet made extraordinary effects. These were very much like the Abstract Expressionist paintings that were being done at that time. I discovered that when paint fell on objects, the result could be dramatic. I used tear-gas for the grand finale of my shooting performances. Performance art did not yet exist but this was a performance.

The smoke gave the impression of war. The painting was the victim. WHO was the painting? Daddy? All Men? Small Men? Tall Men? Big Men? Fat Men? Men? My brother JOHN? Or was the painting ME? Did I shoot at myself during a RITUAL which enabled me to die by my own hand and be reborn? I was immortal!

The new bloodbath of red, yellow, and blue splattered over the pure white relief metamorphosized the painting into a tabernacle for DEATH and RESURRECTION. I was shooting at MYSELF, society with its INJUSTICES. I was shooting at my own violence and the VIOLENCE of the times. By shooting at my own violence, I no longer had to carry it inside of me like a burden. During the two years I spent shooting I was not sick one day. It was great therapy for me.

The ritual of painting a relief over and over again in immaculate virginal white was very important to me. The theatricality of the whole performance appealed to me immensely.

It was late Spring 1961 that I met Jasper Johns and Robert Rauschenberg. They had already met Jean Tinguely at the time of his homage to New York at the MoMA. We soon became friends. I found both of them gorgeous and was fascinated by their being a couple. They had a grace that comes with beauty allied with exceptional talent and intelligence. It was electrifying being with them.

I made an homage to Jasper. It was a relief with a target and a light bulb painted in his colors. I asked him to finish it by shooting. He took hours deciding where to shoot the few shots he finally fired at the target. Bob Rauschenberg, however, shot his piece in a few minutes and screamed, "Red! Red! I want more red!"

Bob had a particular way of talking about art and its relationship to life that was expressed with such clarity and passion that it would linger inside of me for many years and become a part of me.

Jasper and Bob invited Jean and me to participate with them in a David Tudor concert which was to be given at the American Embassy. The music was by John Cage. I was very excited and proud to be involved in a project with artists that I admired so much. Jasper decided, after much thought, that he would have a target made of flowers. Bob worked on stage during the entire performance creating a painting the audience never saw; when it was finished he wrapped it up in a sheet and carried it away. David Tudor spent most of the time under the piano.

Jean made a sexy machine called 'Striptease'. Over the course of the musical evening the machine shed various parts until all that was left was the motor. I prepared a shooting painting which was shot at by a professional shooter – David was afraid I might kill him by mistake!

The audience, except for Leo Castelli and a few fans, was not nearly as enthusiastic about the concert as we were. As a matter of fact, they hissed and booed and a lot of people left before the end. We found the hostility and the anger stimulating.

I think it was around February or March of 1960 that I met you, Pontus. Jean had told me a great deal about you and I also knew that you were the director of the Moderna Museet in Stockholm so I was in awe of meeting you. You quickly put me at ease. Whenever there was something to twiddle or play with, like a piece of string lying on the table, it was irresistible to you and you would pick it up and play with it for hours. I understood you were one of us.
Your enthusiasm for the shooting paintings was a great support to me. At the time I was being attacked by the newspapers constantly.

The first time you visited my studio in rue Alfred Durand Claye, you spent hours looking at my old paintings. I had disowned them thinking they were no longer interesting. We argued about this but I was secretly very pleased that you liked them. A few years later you would buy one for the museum.

It was June 1961 that I had my first one-man show in Paris at the Galerie J. I was finishing 'The Shooting Stand' on the day of the show. Visitors would be allowed to shoot at a painting. Three reliefs would be prepared and shot at during the show. Jean had put a big sheet of rusty iron behind the reliefs to protect the wall and a contraption to catch the paint that ran down from the painting so that it wouldn't drip to the floor. Jeannine de Goldschmidt, the gallery owner and Pierre Restanys' wife, stayed marvelously calm during the proceedings and it seemed not to bother her at all that there would be shooting every day in her gallery with a .22 long rifle (by that time we had found the money to buy a gun).

An hour before the show opened an elderly man with a degenerate face came in and asked, "When can I shoot?" I explained he would have to wait a bit until we had finished hanging the show.
"Why don't you come back in a little while?"
"No, I'm not going to leave. I'm going to stay right here until I can shoot."
Every ten minutes he would ask, "Can I shoot Now?" I finally got annoyed and went over quietly to Jeannine and implored, "Can't you find some nice way of getting rid of that guy. He's a nuisance." Jeannine declared, "Are you kidding? That is Fautrier!" I was a fan of Fautrier's work even though his preoccupation with paint and space were very far from mine. I came back to him and said, "O.K. you can start shooting." Later, when the crowd started arriving, he had difficulty giving up the gun. He kept shooting at the center and was trying to make one of his own paintings out of the shooting. When someone else was taking a shot he would scream, "The center, the center! Shoot at the center!"

My other fellow artists were also fascinated by the fact that by shooting at a painting they could finish a work of art. They, too, were caught up in the spellbinding dynamics of the shooting paintings, a feeling as indescribable as making love. Bob Rauschenberg thrilled me by buying a sculpture of mine at the opening night show.

Autumn 1961, Larry Rivers moved into one of the studios at l'Impasse. He was there with his new bride, Clarice. I would go and chat with them often. Jean was suspicious of these people he didn't know and refused to meet them. When Jean felt I had been chatting with them too long, he would take my gun and start shooting in the air. I knew it was time to come home. One day he could no longer resist the smell of Clarice's homemade soup which won him over; after that we had lunch with them everyday. We almost lost their friendship, however, by forgetting to warn them that we were going to use the front of their house to shoot at my new relief with a small cannon Jean had just built. By mistake, Jean mixed in a little too much gunpowder with the paint in the cannon. When the cannon hit the relief, the entire house shook. Larry came out screaming, "What are you trying to do, kill us?" After much apologizing, our friendship was saved and we continued to enjoy our great lunches together.

Why did I give up the shooting after only two years? I felt like a drug addict. After a shoot-out I felt completely stoned. I became hooked on this macabre yet joyous ritual. It got to the point where I lost control, my heart was pounding during the shoot-outs. I started trembling before and during the performance. I was in an ecstatic state.

I don't like losing control. It scares me and I hate the idea of being addicted to something – so I gave it up. I was tempted to return to shooting when I suffered extreme depression and also while I had rheumatoid arthritis and could hardly walk.

I wanted to shoot my way out of the disease. I decided against it because I wasn't able to think of a new way to make the shooting paintings and I didn't want to do the same thing I had already done. IT HAD TO BE NEW OR NOT BE, so I gave up the idea.

It was also hard to give up all the attention in newspapers and newsreels I was getting from the shooting. Here I was, an attractive girl (if I had been ugly, they would have said I had a complex and not paid any attention) screaming against men in my interviews and shooting with a gun. This was before the women's liberation movement and was very scandalous.

It was not surprising that hardly anyone bought these works and they mainly belong to me today. Bill Seitz from the MoMA made a statement that my attitude was harmful to art and that I had set back modern art by 30 years!

From provocation, I moved into a more interior, feminine world. I started making brides, hearts, women giving birth, the whore – various roles women have in society.

A new adventure had started.

Autumn 1966

Dear Clarice

PAGAN GODDESS

THE GREAT MOTHER

(THE HON)

Dearest Clarice,

You asked me what it was like working and making the HON, the BIGGEST NANA I ever made. She was 90 feet long, 18 feet high, 27 feet wide. Pontus Hulten, director of the Moderna Museet in Stockholm asked me to go there in the Spring of 1966 with Tinguely, Martial Raysse and Oldenburg to build a monumental sculpture in the big hall of the museum. Martial Raysse declined the invitation. Oldenburg couldn't come at the last moment and Jean had just started some new work in Soisy and wasn't in the mood. It looked as though the whole project would fall through, but a secret voice kept telling me that I must go, that it was important. I listened.

The first few days we met in Stockholm were unsatisfactory. My enthusiasm convinced Jean to come also and many ideas were tossed about by Jean, Pontus, myself and the Swedish artist who joined us, Per Olof Ultvedt. Pontus suggested we all go to Moscow for a few days (Jean and I had never been there) and either the city or the vodka would inspire us. We were about to buy our tickets when Pontus had a brainstorm. EUREKA! He suggested we build a huge, penetrable Nana that would be so large she would take up the entire hall of the museum. We suddenly became very excited. We knew we were entering the sacred land of myth. We were about to build a goddess. A great PAGAN goddess.

As you, Clarice, were the original Nana, consider yourself the model for the GREAT GODDESS.

Jean assumed the technical direction of a team of volunteers that Pontus found for us. One of them was Rico Weber, a young Swiss artist, who was to remain afterwards as assistant collaborator for Jean and me for many years. Rico was working as cook at the snack bar of the museum. We had six weeks to produce our huge giantess and must have worked 16 hours a day. We named our Goddess HON which means SHE in Swedish. I made the original small model that gave birth to the goddess. Jean, by measuring with eyes only, was able to enlarge the model in an iron frame and have it look exactly like the original. After the chassis had been welded, chicken wire was attached to the immense surface of the Goddess. I cooked, in huge pots, a mass of stinking rabbit skin glue on small electric heaters. Yards of sheet material were mixed with the glue and then placed on the metal skeleton. Several layers were necessary to hide the frame. I often felt like a medieval witch brewing this glue. When the sheets dried and were stuck to the metal, we painted the body of the Goddess white. I then made my design using the original model with some modifications. Later, with the help of Rico Weber, I painted the sculpture. Pontus worked night and day sawing and hammering and participating in every way he could with us. Meanwhile, Jean and Ultvedt were occupied with filling the inside of the body of the Goddess with all kinds of entertainment. Jean made a planetarium in her left breast and a milk bar in the right breast. In one arm was shown the first short movie starring Greta Garbo, and in a leg was a gallery of fake paintings (a fake Paul Klee, Jackson Pollock, etc.)

The reclining Nana was pregnant and by a series of stairs and steps you could get to the terrace from her tummy where you could have a panoramic view of the approaching visitors and her gaily painted legs. There was nothing pornographic about the HON even though she was entered by her sex.

Pontus knew he had embarked on a perilous venture with this great lady and decided to keep the entire project secret. Otherwise, the authorities might hear distorted rumors and shut the show before it opened. We constructed a giant screen, behind which we worked; no one was allowed to see what we were doing.

I remember laughing with Pontus many times about enjoying his last moments at the museum before he was asked to leave by an outraged Cultural Minister. He was willing to take the risk as he always does when he believes in something. Pontus Hulten had already brought many innovative artists to Stockholm. He was the first to show Jasper Johns, he bought Rauschenberg's "Goat". He arranged for Jackson Pollock to be seen in Sweden and for John Cage to give his first concert which everyone left horrified.

During this time I was painting the HON like an Easter egg with the very bright, pure colors I have always used and loved. She was like a grand fertility goddess receiving comfortably in her immensity and generosity. She received, absorbed, and devoured thousands of visitors. It was an incredible experience creating her. This joyous, huge creature represented for many visitors and me the dream of the return to the Great Mother. Whole families flocked together with their babies to see her.

The HON had a short but full life. She existed for three months and then was destroyed. The HON took up all the space of the big hall of the museum and was never meant to stay. Wicked tongues said she was the biggest whore in the world because she had 100,000 visitors in three months.

A Stockholm psychiatrist wrote in the newspaper that the HON would change people's dreams for years to come. The birth rate in Stockholm went up that year. This was attributed to her.

The HON had something magical about her. She couldn't help but make you feel good. Everyone who saw her broke into a smile.

Chére
MARINA
champagne
suicide
glacieR
floweR

Dear Marina,

During these years in St. Moritz I fell in love with a glacier. I cannot remember the name of it anymore but I remember exactly what it looked like. Maybe you remember there are many glaciers in Switzerland and this particular one struck my fancy.

It took about an hour's walk to get to it. I must have walked there a hundred times. Then I wrote a film script about it. The subject was an artist and his preoccupation with time, accelerated time, metaphysical time, the merging of times.

In the end the artist walks in the glacier knowing his youth there will be both captured and eternal.

I became fascinated with the idea of committing the perfect suicide, the way someone in an Agatha Christie novel would feel fascinated by committing the perfect crime. I would prepare a picnic. I went for days fantasizing on what would be my last meal. I would take great care in wearing lots of very warm clothing, makeup, have my hair done in the afternoon. Bring a very pretty blanket, a flashlight, the Duino Elegies and no one would ever know (my plan had to be diabolically clever otherwise Eva or Jean or you might guess and feel awful).

It must be beautiful. A work of art.

So in my pocket I would slip in just a few sleeping pills, the glacier would do the rest. I would be found fast asleep and frozen in the morning. And I would look beautiful in the morning when they found me.

My plan was to go out to the glacier around midnight. Have a last meal, I had finally decided on caviar and Dom Perignon, pop the sleeping pills in my mouth, read with the help of my flashlight the 4th Duino Elegy and join the stars.
Those that loved me knowing how crazy I was about the glacier would just think Niki had gone there for a midnight snack and fallen asleep drinking champagne. They wouldn't be surprised.

Two days before THE FINAL DAY I came down with pneumonia and was taken to hospital in Bern.

You came to see me. I couldn't talk for three days I was so depressed. My search for infinity brought me to the edge of the precipice.

Living alone high in the Engadine mountains I spent my time reading Nietzsche and Bachelard.

There was no reason to live alone. I chose this Spartan existence which went against my rather accessible, open and gay nature and I started to burn like a fire. My solitude gave me an ecstatic drunkenness. Passion was more than Existence.

Like the phoenix that needs to go through the destructive fire with his body to be reborn so I tormented myself with my will to go to the end of the experience.

Not only my mind, but my body took fire. Only through suffering and sacrifice did I feel free. I wanted to fly like a bird and discover infinity.

I have always chosen moments of great intensity instead of durability.

My art as my love will be sacrificed on the infernal burning altar. Remember? Your hair turned into snakes.

June 1990
Dearest Chère, Marella,
le magicien
the MAGiCiEN
le JARDiN DES TAROT
CARd NO. 1
The tarot garden
MiROiRS, VERRE, CERAMiQUE

Dear Marella,

Whoever would have guessed that meeting you and liking you in 1950 when you were the assistant of Bloomenfeld the photographer was the secret beginning of the TAROT GARDEN.

We lost sight of each other and 25 years later met again high up in the Engadine mountains. There our friendship renewed itself. I was recuperating from lungs damaged from working with plastics.

How well I remember our long winter walks amidst the pine trees. Do you remember our five o'clock Russian teas in front of the fire while we took turns reading the poems of Kavavy and Aknatova?

It was there, one day, while walking toward the glacier that I told you about my LIFELONG DREAM of building a garden that would be a dialogue between sculpture and nature. A place to dream in. A garden of joy and fantasy.

I wanted to build it in ITALY and I asked you to find someone in TUSCANY who would let me build my Sculpture Garden on their property. (At my expense, of course!) By BUILDING on someone's property, my work would be protected against vandalism.

You told me that your brothers, Carlo and Nicola Caracciolo, were enthusiastic about the project. A few weeks later I arrived at the Roma Termini station with my bulky maquette. Carlo was there to drive me to the beautiful Tuscan countryside of Garavicchio. Your brothers were enthusiastic and the die was cast!

THE BIGGEST ARTISTIC ADVENTURE OF MY LIFE HAD BEGUN.

I would spend most of the next ten years, beginning in 1980, entirely devoted to the realization of the Garden. If I had not concretized my dreams into sculptures, I might have become possessed by them and ended up in a psychiatric hospital – a victim of my own inner visions.

At last, my lifelong desire to live inside a sculpture would come true. An undulating round space without any right angles to threaten and attack me.

You took wonderful photos, Marella, when you came to visit me in Garavicchio in 1981 while JEAN TINGUELY, Rico Weber, and Sepp Imhof were welding the metal structure that was to be my home. Jean would take in his hands the model I made, absorb it in his ELECTRIC SOUL, then we'd hear him shout as he pointed to the sky, "Seppi, weld there!" How I loved watching this process. My house appeared almost overnight like a huge mushroom rising after a good rain, the iron frame a much larger duplicate of my model. Jean had taken no measurements – he built with his eye only.

He seemed like SUPERMAN to me, and likewise, I was WONDERWOMAN for having the nerve to embark on such a mad adventure. Our mutual admiration stimulated each other. We were in competition to amaze one another.

After the iron structure was finished, wire mesh was attached to the frame to catch the cement which was sprayed on by noisy machines. The Sphinx became gray and melancholy in her cement dress. I knew that she needed a new costume, and I was going to give her one that would be spectacular. Little by little she was covered with colored glass that I had ordered especially from Venice. Mainly, however, her apparel was made of molded ceramics and mirrors.

I had made my first NANA house in 1967. It was a doll's house for adults – just big enough to sit and dream in.

I WANTED TO INVENT A NEW MOTHER, A MOTHER GODDESS, AND IN THESE FORMS BE REBORN.

A breast. I would sleep in a breast. My kitchen would be in the other breast.

I found myself far from my origins, far from my family and friends in a new culture besieged by a lot of technical and financial problems. These problems enlarged my vision of things.

I had to learn to direct the local workers, the electricians and the masons, who were involved in the making of the sculpture. This was not my usual working relationship with artists; these were my partners.

The workers knew nothing about Modern Art. The women we hired had all been cleaning ladies. It took many years before they would feel a part of this adventure and it took a while for me to establish a real contact with them. In the beginning, when Jean welded the steel frames for my forms, the workers would watch me go into ecstasy in front of the welded iron and they would wonder what was going on. Today, however, they are very proud of being a part of the Garden and are uniquely skilled artisans.

To avoid the macho problem (the first few years I only had men working for me, no women showed up) I instinctively became the MOTHER. Italians are used to taking orders from Mother. I prepared coffee for them and tea for me. Today almost all of them have become tea drinkers. We took our morning break in the stomach of the Sphinx.
I had no privacy because the workers were continuously finding excuses to PENETRATE the Mother. There was only one huge space inside the Sphinx with an alcove for my bed. There was no space for me to hide and I felt devoured by my own Mother and my children, the workers.

The Mother sculpture emanates a FATAL ATTRACTION. The Sphinx Mother has an extraordinary power not only on me but on all who enter. Everyone who comes inside wants to stay.

Twenty years earlier I had left my children for my Art. Here I was mothering my adopted children, the workers, and living inside a Mother sculpture I had created! It was during these years, while living inside of the Mother, that I got close again to my own children, Laura and Philip.

The accommodation inside the Empress was rather primitive when I first began living there in 1982. I used all my money to make additional sculptures for the Garden. I enjoyed living like a monk, but it wasn't always pleasant. There was a big hole in the ground where I used to keep my food and I cooked on a tiny little gas heater. Each hot night, like in a child's nightmare, I would wake up surrounded by hundreds of insects from the marsh. I spent hours trying to KILL them with books or shoes. Their bloody cadavers DISGUSTED me. Sometimes I watched the legs of these dying little spiders while they were AGONIZING. I was SCARED that one day they would devour the Empress and me.

I was RESCUED by my Argentinian friend, Sylvia. Terrified by these nocturnal visitors, she decided to leave right away, but not before giving me a check destined to save me from these horrible beasts. That same day I ordered screen doors. It hadn't occurred to me before, something so simple!

The following summer, Sylvia came back. She said the heat was unbearable inside this sculpture which was made of cement over an iron frame. The cement absorbed all the heat. Shortly after, Sylvia sent me a big electric ventilator which is still on my ceiling.

My first years in the Empress were marked by PAIN. When I started working on the Tarot Garden I was struck with rheumatoid arthritis, an extremely painful disease. For reasons that are incomprehensible to me today, for two years I didn't want to see a traditional doctor. I was going to conquer the pain. I didn't even take an aspirin. I liked the idea of healers and I was convinced that with my WILL POWER I would cure myself. The experience of pain became very important.

I started limping. I could hardly hold anything in my hands. Jean invented a system which permitted me to open the water taps without any pressure. At night I would wake up screaming. Jean calls this period of my life "CALVARY".

If I could CONQUER this unbearable pain, I would be stronger, stronger than DEATH. This great lady, death, who fascinates and frightens me. She doesn't exist.

Do I exist? If I suffer so much, I exist.

Hell. The attraction of hell. The beauty of horror. My hands start becoming deformed. I watched the disease progress each day. I couldn't sculpt anymore. Jean cries when he looks at my hands. I lose twenty pounds. I become the transparent shadow of myself. I wanted to live at any price. The cost didn't matter. But live. Suffering is also living.

My intelligence remained, along with my imagination and my eyes. I would learn how to direct others, since I no longer was able to work myself.

One day I found myself in a hospital, vanquished by pain. I couldn't walk anymore. The pain had proven stronger than me. At last I'd found my master.

I accepted the cocktail of drugs that the doctors prescribed for me.

The next few years I was STONED most of the time with heavy medications but I was able to continue working on my Garden. The Garden profited from my health problems because it made me stay put; I didn't take any trips. I was soldered to the sculpture more than ever.
The drugs, especially the cortisone, changed my character, I was very nervous. Usually I have an

even character. My new SPEEDY personality made me look after a million details which was good for the Garden. However, it wasn't a very happy time for my close collaborators.

I refused to go anywhere. I was stuck there. One New Year's Eve, one of the workers, Estelvio, came to get me to celebrate the New Year with his family. He didn't like the idea of me being there all alone. I was touched by his gesture but I was incapable of leaving the Sphinx. These were years of great SOLITUDE.

At the beginning of the 80's, Carlo and Nicola, my friends and owners of the land on which the Tarot Garden was built were worried about my safety, as some notorious bandits had come to the area. They spoke about this to Jean Tinguely who, immediately, had his assistant, Sepp Imhof, come and make some iron doors with an easy, mechanical way of opening. So during the day the Sphinx was open, hospitable. At night, it became a bunker, a fortress. I didn't like locking myself up like that; I wasn't scared. But out of respect for Jean's effort, I always shut the iron doors.

Inside my nocturnal prison I listened to music very late into the night. The acoustics of the Sphinx are extraordinary. The music pierced my heart here as it hasn't anywhere else. I often thought of the cathedrals, my first architectural love.

I had to earn the money to finance this vast adventure. I continually found myself in the difficult situation of having enough money for only one or two months to pay the workers. I never mentioned this to them. Why worry them?

I BECAME JEALOUS OF MY MASTER, GAUDI. He was lucky to have his Duke support him in making a miraculous park. I, a woman, was making the largest sculpture garden since Gaudi. Maybe this is why I met so much resistance.

Once, a woman in the nearest village asked Venera, the ceramist, "Do you work for that crazy French woman who spends all her money making the hill more and more beautiful?

Constantine Mulgrave, a writer I lived with from 1976 to 1980, had secretly saved enough money, which he gave to me, to start the Garden. Also, the Gimpel Gallery sold sculpture models of the Tarot Cards which helped contribute towards some expenses.

When things were very tough, Jean came to my rescue. He bought from me, at gallery prices, sculptures of mine that he really liked. One day he bought me a huge ceramic oven.

A few years ago Marella you bought some sculpture models of the Tarot from JGM. Gallery in Paris and that money also went into the Garden.

Recently, Harry Mathews gave me some money to plant bushes, trees and flowers to embellish the Garden.

The money problems obliged me to find new resources inside myself. I got the idea to make some vases and furniture. My decorative art was successful and sold well in the art galleries.

I was asked to create a perfume that would be contained in a sculpture of mine. I decided to make the container a sculpture of two snakes. Remember, Marella, when for several months you carried around the scent of the last two to be tested? I chose the one you liked best. The perfume paid for one-third of the Garden!

The final cost of my Garden would be between 4 and 5 million dollars.

TO BE MY OWN BENEFACTOR HAD MANY ADVANTAGES. I was master of my own ship. I didn't have to cater to patrons. I could work at my pace, in my way, which wasn't always logical. Sometimes I would start two or three sculptures at once. I could start again, change my mind, there were no dates. This was complete freedom.

Today, I believe THESE DIFFICULTIES WERE NECESSARY. Every fairy tale contains a long quest before you find the treasure. The treasure here has been the privilege of making the Garden, and my UNSHAKABLE FAITH in the necessity to build it. There are 22 cards in the Tarot and the Sphinx is one of them. 18 of the 22 cards are now completed.

A nuclear plant was being built at the same time as the Garden and directly opposite it. I ardently wished for it to stop. Two years ago the Italian people had the right to choose whether or not they wanted to have nuclear plants in their country. They voted against it. Was this the result of the magic power of the Tarot?

One thing that helped me enormously during these years was my great love for Italy. It is now my second home.

During this time, Ricardo Menon, my assistant-collaborator, cook, chauffeur, welder, (he did everything!) stayed by my side. He had an incredible intuition about when I was in danger, and he'd look after me with the jealousy of a tiger. His love and devotion gave me the courage to finish the Garden.

Ricardo was young and handsome. He had enough charm to seduce the Angel Gabriel. He left Paris, which he adored, to come and work with me in the middle of an ex-swamp. This wasn't easy for him. NEVER, during those terrible years of my arthritis when my friends no longer liked to come and see me (who wants to see someone you admire a cripple?) did he ABANDON me. Ricardo often brought his friends to visit. He even carried me in his arms, to my bathtub, when I couldn't walk.

Ricardo, who was the healthiest man in the world, was carried away two years ago by AIDS. In the chapel of Temperance, one of the Tarot Cards, on the altar of the Black Madonna, there is a photo of Ricardo. Very often I go there; I STILL FEEL HIS PROTECTION.

In 1983 I asked Ricardo to find a ceramist to assist me. I wanted to take risks in this medium. Three days later, Venera Finocchiaro made her appearance and she would prove to be indispensable. Venera was ready to start a color one hundred times to get it just the way I wanted it and some days she worked 16 hours at our 5 ovens. She worked with PASSION AND LOVE for the Garden and for me. Venera brought great technical knowledge with her and was able to resolve complex problems that ceramists are never faced with. Giorgio her fiancé calls the Tarot Garden her second love.

In the beginning, Venera used to sleep downstairs in the Sphinx on the sofa while Ricardo slept in the Tower of Babel (another structure in the Garden that could be lived in – and another Tarot Card). Ricardo, Venera, and I used to spend quite a few evenings playing canasta, poker, or gin rummy; we laughed a lot. On crisp autumn days we burned wood in the fireplace which was covered with mirrors. Sometimes I would read their Tarot Cards for them.

I felt part of the space. I couldn't leave her, this mother refound. There were two big portholes in the stomach of my Mother and I used to spend hours looking from the inside of the Mother's stomach to the outside world. I spent long moments watching the wind play with the leaves of the olive trees. WHAT A LUXURY TO BE INSIDE MY MOTHER AND ABLE TO LOOK OUTSIDE!

In the magic space I lost all notion of time and the limitations of normal life were abolished. I felt comforted and transported. Here everything was possible. But there was a dark side also.

I would feel every second of the night tick by and during my long bouts of insomnia, the idea came to me that God really loved me and chose me to make this Garden.

Sometimes I had visions of thousands of shiny, little black devils with horrible wings. Disgusting, revolting devils coming out of all my orifices; could I get rid of them? I would open the doors of the Sphinx in the middle of the night and they would fly away. The demons would be gone for now.

Last year, I felt an imperative desire to be alone with my Mother, the Sphinx.

I chased away all my children, the workers. I wouldn't let them in anymore. I wouldn't prepare tea or coffee for them. I bought them a coffee machine.

I FINALLY HAD TO HAVE MOTHER ALL TO MYSELF. When I did, IT WAS UNBEARABLE.

I had to leave my Mother! – or was it she who decided to EXPULSE ME?

In 1988, I left my Mother, the Sphinx, in peace and not with violence (the way I left my family when I was 18). Reborn? How many times can one be reborn?

Jean was afraid that if I left the Sphinx, I would stop working on the Garden and he also felt that I was close to a nervous breakdown. I was living on tranquilizers. He suggested a very ingenious solution: build a studio beneath the ground. He felt I needed a large studio in a normal rectangular space to work in. Actually it resembles a New York loft – in the middle of Tuscany.

There was a big hole under the Sphinx and one side of the studio would be in glass, and the rest would be covered with earth. My roof was my Garden.

I'm practically a mole. I now live in a structure three-quarters under ground.

I became calm for a short time, however, in my artistic haste, I forgot to get a building permit. The BUREAUCRACY is now after me. This is a bigger NIGHTMARE than the IRRATIONALITY of the Mother.

Marella, I am really worried. They are threatening to shut the entire Garden. Let's pray it will all turn out well.

A Big Kiss
From Your Niki

you had great charm
Mother
you believed in womens roles I didn't
marriage children husbands $
I wanted to exist for myself
conquer the world
DEAR MOTHER
chère MAMAN
je vous Aime
PERFUME
MIRROR MIRROR ON THE WALL WHO IS THE FAIREST OF THEM ALL?
how beautiful you were
think of the poor starving
CHINESE
EAT EVERYTHING ON YOUR PLATE
don't CROSS YOUR legs

Dear MOTHER,

When I was born in Paris on October 29, 1930, the umbilical cord was tied twice around my neck. You told me the doctor saved my life by slipping his hand between the cord and my neck. Otherwise, I would have been born strangled.

Danger was present from the first moment. I would learn to love DANGER, RISK, ACTION. I would also be plagued all my life by asthma and respiratory problems.

My astrological sign is double Scorpio. A chart to overcome all obstacles – to love obstacles.

You told me that when I was born you lost all your money in the crash. It was when you were expecting me that you found out about my father's first infidelity. I BROUGHT trouble.

After the first 3 months we were separated. You sent me to my grandparents in the Nievre and you went to New York. I spent my first three years there. Mother, Mother where are you? Why did you leave me?

Will you ever come back?

Everything is my fault.

Every woman became you. Maman. Maman.

I don't need you. I will manage without you. Your bad opinion of me, Mother, was extremely painful and useful to me.
I learned to rely on myself. Other people's opinions of me wouldn't matter. That gave me a tremendous LIBERTY. The liberty to be myself.

I would REJECT your system of values and invent my own.

I decided early to become a heroine. Who would I be? George Sand? Joan of Arc? Napoleon in drag?

At 15 I won a poetry prize. Maybe I would write?

Whatever I decided to do, I wanted it to be difficult, exciting, grand.

I WASN'T GOING TO BE LIKE YOU, MOTHER. You accepted what had been handed down to you by your parents. Your religion, masculine and feminine roles – your ideas about society and security.

I would spend my life questioning. I would fall in love with the question mark.

?

Mother, I conquered the world for you. You were the mother I needed, I'm a fighter. What would I have done with a mother who smothered me in love?

You used to come and visit my studio when I was 25 and living with Harry Mathews; you would hide your eyes with your hands so as not to see my horrible paintings.

How stimulating it was!

You hated Harry. You felt he was stealing my feminine role when you found him vacuum cleaning the apartment one day. You couldn't understand. It was great.

You were very beautiful, Mother. Your beauty and your charm (when you wanted to turn it on) were magic.

You would have made a great actress, Mother. How theatrical you were!

Remember the first time I introduced you to Jean Tinguely and we went to the Coupole to have lunch? You shut your beautiful eyes and in a very dramatic way said, "I won't eat with my daughter's lover. Why can't you stay with your husband and have a lover SECRETLY like everyone does?" Jean was highly amused by you but I left the table, enraged.

From then on, every time you saw Jean he flirted with you and you loved it.

You were never the big Saint you pretended to be. I remember very well several of your lovers when I was a teenager. There was one redheaded, attractive journalist I particularly hated.

Everything had to be hidden for you.

I would show. I WOULD SHOW EVERYTHING. My heart, my emotions. Green – red – yellow – blue – violet. Hate love laughter fear tenderness.

I wish you were still around, Mother. I would love to take you by the hand and show you the Tarot Garden. You might not have such a bad opinion of me today. Who knows?

Thank you. What a boring life I would have had without you.

I MISS YOU.

Artworks 1953–1992

Classe de Ballet
1953/54
80 x 100 cm

La fête
1954/55
125 x 176 cm

Entre la ville et la fleur
1955
161 x 113 cm

The Round Room
1956
200 x 139 cm

Le château
1956
194 x 130 cm

Composition
1956
190 x 130 cm
Moderna Museet
Stockholm

Untitled
1958
55 x 65 cm

Bouche d'incendie
1959
54 x 43 cm

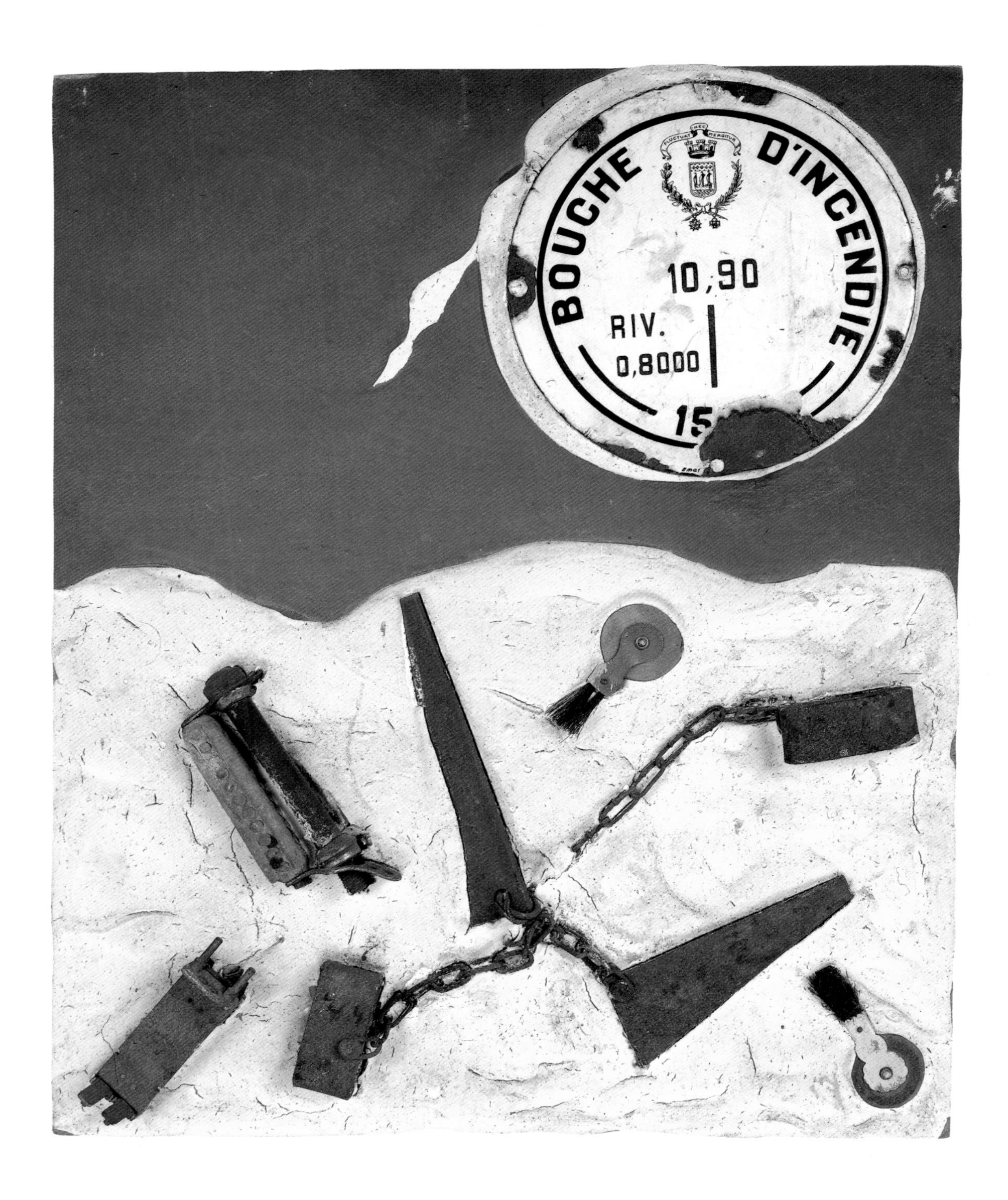

Two guns and
one knife
1960
50 x 60 x 30 cm

Untitled
1960
100 x 160 cm

Le hachoir
1960
65 x 50 cm

Saint-Sébastien or
Portrait of my Lover
1961
72 x 55 x 7 cm

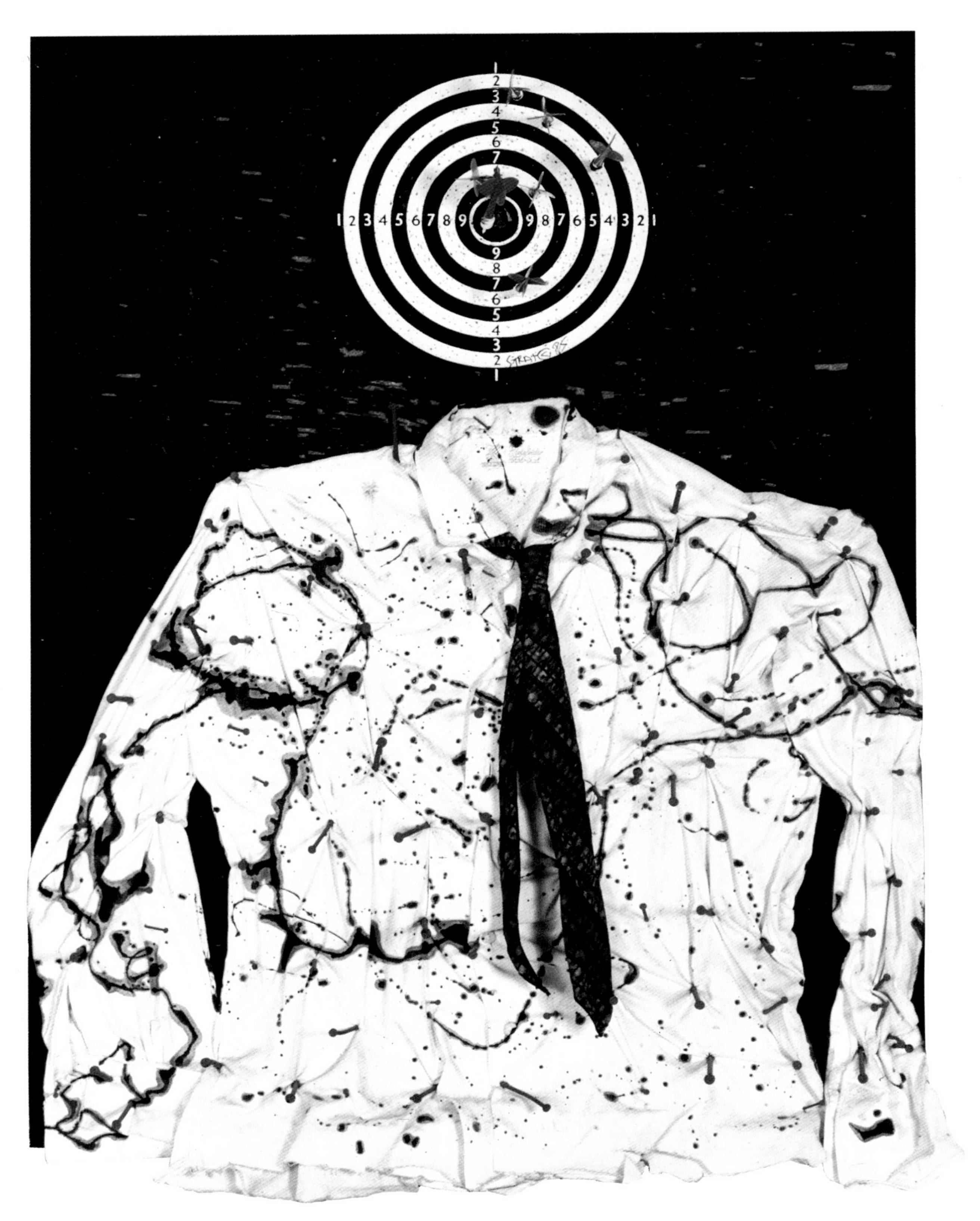

Tir de Bob Rauschenberg
1961
188 x 55 x 36 cm
Galerie de France
Paris

Tir de Jasper Johns
1961
117 x 59 x 26 cm

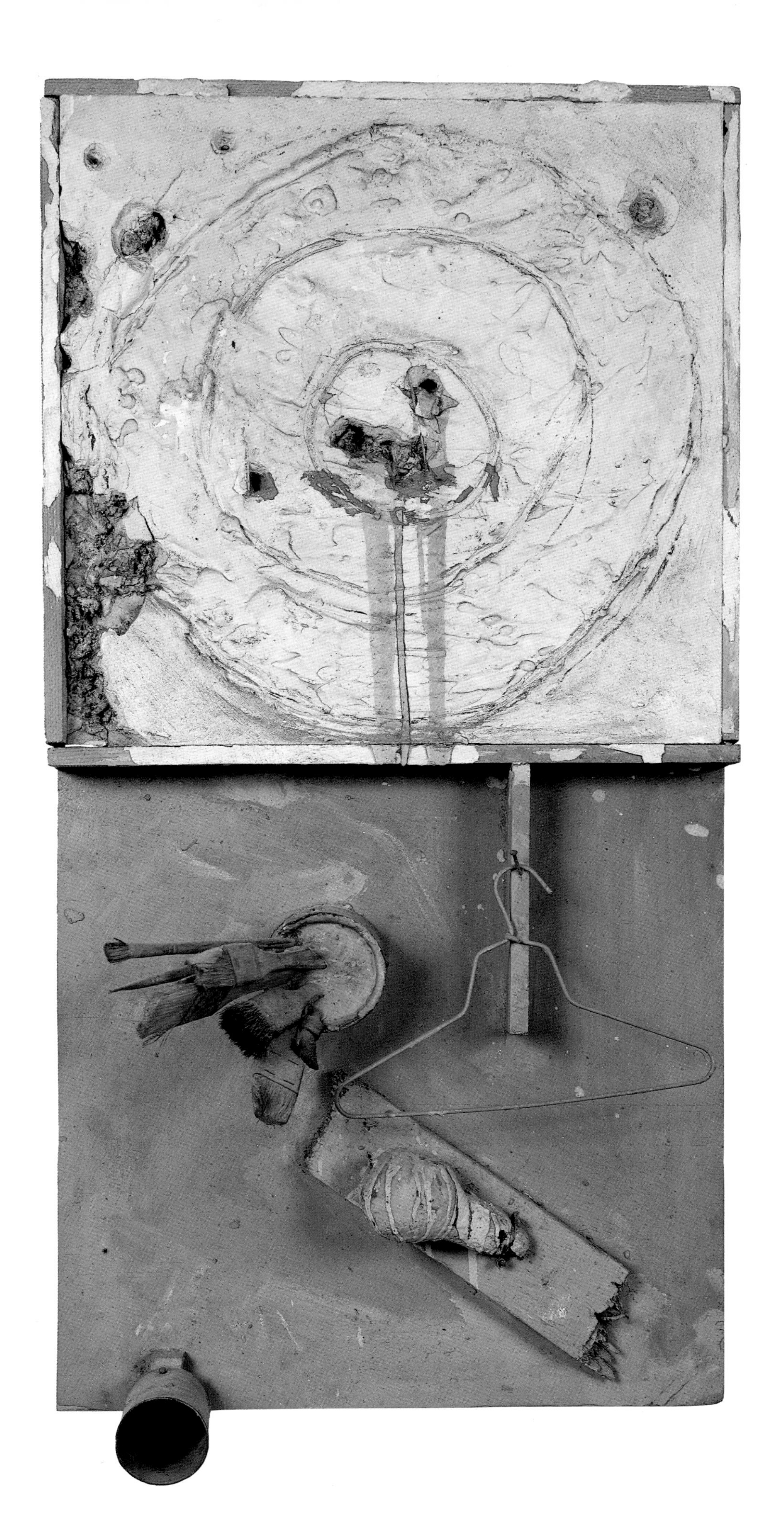

Tir première séance
1961
130 x 73 x 28 cm

Tir de l'Ambassade Américaine
1961
245 x 66 x 22 cm
JGM. Galerie
Paris

My Shoes
1962
85 x 38 x 11 cm
Galerie de France
Paris

Tir dragon
(Tyrannosaurus Rex)
Study for King Kong
1962
198 x 122 x 23 cm
JGM. Galerie
Paris

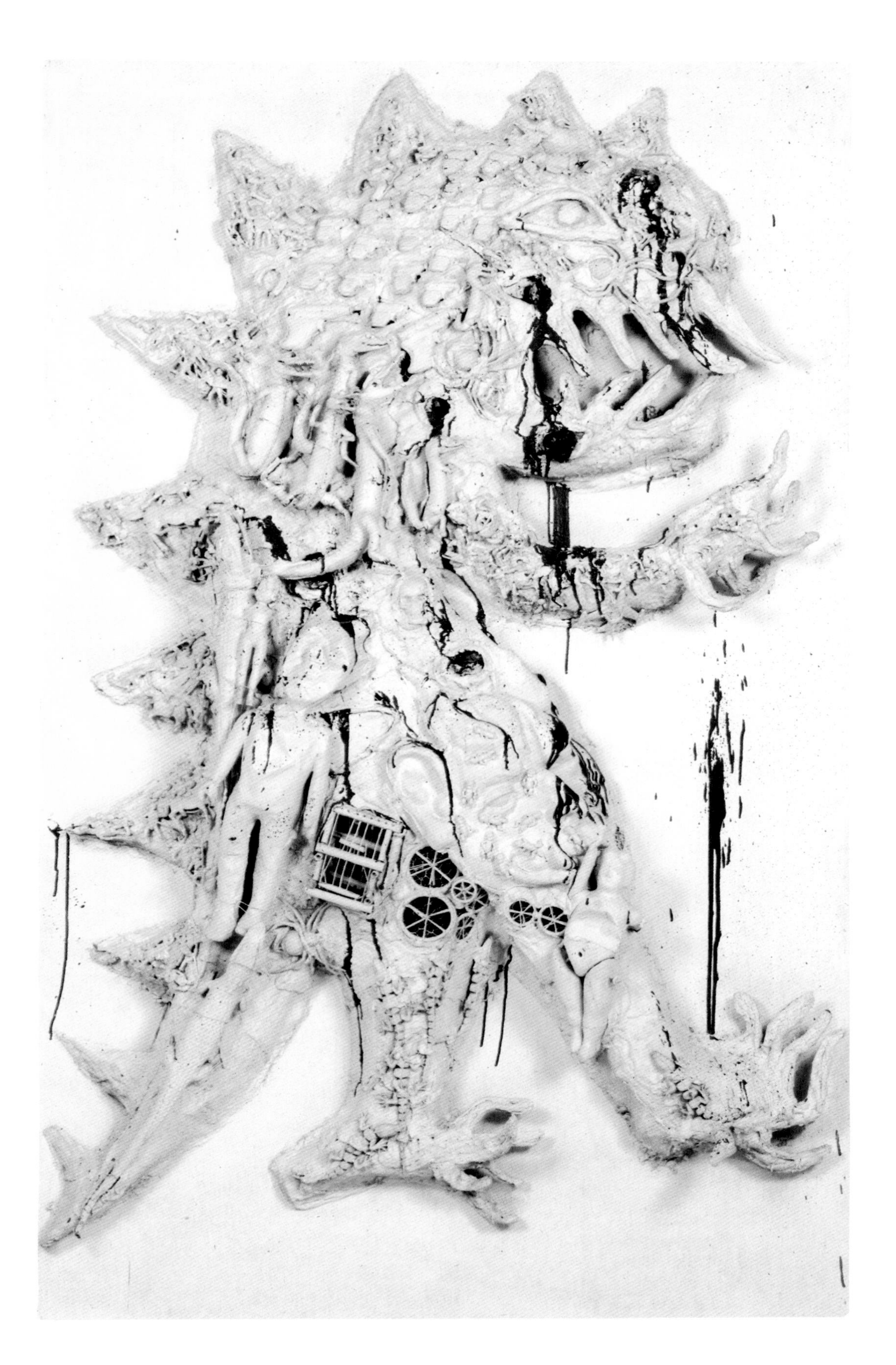

Pirodactyl de New York/
The New York Alp
1962
250 x 310 x 30 cm
Galerie de France
Paris

L'autel des politiques
Study for King Kong
1962
125 x 250 cm

Autel du chat mort
1962
286 x 250 x 79 cm

O.A.S.
1962
252 x 241 x 41 cm
Galerie de France
Paris

Vénus de Milo
1962
193 x 64 x 64 cm

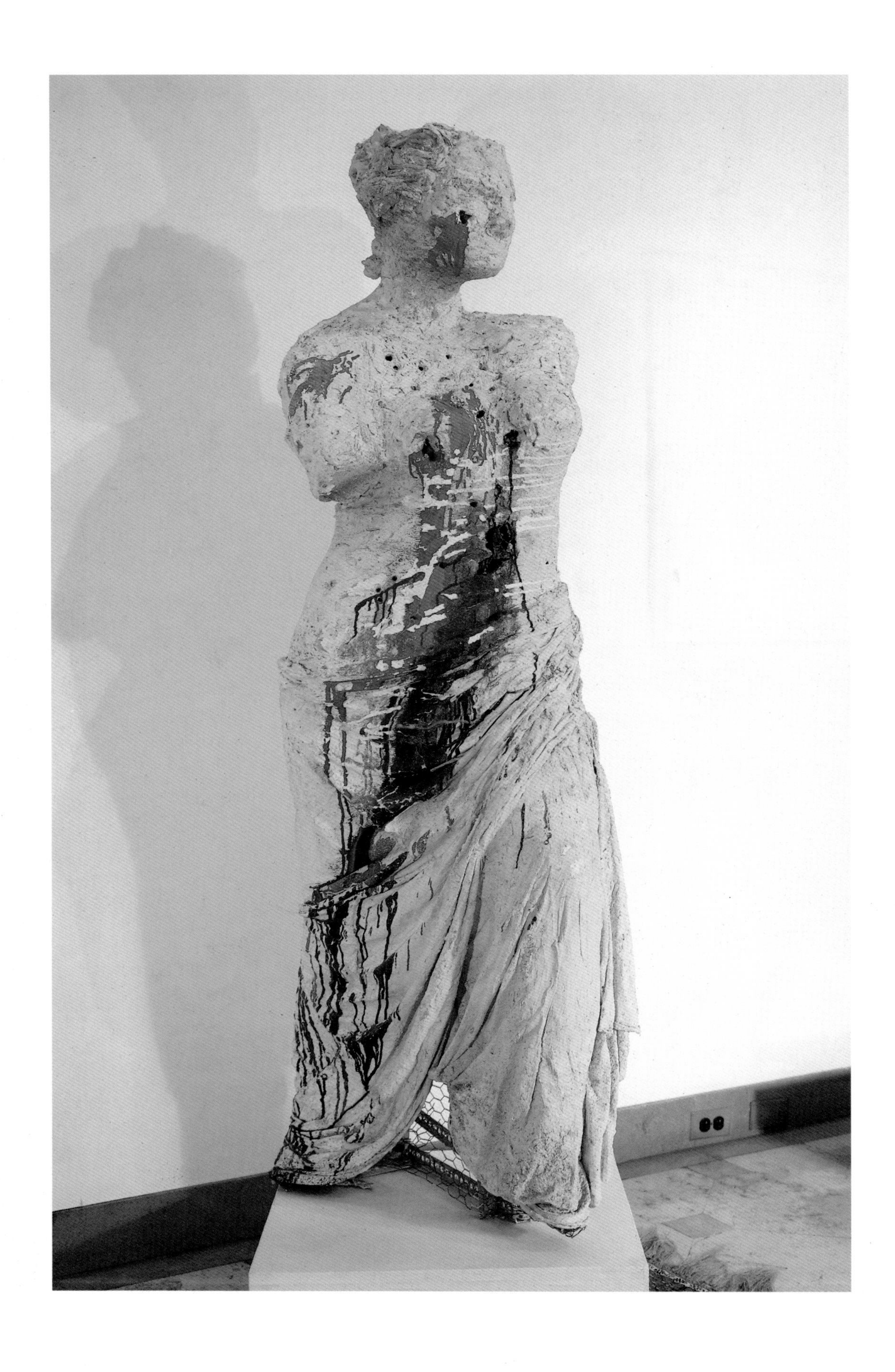

Le monstre de Soisy
1962/63
253 x 161 x 190 cm

Pink Heart
1962
110 x 123 cm

La mort du patriarche
1962/1972
230 x 110 x 30 cm
JGM. Galerie
Paris

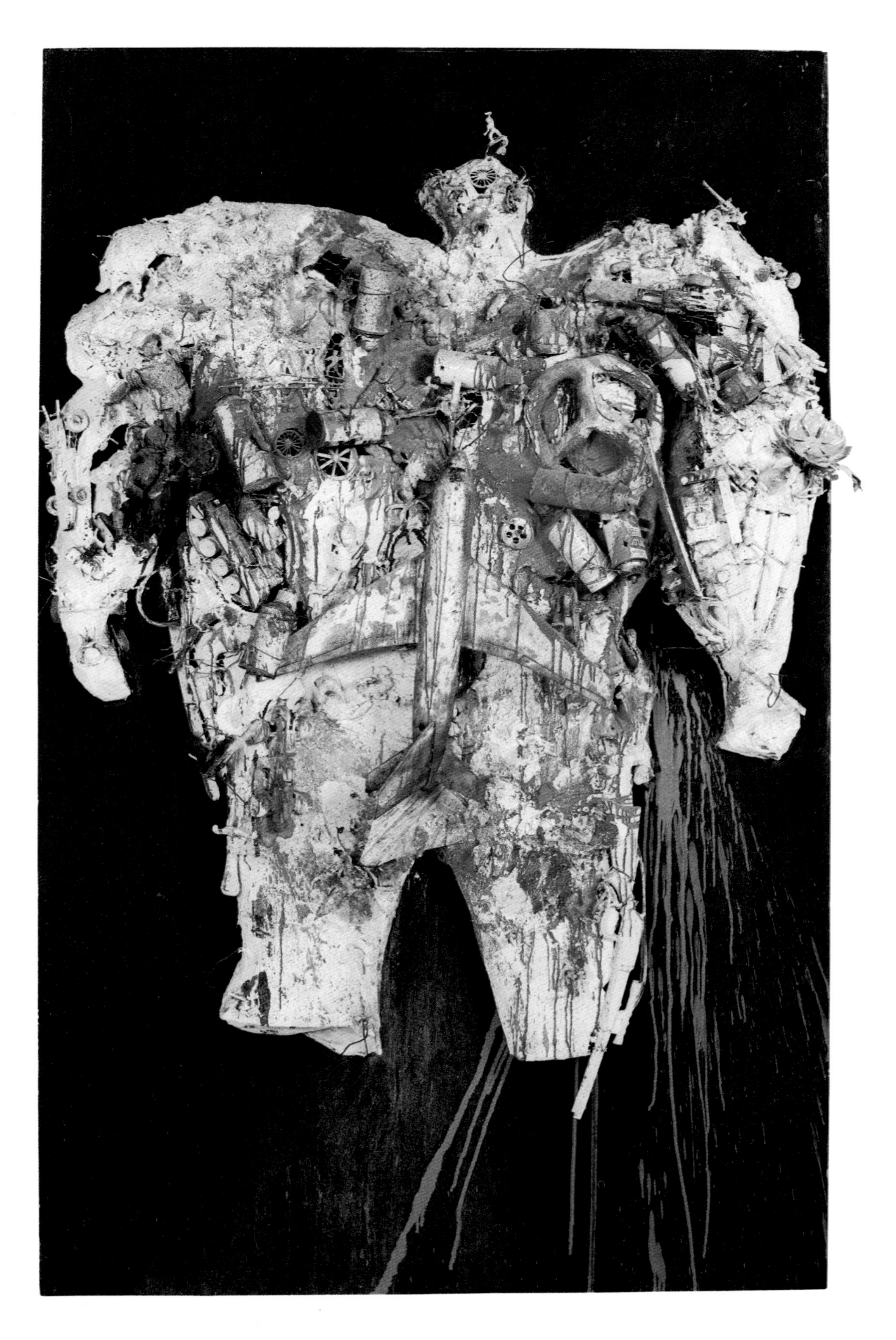

New England Church
1963
200 x 130 cm
JGM. Galerie
Paris

La femme éclatée
ou l'accouchement
du taureau
1963
190 x 122 x 34 cm
Galerie de France
Paris

Tir à la moto
1963
198 x 122 x 23 cm
Laura Condominas

Autel des femmes
1963
250 x 305 x 37 cm

La mariée sous l'arbre
1963/64
228 x 200 x 240 cm
Galerie de France
Paris

Le cheval et la mariée
1963/64
235 x 300 x 120 cm

Crucifixion
1963/64
245 x 160 x 50 cm
Musée National d'Art Moderne
Centre Georges Pompidou
Paris

L'accouchement rose
1964
219 x 152 x 40 cm
Moderna Museet
Stockholm

Figure
1963/64
Length: 62 cm

Cœur rose
1964
65 x 80 x 13 cm
JGM. Galerie
Paris

La tête aux roues
1964
110 x 60 x 35 cm

Gilles de Rais
1964
125 x 80 x 37 cm
JGM. Galerie
Paris

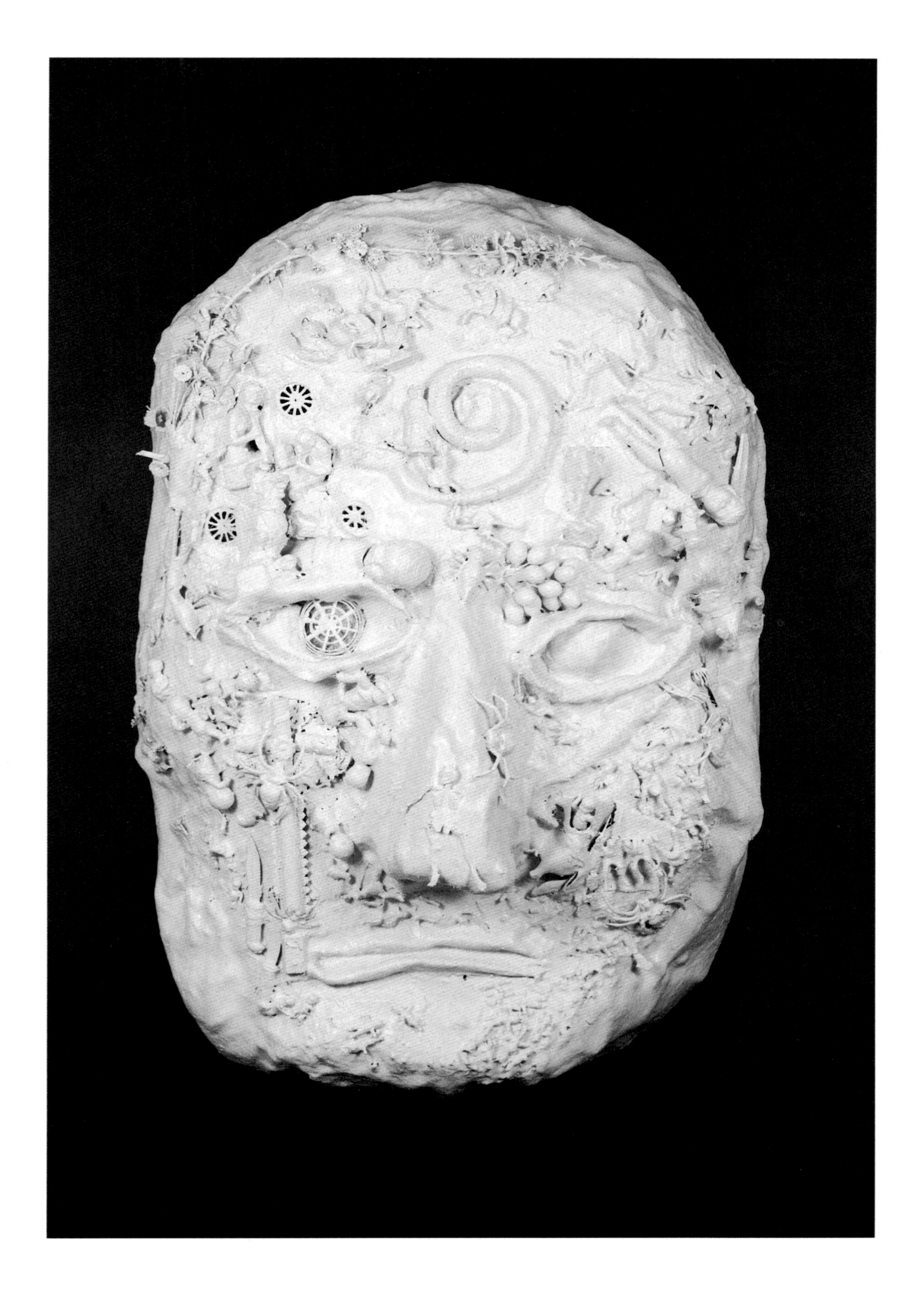

Clarice again
1965/1967
190 x 140 x 125 cm
Philip Mathews
New York

Nana Maison
1967/68
375 x 400 x 300 cm

La Waldaff
1965
268 x 157 x 66 cm
Musée National
d'Art Moderne
Centre Georges
Pompidou
Paris

Bénédicte
1965
80 x 104 x 87 cm

Black Rosy
1965/66
225 x 150 x 85 cm

Black Venus
1965/1967
280 x 89 x 61 cm
Whitney Museum
of American Art
New York

Dancing Nana "Anna"
1966
Height: 123 cm

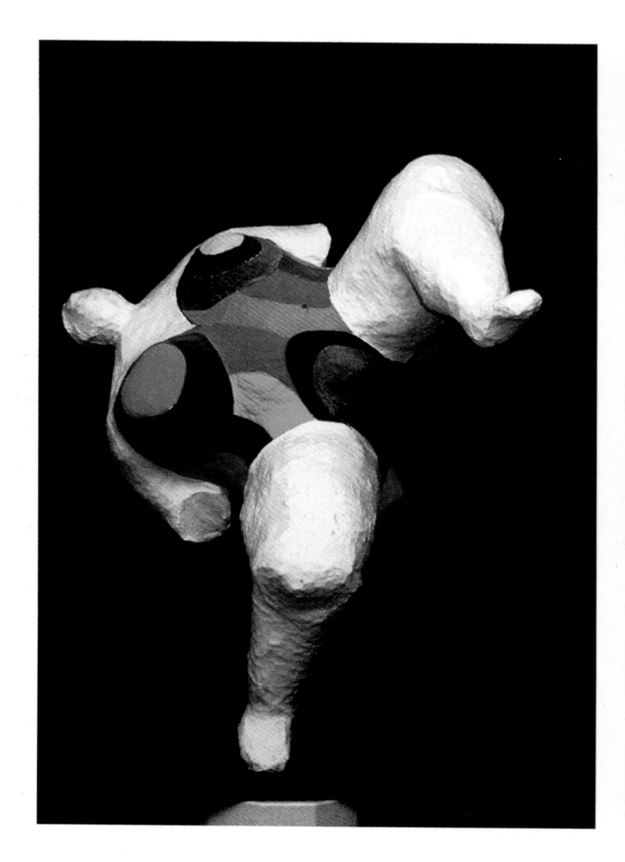

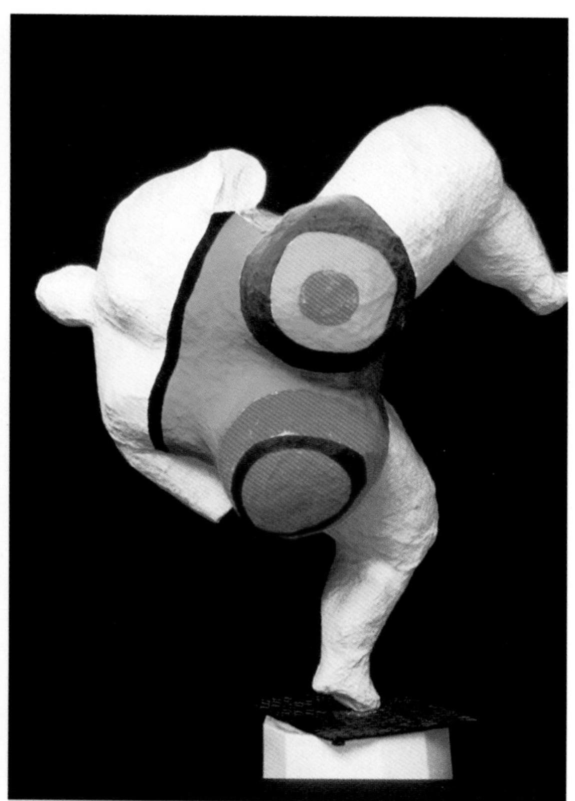

Gwendolyn
1966/1990
262 x 200 x 125 cm

Upside-down Nana
1967
188 x 128 x 95 cm
Clarice Rivers
New York

Nana verte à sac noir
1969
250 x 150 x 100 cm
Collection R. J. Schneider
Paris

Devouring Mothers
1970
White woman: 90 x 60 x 60 cm
Yellow woman: 84 x 78 x 70 cm
Table: 22 x 55 x 40 cm

Chien écrasé
1970
84 x 100 x 55 cm

Le rêve de Diane
1970
7 sculptures
in various sizes

Le témoin
1970/71
240 x 255 x 110 cm
Galerie de France
Paris

Grande tête
1970
240 x 200 x 85 cm

Tea Party, ou le
thé chez Angelina
1971
Red woman:
173 x 180 x 110 cm
Green woman:
194 x 120 x 100 cm
Table with objets
Height: 130 cm
Diameter: 125 cm
Stiftung Ludwig
Vienna

Les funérailles du père
1971
Woman: 230 x 180 x 100 cm
Coffin: 70 x 200 x 120 cm
Cross: 250 x 160 x 40 cm

L'aveugle dans la prairie
1974
Cow: 184 x 307 x 107 cm
Man: 120 x 118 x 117 cm
Musée National d'Art Moderne
Centre Georges Pompidou
Paris

Grand oiseau amoureux
1974
310 x 295 x 105 cm
Collection Linda
and Guy Pieters
St.-Martens-Latem
Belgium

Nana fontaine
1974/1991
Diameter: 225 cm
Height: 55 cm
Collection Mylène
and Francis de Puydt
Ghent

Arche de Noé
(Maquette)
1978
39 x 60 x 27 cm
The Jerusalem
Foundation

Le fil du discours
1979
128 x 50 x 35 cm
JGM. Galerie
Paris

La déesse de la lumière
1980
163 x 85 x 31 cm

Bon appétit
1980
Woman: 180 x 120 x 70 cm
Table: 80 x 120 x 125 cm
Dog: 75 x 35 x 50 cm

Charley chaise homme
1981/82
135 x 120 x 80 cm
Collection Micheline
and Charley Szwajcer
Antwerp

Clarice chaise femme
1981/82
120 x 114 x 74 cm
Collection Micheline
and Charley Szwajcer
Antwerp

La main
1983
94 x 48 x 30 cm

Le rossignol
1983
203 x 252 x 146 cm
Courtesy
Galerie Bonnier
Geneva

New man is coming
1980
216 x 174 x 12 cm
Bloum Condominas

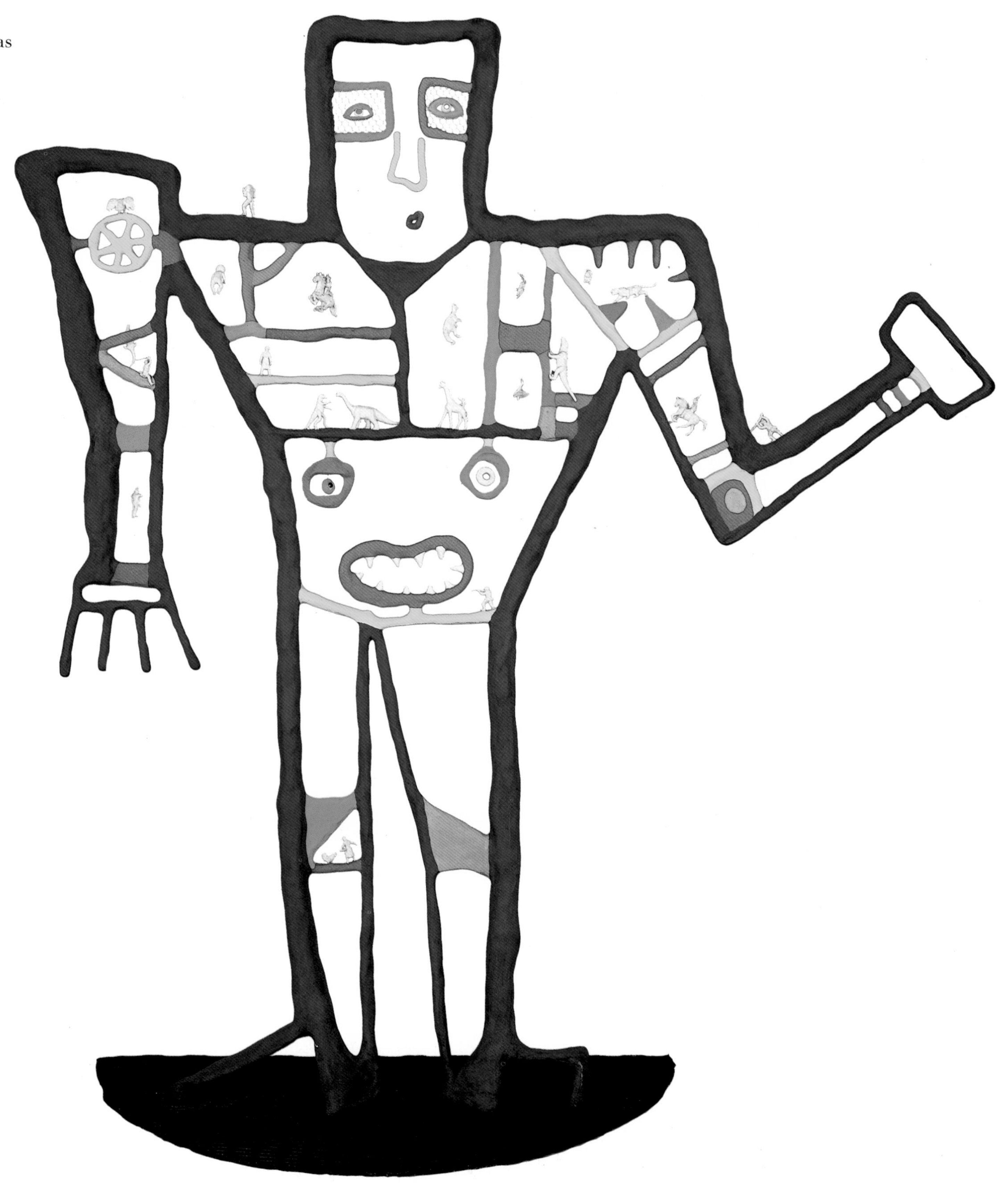

Femme bleue
1984
208 x 127 x 5 cm
Gimpel Fils
London

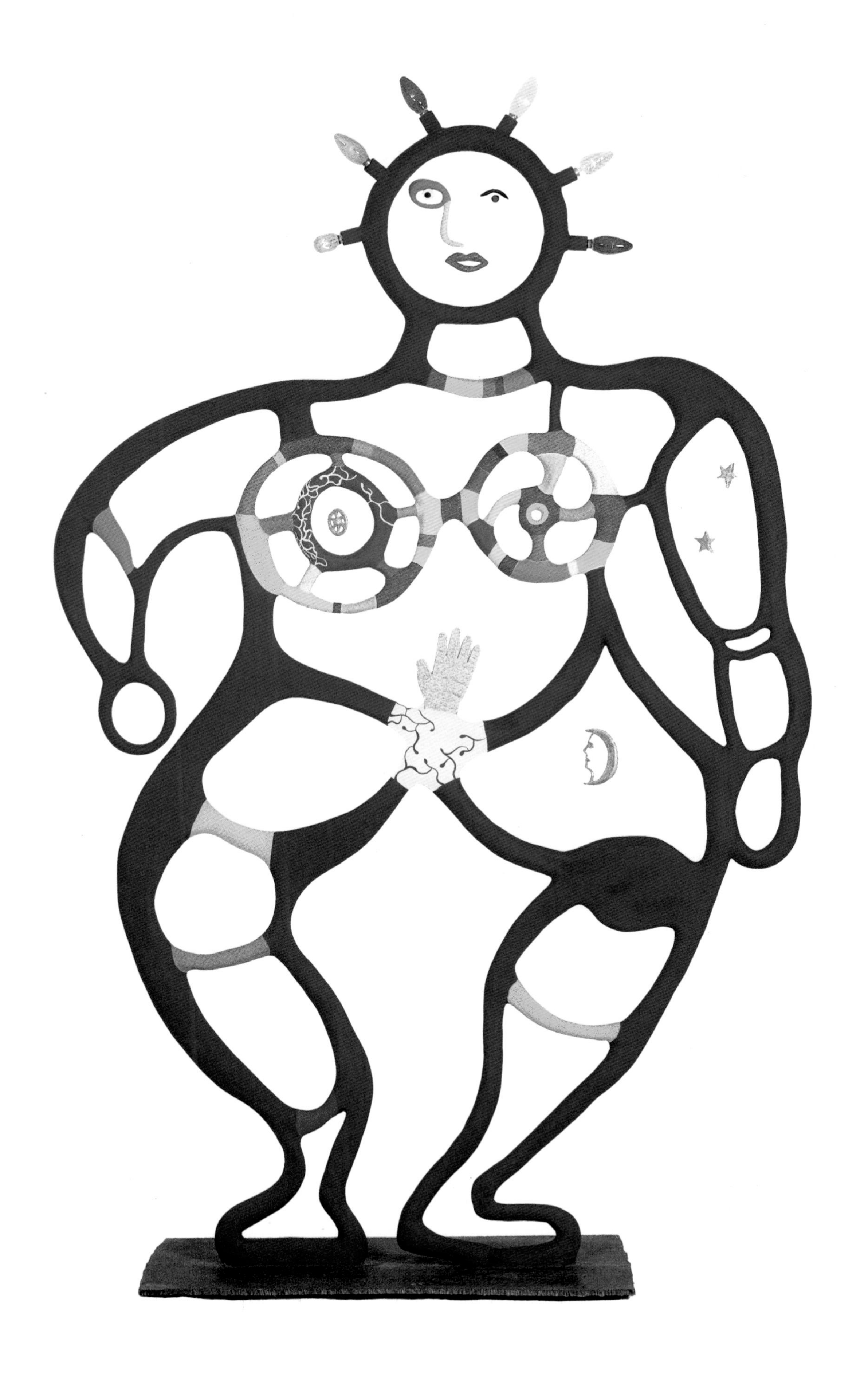

La tempérance
1984
240 x 155 x 65 cm
Courtesy: Galerie
Hans Mayer
Düsseldorf

La lune
1985/1992
300 x 121 x 103 cm

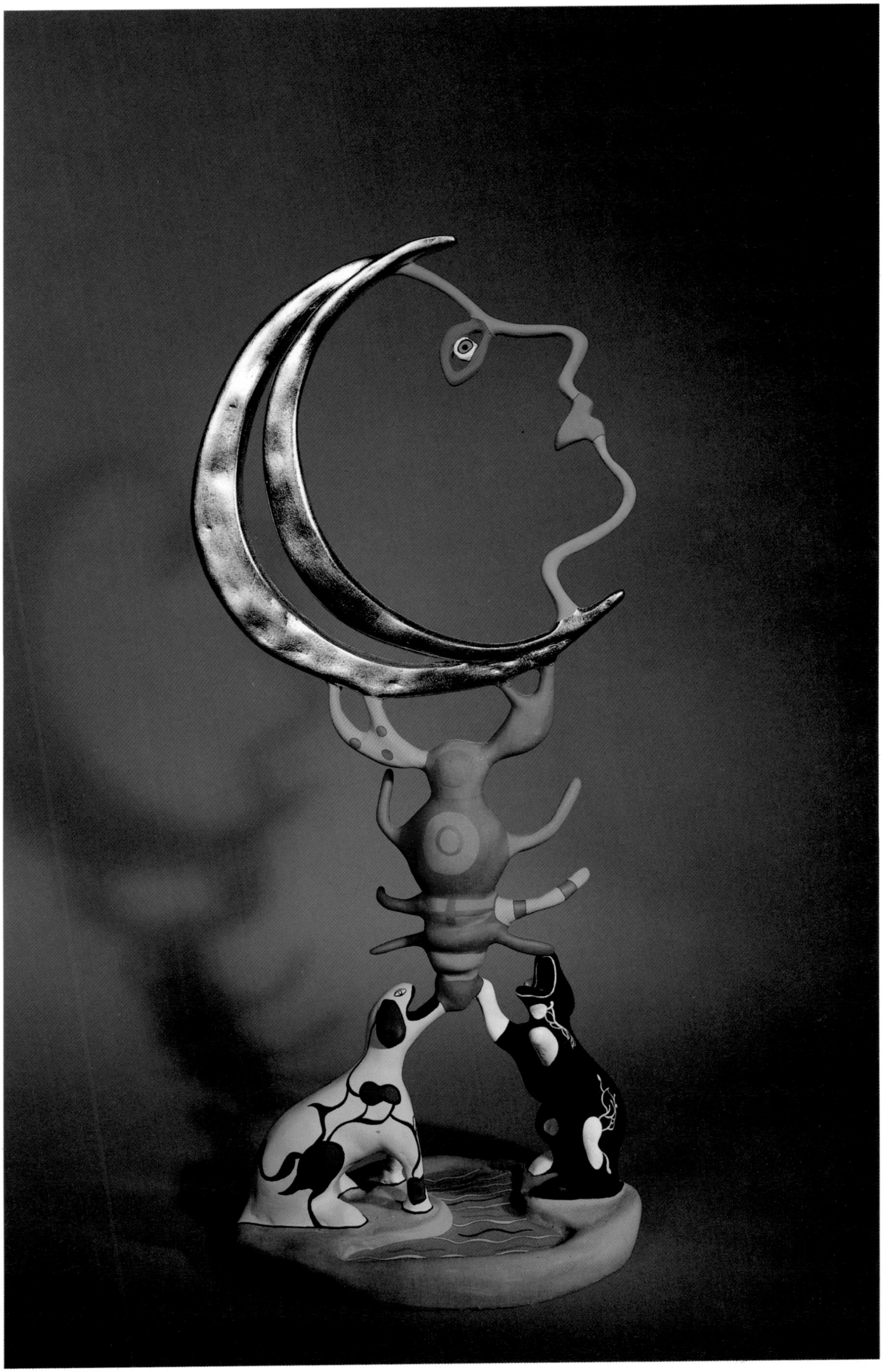

Le grand diable
1985
250 x 150 x 96 cm

Adam et Eve
1985/1989
170 x 200 x 150 cm

La mort
1985
34 x 43 x 28 cm
Gimpel & Weitzenhoffer
New York

La grande tête
1988
255 x 225 x 140 cm
Galerie de France
Paris

L'arbre fontaine
1987/1989
260 x 295 x 200 cm
Gimpel & Weitzenhoffer
New York

L'ermite
1988
233 x 110 x 85 cm
Gimpel Fils
London

Le pendu
1988
250 x 100 x 10 cm
Galerie de France
Paris

Le banc
1989
161 x 140 x 110 cm

Le champignon magique
1989
300 x 210 x 170 cm
Galerie de France
Paris

Le sphinx
1989
28 x 43 x 32 cm

Le monde
1989
425 x 140 x 160 cm

Tête de mort
(Room of meditation)
1990
230 x 310 x 210 cm

Blue Goddess
1990
90 x 31 x 37 cm
JGM. Galerie
Paris

Green Goddess
1990
90 x 31 x 37 cm
JGM. Galerie
Paris

Horus
1990
230 x 140 x 160 cm
Collection Yoko Masuda
Tokyo

Anubis
1990
245 x 100 x 160 cm
JGM. Galerie
Paris

Thoëris
1990
225 x 100 x 145 cm
JGM. Galerie
Paris

Le fou
1990
218 x 165 x 150 cm
Gimpel Fils
London

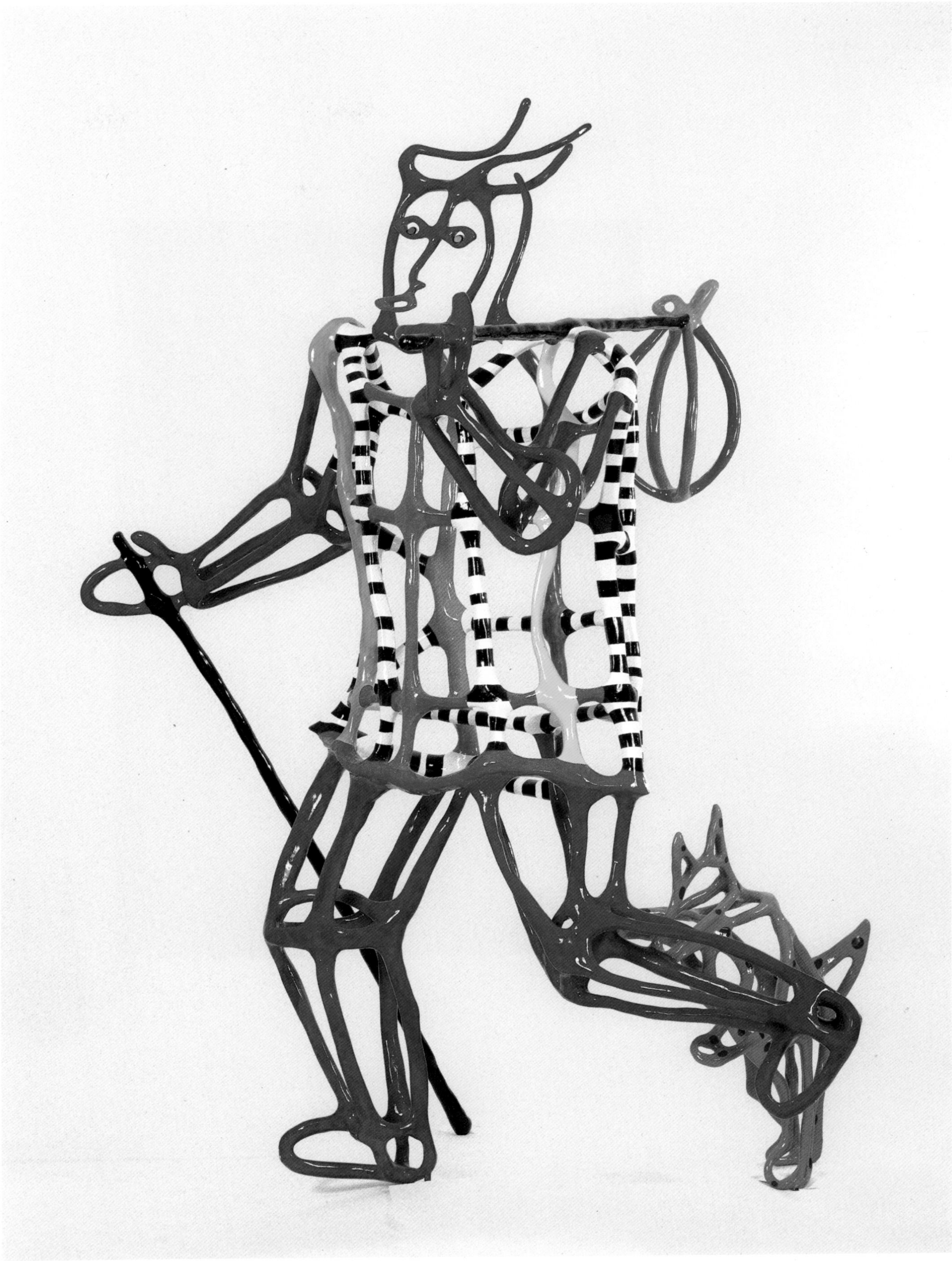

Le prophète
1990
270 x 70 x 70 cm
Galerie de France
Paris

Le temple idéal
(Eglise pour toutes
les religions)
1991
400 x 380 x 340 cm
Artist's collection

Gilgamesch
1991
240 x 155 x 10 cm
JGM. Galerie
Paris

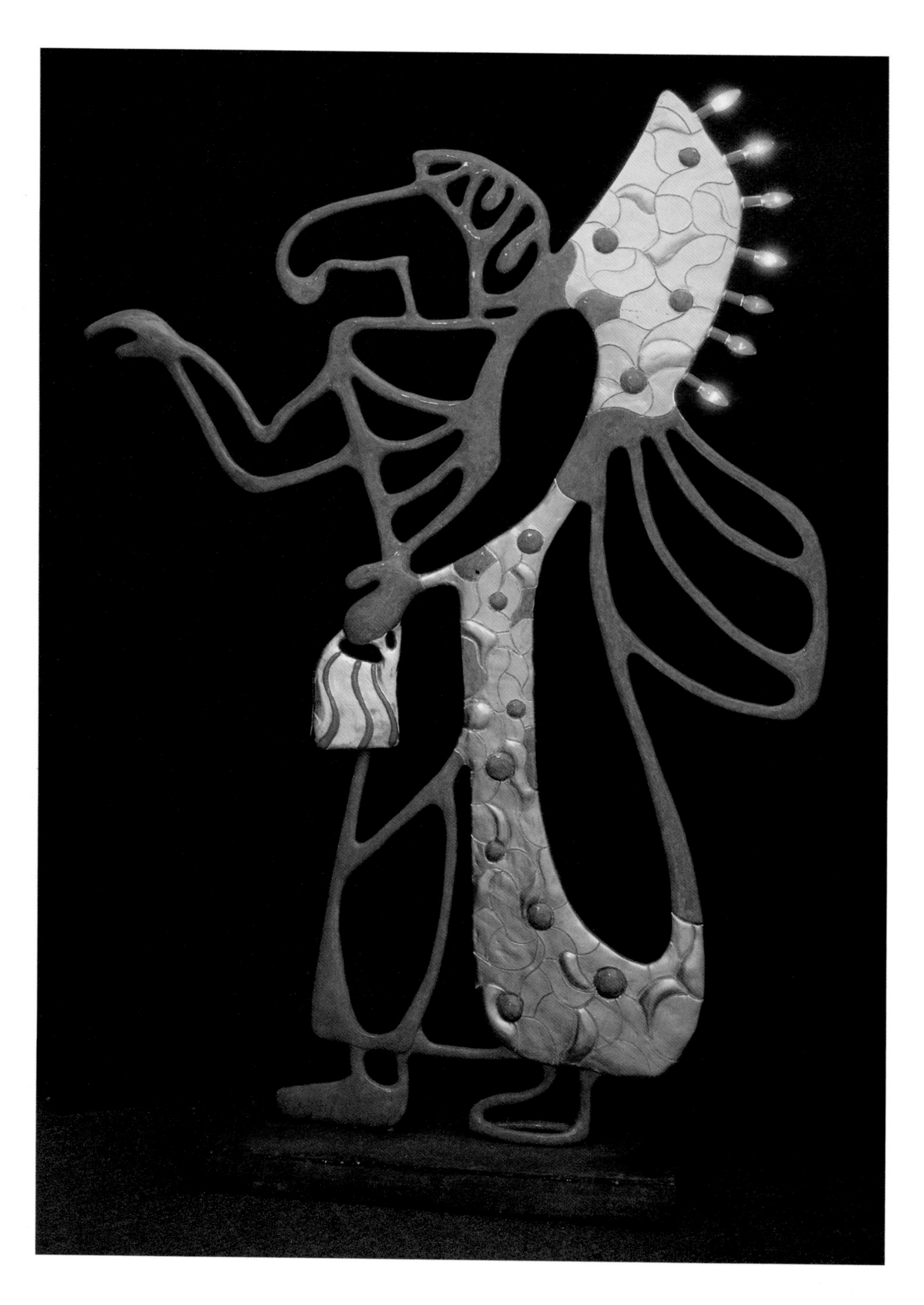

Lampe angulaire
1991
185 x 124 x 30 cm
JGM. Galerie
Paris

The wise man
1991/92
500 x 190 x 150 cm
Artist's collection

Obélisque
1992
Height: 400 cm
Artist's collection

Méta-Tinguely
1992
155 x 125 x 40 cm
Artist's collection

List of illustrations

page 188
Classe de Ballet
1953/54
oil on canvas
80 x 100 cm

page 189
La fête
1954/55
oil on canvas
125 x 176 cm

page 190
Entre la ville et la fleur
1955
oil on canvas
161 x 113 cm

page 191
The Round Room
1956
oil on canvas
200 x 139 cm

page 192
Le château
1956
oil on canvas
194 x 130 cm

page 193
Composition
1956
oil on canvas
190 x 130 cm
Moderna Museet
Stockholm

page 194
Untitled
1958
wood, plaster of Paris,
fragments, misc. objects
55 x 65 cm

page 195
Bouche d'incendie
1959
wood, plaster of Paris
color, misc. objects
54 x 43 cm

page 196
Two guns and one knife
1960
wood, plaster of Paris
misc. objects
50 x 60 x 30 cm

page 197
Untitled
1960
wood, plaster of Paris
misc. objects
100 x 160 cm

page 198
Le hachoir
1960
wood, plaster of Paris
misc. objects
65 x 50 cm

page 199
Saint-Sébastien or
Portrait of my Lover
1961
wood, shirt, tie, practice
target, arrows, color
72 x 55 x 7 cm

page 200
Tir de Bob Rauschenberg
1961
wood, misc. objects
plaster of Paris, color
188 x 55 x 36 cm
Galerie de France
Paris

page 201
Tir de Jasper Johns
1961
wood, misc. objects
plaster of Paris, color
117 x 59 x 26 cm

page 202
Tir première séance
1961
wood, misc. objects
plaster of Paris, color
130 x 73 x 28 cm

page 203
Tir de l'Ambassade Américaine
1961
wood, misc. objects
plaster of Paris, color
245 x 66 x 22 cm
JGM. Galerie
Paris

page 204
My Shoes
1962
wood, misc. objects
plaster of Paris, color
85 x 38 x 11 cm
Galerie de France
Paris

page 205
Tir dragon
(Tyrannosaurus Rex)
Study for King Kong
1962
wood, misc. objects, color
198 x 122 x 23 cm
JGM. Galerie
Paris

page 206
Pirodactyl de New York/
The New York Alp
1962
wood, misc. objects
plaster of Paris, color
250 x 310 x 30 cm
Galerie de France
Paris

page 207
L'autel des politiques
Study for King Kong
1962
wood, misc. objects
plaster of Paris, color
125 x 250 cm

page 208
Autel du chat mort
1962
wood, misc. objects
plaster of Paris, color
286 x 250 x 79 cm

page 209
O.A.S.
1962
Catalogue: wood, misc.
objects, gold bronze paint
Exhibit: cast bronze
252 x 241 x 41 cm
Galerie de France
Paris

page 210
Vénus de Milo
1962
Plaster of Paris on chickenwire
construction, color
193 x 64 x 64 cm

page 211
Le monstre de Soisy
1962/63
Plaster of Paris on chickenwire
construction, color, misc. objects
253 x 161 x 190 cm

page 212
Pink Heart
1962
wood, color
misc. materials
110 x 123 cm

page 213
La mort du patriarche
1962/1972
wood, misc. objects
plaster of Paris, color
230 x 110 x 30 cm
JGM. Galerie
Paris

page 214
New England Church
1963
wood, yarn, plaster of Paris, color
200 x 130 cm
JGM. Galerie
Paris

page 215
La femme éclatée ou
l'accouchement du taureau
1963
wood, color, misc. objects
190 x 122 x 34 cm
Galerie de France
Paris

page 216
Tir à la moto
1963
wood, misc. objects
plaster of Paris, color
198 x 122 x 23 cm
Laura Condominas
Paris

page 217
Autel des femmes
1963
wood, color, misc. objects
250 x 305 x 37 cm

page 218
La mariée sous l'arbre
1963/64
misc. objects and fabric on
chickenwire construction, color
228 x 200 x 240 cm
Galerie de France
Paris

page 219
Le cheval et la mariée
1963/64
misc. objects and fabric on
chickenwire construction, color
235 x 300 x 120 cm

page 220
Crucifixion
1963/64
misc. objects on chickenwire
construction, color
245 x 160 x 50 cm
Musée National d'Art Moderne
Centre Georges Pompidou
Paris

page 221
L'accouchement rose
1964
misc. objects on chickenwire
construction, color
219 x 152 x 40 cm
Moderna Museet
Stockholm

page 222
Figure
1963/64
yarn on chickenwire
construction
length: 62 cm

page 223
Cœur rose
1964
wood, color, misc. objects
63 x 80 x 13 cm
JGM. Galerie
Paris

page 224
La tête aux roues
1964
misc. objects and yarn on
chickenwire construction
color
110 x 60 x 35 cm

page 225
Gilles de Rais
1964
misc. objects on
chickenwire construction
color
125 x 80 x 37 cm
JGM. Galerie
Paris

page 226
Clarice again
1965/1967
polyester, painted
190 x 140 x 125 cm
Philip Mathews
New York

page 227
Nana Maison
1967/68
polyester, painted
375 x 400 x 300 cm

page 228
La Waldaff
1965
fabric and wool on bamboo
and chickenwire construction
268 x 157 x 66 cm
Musée National d'Art Moderne
Centre Georges Pompidou
Paris

page 229
Bénédicte
1965
fabric and wool on
chickenwire construction
80 x 104 x 87 cm

page 230
Black Rosy
1965/66
fabrik and wool on bamboo
and chickenwire construction
225 x 150 x 85 cm

page 231
Black Venus
1965/1967
polyester, painted
280 x 89 x 61 cm
Collection of the
Whitney Museum
of American Art
Gift of the
Howard and Jean
Lipman Foundation

page 232
Dancing Nana "Anna"
1966
papier-maché, painted
Height: 123 cm

page 233
Gwendolyn
1966/1990
polyester, painted
262 x 200 x 125 cm

page 234
Upside-down Nana
1967
polyester, painted
188 x 128 x 95 cm
Clarice Rivers
New York

page 235
Nana verte à sac noir
1969
polyester, painted
250 x 150 x 100 cm
R. J. Schneider Collection
Paris

page 236
Devouring Mothers
1970
papier-maché, painted
White woman: 90 x 60 x 60 cm
Yellow woman: 84 x 78 x 70 cm
Table: 22 x 55 x 40 cm

page 237
Chien écrasé
1970
polyester, painted
84 x 100 x 55 cm

page 238
Le rêve de Diane
1970
polyester, painted
7 sculptures in
various sizes

page 239
Le témoin
1970/71
polyester, painted
240 x 255 x 110 cm
Galerie de France
Paris

page 240
Grande tête
1970
polyester, painted
240 x 200 x 85 cm

page 241
*Tea Party, ou le thé
chez Angelina*
1971
polyester, painted
Red woman: 173 x 180 x 100 cm
Green woman: 194 x 120 x 100 cm
Table with objects, height: 130 cm
Diameter: 125 cm
polyester, painted
Museum moderner Kunst
Stiftung Ludwig

page 242
Les funérailles du père
1971
polyester, painted
Woman: 230 x 180 x 100 cm
Coffin: 70 x 200 x 120 cm
Cross: 230 x 160 x 40 cm

page 243
L'aveugle dans la prairie
1974
polyester, painted
Cow: 184 x 307 x 107 cm
Man: 120 x 118 x 117 cm
Musée National d'Art Moderne
Centre Georges Pompidou
Paris

page 244
Grand oiseau amoureux
1974
polyester, painted
310 x 295 x 105 cm
Linda and Guy Pieters
Collection
St-Martens-Latem
Belgium

page 245
Nana fontaine
1974/1991
Diameter: 225 cm
Height: 55 cm
Spring: polyester, painted
Mylène and Francis
de Puydt Collection
Ghent

page 246
Arche de Noé
(Maquette)
1978
polyester, painted
39 x 60 x 27 cm
The Jerusalem Foundation

page 247
Le fil du discours
1979
polyester, painted
light bulbs
128 x 50 x 35 cm
JGM. Galerie
Paris

page 248
La déesse de la lumière
1980
polyester, painted
163 x 85 x 31 cm

page 249
Bon appétit
1980
polyester, painted
Woman: 180 x 120 x 70 cm
Table: 80 x 120 x 125 cm
Dog: 75 x 35 x 50 cm

page 250
Charley chaise homme
1981/82
polyester, painted
135 x 120 x 80 cm
Micheline and Charley
Szwajcer Collection
Antwerp

page 251
Clarice chaise femme
1981/82
polyester, painted
120 x 114 x 74 cm
Micheline and Charley
Szwajcer Collection
Antwerp

page 252
La main
1983
polyester, painted
wrought-iron base
94 x 48 x 30 cm

page 253
Le rossignol
1983
polyester, painted
iron base
203 x 252 x 146 cm
Courtesy of the
Galerie Bonnier
Geneva

page 254
New man is coming
1980
polyester, painted
216 x 174 x 12 cm
Bloum Condominas

page 255
Femme bleue
1984
polyester, painted
light bulbs
208 x 127 x 5 cm
Gimpel Fils
London

page 256
La tempérance
1984
polyester, painted
240 x 155 x 65 cm
Courtesy of the
Galerie Hans Mayer
Dusseldorf

page 257
La lune
1985/1992
polyester, painted
300 x 121 x 103 cm

page 258
Le grand diable
1985
polyester, painted
250 x 150 x 96 cm

page 259
Adam et Eve
1985/1989
polyester, painted
170 x 200 x 150 cm

page 260
La mort
1985
polyester, painted
34 x 43 x 28 cm
Gimpel & Weitzenhoffer
New York

page 261
La grande tête
1988
polyester, painted
light bulbs, iron base by
Jean Tinguely
255 x 225 x 140 cm
Galerie de France
Paris

page 262
L'arbre fontaine
1987/1989
Spring: polyester, painted
260 x 295 x 200 cm
Gimpel & Weitzenhoffer
New York

page 263
L'ermite
1988
polyester, painted
light bulb
233 x 110 x 85 cm
Gimpel Fils
London

page 264
Le pendu
1988
polyester, painted
250 x 100 x 10 cm
Galerie de France
Paris

page 265
Le banc
1989
polyester, painted
mirror mosaic
161 x 140 x 110 cm

page 266
Le champignon magique
1989
polyester, iron
mirror mosaic
300 x 210 x 170 cm
Galerie de France
Paris

page 267
Le sphinx
1989
polyester, painted
28 x 43 x 32 cm

page 268
Le monde
1989
polyester, painted
iron base by
Jean Tinguely
425 x 140 x 160 cm

page 269
Tête de mort
(Meditation Room)
1990
glass and mirror mosaic
ceramic
230 x 310 x 210 cm

page 270
Blue Goddess
1990
polyester, painted
light bulbs
90 x 31 x 37 cm
JGM. Galerie
Paris

page 271
Green Goddess
1990
polyester, painted
light bulbs
90 x 31 x 37 cm
JGM. Galerie
Paris

page 272
Horus
1990
bronze, painted
iron base
230 x 140 x 160 cm
Collection Yoko
Shizue Masuda
Tokyo

page 273
Anubis
1990
bronze, painted
iron base
245 x 100 x 160 cm
JGM. Galerie
Paris

page 274
Thoëris
1990
bronze, painted, light
bulbs, iron base
225 x 100 x 145 cm
JGM. Galerie
Paris

page 275
Le fou
1990
polyester, painted
218 x 165 x 150 cm
Gimpel Fils
London

page 276
Le prophète
1990
polyester, painted
gold leaf
270 x 70 x 70 cm
Galerie de France
Paris

page 277
Le temple idéal
(A Church for all Religions)
1991
polyester, painted
400 x 380 x 340 cm
Artist's collection

page 278
Gilgamesch
1991
polyester, painted
240 x 155 x 10 cm
JGM. Galerie
Paris

page 279
Lampe angulaire
1991
polyester, painted
light bulbs
185 x 124 x 30 cm
JGM. Galerie
Paris

page 280
The wise man
1991/92
mirror mosaic
500 x 190 x 150 cm
Artist's collection

page 281
Obélisque
1992
glass and mirror mosaic
Height: 400 cm
Artist's collection

page 282
Méta-Tinguely
1992
wood, metal, electrical
motors, color
155 x 125 x 40 cm
Artist's collection

The works above that have
not been attributed to a
particular museum or
gallery are held in
private collections

Appendix

1930
Catherine Marie-Agnès Fal de Saint Phalle is born at Neuilly- sur-Seine at 6:40 on the morning of 29 October. Her birth sign is Scorpio (with Scorpio in the ascendant). She is the second of five children born to Jeanne Jacqueline *née* Harper and André Marie-Fal de Saint Phalle. Her father is one of seven brothers with a share in the family's banking house. He had become manager of its New York branch in 1927 but when the stock- exchange collapsed in 1930 he lost both the business and his entire fortune. Marie-Agnès and her brother John are sent to their paternal grandparents in France and spend the next three years in Nièvre.

1933
Marie-Agnès and John return to their parents in Greenwich, Connecticut. Every year they spend their summer holidays at the Château of Filerval, which had been built by Le Nôtre and which now belongs to their American grandfather.

1937
The family moves into an apartment on East 88th Street, New York. Marie-Agnès, now known as Niki, attends the Convent School of the Sacred Heart on East 91st Street.

1941
Niki de Saint Phalle is expelled from the Convent School. She moves to Princeton, New Jersey, to live with her grandparents, who have left France during the Second World War. She attends the local public school.

1942
Niki de Saint Phalle returns to her parents' home and attends Brearley School, New York. She reads Edgar Allan Poe, Shakespeare and Greek tragedies. She takes part in school performances and writes her first poems and plays.

1944
In the opinion of her headmistress, Niki de Saint Phalle's behaviour is such that she should either have psychiatric treatment or leave school. Her parents send her to a Convent School at Suffern, New York State.

1947
Niki de Saint Phalle graduates from Oldfield School, Maryland

1948/1949
She works as a model. Photographs of her appear in *Vogue*, *Harper's Bazaar* and on the cover of *Life* magazine. In June Niki de Saint Phalle, 18, elopes with Harry Mathews, 19, a US marine.

1950
Niki de Saint Phalle and Harry Mathews settle in Cambridge, Massachusetts. He studies music at Harvard University, she begins to paint. She produces her first oils and gouaches.

1951
Their daughter, Laura, is born in Boston.

1952
Niki, Harry and Laura Mathews leave Boston and move into an apartment in the Rue Jean Dolent in Paris. Harry Mathews studies music in the hope of becoming a conductor. Niki Mathews studies drama. They both take charge of their daughter's education. The family spends the summer months in the South of France, Spain and Italy.

1953
Niki de Saint Phalle suffers a severe nervous breakdown and is treated as an in-patient in Nice. Since painting helps her to overcome this crisis in her life, she decides to give up acting and become an artist. At the same time Harry Mathews abandons his music studies and writes his first novel.

1954
In March Niki and Harry Mathews buy their first car in Nice. They drive back to Paris, where they share a house with Anthony Bonner, an American jazz musician and composer. Niki Mathews is introduced to the American painter, Hugh Weiss, who remains her mentor for five years and who encourages her to retain her autodidactic style. In September Niki, Harry and Laura Mathews move to Deyá on the island of Mallorca.

1955
Their son Philip is born in May. Niki de Saint Phalle visits Madrid and Barcelona, where she discovers Gaudí. The experience changes her life and lays the seeds for her later decision to design her own sculpture park. In August the family returns to Paris and moves into a small apartment in the Rue Alfred Durand-Claye. During 1955 Niki de Saint Phalle meets Jean Tinguely and his wife, Eva Aeppli. She often visits the Louvre and gets to know the work of Paul Klee, Henri Matisse, Pablo Picasso and Henri Rousseau. She also visits Joseph Ferdinand Cheval's fantastic castle *Le Palais idéal* in Hauterives.

1956–1958
The Mathews family lives in Lans-en-Vercors in the French Alps. Niki Mathews produces a series of oil paintings which she exhibits for the first time in St Gallen in 1956. Through her husband she meets many contemporary writers, including John Ashbery and Kenneth Koch.

1959
Niki Mathews visits the Musée d'Art Moderne de la Ville de Paris and is introduced to work by the American artists Jasper Johns, Willem de Kooning, Jackson Pollock and Robert Rauschenberg.

1960
Niki and Harry Mathews are divorced; he moves to the Rue de Varenne with their children, while Niki remains in the Rue Alfred Durand-Claye. She continues her artistic experiments, producing assemblages in plaster and 'target' pictures. At the end of 1960 she and Jean Tinguely move into the Impasse Ronsin, where they share the same studio. Jean Tinguely introduces her to Pontus Hulten, the director of the Moderna Museet in Stockholm. He helps her to take part in important exhibitions which are being held at this time and buys a number of her works for the Moderna Museet.

1961
During February a group exhibition is held at the Musée d'Art Moderne de la Ville de Paris under the title *Comparaison: Peinture Sculpture*. Niki de Saint Phalle exhibits her first work – a 'target' montage titled *Portrait of My Lover*. On 12 February she organises the first of more than twelve 'shootings' which are held in 1961 and 1962. These events involve sculptures and assemblages incorporating containers of paint which, concealed beneath the plaster, spatter their contents over the image when shot with a pistol. The resultant pictures are known as 'shooting paintings'. Among spectactors at the first such event are members of the Nouveaux Réalistes. Pierre Restany invites Niki de Saint Phalle to join the group, which already includes Arman, César, Christo, Gérard Deschamps, François Dufrêne, Raymond Hains, Yves Klein, Martial Raysse, Mimmo Rotella, Daniel Spoerri, Jean Tinguely and Jacques de la Villeglé. In March she takes part in an exhibition, *Bewogen Beweging*, organised by Pontus Hulten at the Stedelijk Museum in Amsterdam. Her works are later shown in the Moderna Museet in Stockholm and the Louisiana Museum in the Danish town of Humlebaek. In June she holds her first one-woman exhibition at Jeannine Restany's Galerie J. Leo Castelli, Robert Rauschenberg and all the Nouveaux Réalistes attend the launch. Rauschenberg buys a 'shooting painting'. On 20 June Jasper Johns, Robert Rauschenberg, Niki de Saint Phalle and Jean Tinguely take part in a concert in the American Embassy in Paris. While David Tudor plays music by John Cage on the piano, other works of art are created on stage.
Pierre Restany organises a Festival of Nouveaux Réalistes at the Galerie Muratore in Nice. For the official opening on the evening of 13 July Niki de Saint Phalle arranges a 'shooting' at the Abbaye Roseland at which at the Nouveaux Réalistes take part. Marcel Duchamp introduces Niki de Saint Phalle and Jean Tinguely to Salvador Dalí. During a trip to Spain in August, both artists are invited to take part in celebrations in honour of Dalí. They create a life-size bull made of plaster and paper which explodes in the Arena at Figueras during a firework display.
In October Niki de Saint Phalle takes part in *The Art of Assemblage* exhibition at The Museum of Modern Art in New York. The exhibition subsequently travels to the Dallas Museum for Contemporary Art and the San Francisco Museum of Art.
Between June and September more than fifty international magazines and journals carry reports on Niki de Saint Phalle's work.

1962
In February Niki de Saint Phalle and Jean Tinguely travel to California and visit Simon Rodia's Watts Tower near Los Angeles. In March Jean Tinguely exhibits at the Everett Ellin Gallery in Los Angeles. With the help of Niki de Saint Phalle he organises a 'happening', *Study for an End of the World Number 2*, in the Nevada Desert. Niki de Saint Phalle stages her first two 'shootings' in the United States: the first is held at Virginia Dwan's beach house at Malibu, the second, assisted by Ed Kienholz, in the hills overlooking Malibu. Niki de Saint Phalle and Jean Tinguely travel to Mexico. In May, Niki de Saint Phalle, Jean Tinguely and several other artists take part in Kenneth Koch's play, *The Construction of Boston*. On stage at the Maidman Playhouse, New York, is her 'shooting sculpture', *Vénus de Milo*. Following her return to Europe she exhibits ten works at a one- woman exhibition at Paris's Galerie Rive Droite. Among the visitors is Alexander Iolas, who invites Niki de Saint Phalle to exhibit in New York the following October. He supports her financially for many years and organises numerous exhibitions for her, even though few of the exhibits are sold. It is Iolas who introduces her to the Surrealist painters, Victor Brauner, Max Ernst and René Magritte.
Yves Klein dies suddenly in June.
In August Niki de Saint Phalle takes part in *DYLABY (Dynamic Labyrinth)*, a large-scale installation at the Stedelijk Museum in Amsterdam, in which Robert Rauschenberg, Martial Raysse, Jean Tinguely and Per Olof Ultvedt are also involved.
In October Niki de Saint Phalle opens her first one-woman exhibition in New York at the Alexander Iolas Gallery. In addition to ten other works, she exhibits her *Homage to Le Facteur Cheval*, a shooting gallery in which members of the public are invited to fire at a complex structure.

1963
In May Virginia Dwan organises a shooting event in Los Angeles at which Niki de Saint Phalle shoots at her monumental sculpture, *King Kong*. From now on Niki de Saint Phalle and Jean Tinguely live at a former auberge, the 'Auberge au cheval blanc', at Soisy-sur-Ecole near Essonne. She confronts the various roles of women in society, producing a series of sculptures depicting women in childbirth, devouring mothers, witches and whores.

1964
At her first one-woman exhibition at London's Hanover Gallery she exhibits brides, woollen heads and dragons. In October Niki de Saint Phalle and Jean Tinguely begin working at New York's Chelsea Hotel, which at that time was a well-known meeting-place for artists.

1965
Niki de Saint Phalle spends the summer at The Hamptons, Long Island, where she creates her first Nanas from wool, cotton thread, papier mâché and wire netting. The following September she shows her Nanas at a one-woman exhibition at Alexander Iolas's Paris gallery. At Iolas's suggestion, Niki de Saint Phalle begins making silk-screen prints.

1966
In collaboration with Martial Raysse and Jean Tinguely, Niki de Saint Phalle designs the scenery and costumes for Roland Petit's ballet, *Eloge de la folie*, performed in March at the Théâtre des Champs-Elysées in Paris.
In June, Niki de Saint Phalle, Jean Tinguely and Per Olof Ultvedt are invited by Pontus Hulten to install a sculpture in the large entrance hall of the Moderna Museet in Stockholm. They decide to create a monumental reclining Nana, 28 metres long, 9 metres wide and 6 metres high. It is called *Hon* (the Swedish pronoun, 'she').
While working in Stockholm, Niki de Saint Phalle and Jean Tinguely meet the young Swiss artist, Rico Weber. He works on *Hon* with them and remains their assistant and colleague for ten years.
In October, Niki de Saint Phalle designs the sets and costumes for Aristophanes's *Lysistrata* in a production by Rainer von Diez at the Staatstheater in Kassel.

1967
Niki de Saint Phalle and Jean Tinguely work on *Le paradis fantastique*, a commission from the French government for the French Pavilion at Expo '67 in Montreal. The commission consists of nine painted sculptures by Niki de Saint Phalle and six black kinetic machines by Jean Tinguely. They are subsequently shown at the Albright-Knox Art Gallery in Buffalo and, for a year, in Central Park, New York. They are now on permanent exhibition in Stockholm, close to the Moderna Museet.
In August, Niki de Saint Phalle's first retrospective is held at the Stedelijk Museum, Amsterdam, under the title *Les Nanas au pouvoir*. For this exhibition she creates her first *Nana Dream House* and her first *Nana Fountain* and plans her first Nana town. The new exhibits are made of polyester, a material in which she has only recently started towork.

1968
In June, Niki de Saint Phalle's first play, *ICH (All About ME)*, is performed at the Staatstheater in Kassel. Her co-author is the director, Rainer von Diez. She herself designs the sets and costumes.
In October, Niki de Saint Phalle exhibits her eighteen-part wall relief, *Last Night I Had a Dream*, at the Galerie Alexandre Iolas in Paris.
Niki de Saint Phalle designs inflatable Nanas, which are marketed in New York. Towards the end of the year she suffers serious breathing difficulties, caused by inhaling polyester fumes and dust.

1969
Following her return from a visit to India, Niki de Saint Phalle begins work on her first architectural project, three houses in the South of France for Rainer von Diez. The Whitney Museum of American Art in New York acquires the sculpture, *Black Venus*, and exhibits it at its April exhibition, *Contemporary American Sculpture, Selection 2*.
Niki de Saint Phalle begins work on *La tête (Le Cyclope)*, a collaborative project in Fontainebleau forest, initiated by Jean Tinguely and involving a large number of artists.

1970
A festival is held in Milan to mark the tenth anniversary of the founding of the Nouveaux Réalistes. At the opening ceremony, Niki de Saint Phalle shoots at an altar assemblage.
A series of seventeen serigraphs is published in Paris under the title *Nana Power*.
Niki de Saint Phalle visits Egypt for the first time in the company of Jean Tinguely.

1971
On 13 July, Niki de Saint Phalle and Jean Tinguely are married in Soisy. They visit Morocco. Their granddaughter Bloum is born on the island of Bali: she is the daughter of Laura and Laurent Condominas.
Niki de Saint Phalle designs her first jewelry.
At the end of the year she begins work on *Golem*, an architectural project for children in Jerusalem's Rabinovitch Park.

1972
From now on Niki de Saint Phalle works with the polyester manufacturer Haligon in order to produce large-scale sculpturesand editions. In July she rents the Château de Mons near Grasse in the South of France.
She begins shooting the first version of *Daddy*, produced in association with Peter Whitehead and shown at London's Hammer Cinema the following November. Niki de Saint Phalle visits Greece.

1973
In January, Niki de Saint Phalle works on a revised version of *Daddy* in Soisy and New York, again with Mia Martin, Clarice Rivers and Rainer von Diez. The world première of the revised version is shown in April as part of the 11th New York Film Festival at the Lincoln Center.
Niki de Saint Phalle designs a swimming pool for Georges Plouvier in Saint-Tropez.
In the Belgian town of Knokke-le- Zoute she builds *The Dragon*, a fully equipped playhouse for the children of Fabienne and Roger Nellens.

1974
Niki de Saint Phalle installs three gigantic Nanas in the city of Hanover.
The Galerie Alexandre Iolas in Paris mounts an exhibition of her architectural projects. She suffers an abscess on her lung, caused by years of working with polyester. After a period in hospital she travels to Sankt Moritz to convalesce and it is here that she meets Marella Caracciolo, an old friend from New York. Niki de Saint Phalle tells her of her dream of designing a sculpture park and Marella Caracciolo's brothers offer her land in Tuscany on which to realise her dream.

1975
Niki de Saint Phalle writes the screenplay for the film, *Un rêve plus long que la nuit*. Many of her artist friends are involved in shooting the film. She designs several pieces of furniture for the sets.

1976
Niki de Saint Phalle spends the entire year in the Swiss mountains, planning her sculpture park.

1977
Together with Constantin Mulgrave, Niki de Saint Phalle designs the sets for the film, *The Travelling Companion*, which is based on a fairy story by Hans Christian Andersen. She visits Mexico and New Mexico. Ricardo Menon becomes her assistant, continuing to work with her for the next ten years.

1978
Niki de Saint Phalle begins laying out her *Giardino dei Tarocchi* on the estates of Carlo and Nicola Caracciolo at Garavicchio in Tuscany. Her designs, which are based on tarotcards, are later used as models for monumental sculptures.

1979
Niki de Saint Phalle spends most of her time in Tuscany, laying the foundations for her Tarot Garden. She invents new sculptures, which she calls Skinnies. In March she holds her first exhibition in Japan at Tokyo's Watari Gallery. Gimpel & Weitzenhoffer of New York hold an exhibition of the models and photographs for her architectural projects. The exhibition, entitled *Monumental Projects*, tours the United States.

1980
In April, Niki de Saint Phalle begins work on the first sculptures for her Tarot Garden, *The Magician* and *The High Priestess*. In Ulm her sculpture, *Le poète et sa muse*, is unveiled on the university campus. The installation coincides with an exhibition of her graphic work, which lasts from May until July. From July to September the Centre Georges Pompidou in Paris devotes a retrospective exhibition to her.
Yoko Masuda organises the first exhibition at Space Niki in Tokyo.
The first edition of furniture by Niki de Saint Phalle is put into production.

1981
Niki de Saint Phalle rents a cottage in the vicinity of her Tarot Garden. She hires assistants from the surrounding farms to help her with her project. Jean Tinguely and his All Star Swiss Team of Sepp Imhof and Rico Weber take on the task of welding the tarot sculptures.
In the spring she paints the exterior of a new twin-engine airplane, the *Piper aérostar 602 P*, for the Peter Stuyvesant Foundation in Amsterdam.

1982
An American firm invites Niki de Saint Phalle to create a new perfume. She uses the proceeds to finance her Tarot Garden. Jean Tinguely receives a commission from the City of Paris to design a fountain for the Centre Georges Pompidou and asks Niki de Saint Phalle to assist him, since he wants to combine his machines with brightly coloured sculptures. The galleries of Gimpel & Weitzenhoffer in New York and Gimpel Fils in London show Niki de Saint Phalle's Skinnies. Work on the Tarot Garden progresses. The Dutch artist Doc Winsen takes over Jean Tinguely's role and works on the steel construction of the sculptures. By the end of the year they are in a position to begin applying cement.
Niki de Saint Phalle suffers her first attack of rheumatoid arthritis. The attacks continue for a period of years.

1983
The Stuart Foundation commissions a sculpture, *Sun God*, for the campus of the University of California at San Diego.
Niki de Saint Phalle moves into *The Empress* in the grounds of her Tarot Garden. The building is designed in the shape of a sphinx. She decides to use ceramics in addition to mirrors and glass for the sculptures. Ricardo Menon discovers Venera Finocchiaro, a ceramics teacher in Rome, who produces all their ceramics from now on.

1984
Niki de Saint Phalle works full-time on her Tarot Garden.

1985
The buildings *The Magician*, *The Tower*, *The Empress* and *The High Priestess* are completed. Jean Tinguely constructs a machine for *The Tower of Babel*.

1986
Niki de Saint Phalle spends most of the year at Garavicchio, where more sculptures are installed in her Tarot Garden.
Together with Professor Silvio Barandun she writes and illustrates a book, *AIDS: You Can't Catch It Holding Hands*, which is later published and translated into five different languages. Ricardo Menon returns to Paris to attend drama school. He introduces Niki de Saint Phalle to Marcelo Zitelli, who becomes her assistant. She works on a series of polyester vases in the shape of animals.

1987
In March, the Kunsthalle der Hypo-Kulturstiftung in Munich holds a major exhibition of Niki de Saint Phalle's work, *Niki de Saint Phalle – Bilder – Figuren – Phantastische Gärten*. Her first retrospective in America is held at the Nassau County Museum of Fine Art in Roslyn, Long Island, under the title, *Fantastic Visions: Works by Niki de Saint Phalle*

1988
Niki de Saint Phalle and Jean Tinguely receive a commission from President Mitterrand to design a fountain for Château-Chinon, where he had been mayor for many years. Mitterrand himself unveils the fountain, in front of the town hall, in March.
Helen Schneider commissions a fountain for the Schneider Children's Hospital on Long Island. Niki de Saint Phalle designs a snake tree 5.50 metres in height.

1989
Niki de Saint Phalle has a twin exhibition in the JGM. Galerie and the Galerie de France under the title *Œuvres des années 80*. She works in bronze for the first time and designs a series of Egyptian gods, which are intended to be cast. Ricardo Menon dies of AIDS. Together with her son, Philip Mathews, she produces a cartoon film, which is based on her book, *AIDS: You Can't Catch It Holding Hands*.

1990
In June, Niki de Saint Phalle exhibits work from the 1960s at both the Galerie de France and the JGM. Galerie in Paris. The exhibition is titled *Tirs ... et autres révoltes 1961-1964*.
In November she presents her film about AIDS at the Musée des Arts Décoratifs in Paris. To coincide with the presentation, the museum mounts an exhibition of drawings for the film and for the revised version of the book. *Le sida: Tu ne l'attraperas pas* is published by the Agence française de lutte contre le sida and distributed to schoolchildren throughout the whole of France.

1991
Niki de Saint Phalle works on an enlarged model in the scale 1:4 of her *Temple Idéal*, an interdenominational church first planned in 1972. The building will be 16 metres high and will be built in Nîmes in the autumn of 1992 under the patronage of the mayor, Jean Bousquet.
Jean Tinguely dies in August. Niki de Saint Phalle produces her first kinetic sculpture and calls it *Méta-Tinguely*.

One-Woman Exhibitions

1956

St Gallen, Galerie Restaurant Gotthard. *Niki Mathews New York Gemälde, Gouachen*. 28 April – 19 May. First exhibition.

1961

Paris, Galerie J. *Feu à Volonté*. 30 June – 12 July. Organised by Pierre Restany. Booklet with essay by Pierre Restany. First one-woman exhibition with 'shooting paintings'.
Copenhagen, Køpcke Gallery. *Niki de Saint-Phalle*. Officially opened on 15 September.

1962

Los Angeles, Everett Ellin Gallery sponsors Niki de Saint Phalle's shooting session at 4:00 pm on Sunday 4 March. The target is 6 metres away. Jean Tinguely and Ed Kienholz also take part. Niki de Saint Phalle's first public shooting session in the USA.
Malibu Hills, California. A shooting session involving two targets – one 2.4 metres high at a distance of 5 metres, the other somewhat smaller. Sunday afternoon, late March or early April.
Paris, Galerie Rive Droite. *Niki de Saint-Phalle*. 15 June – 15 July. Catalogue.
New York, Alexander Iolas Gallery in association with Jean Larcade, Paris. *Niki de Saint Phalle*. 15 October – 3 November. Booklets. Clockwork action for a shooting gallery, *Homage to Le Facteur Cheval*, by Jean Tinguely.

1963

Los Angeles. The Dwan Gallery sponsors *King Kong*, a monumental 'shooting painting' produced during the summer.

1964

Los Angeles. The Dwan Gallery in association with the Alexander Iolas Gallery. *Niki de Saint Phalle*. 5 – 31 January.
Geneva, Galerie Alexandre Iolas. *Niki de Saint-Phalle*. 1 – 22 April. Booklet with text by Georges Peillex.
London, Hanover Gallery. *Niki de Saint Phalle: You are my Dragon*. 23 September – 17 October.

1965

New York, Alexander Iolas Gallery. *Niki de Saint Phalle*. 16 April – 1 May.
Paris, Galerie Alexandre Iolas. *Niki de Saint Phalle*. 30 September – 30 October. Livre d'artiste. First Nanas exhibited.

1966

New York, Alexander Iolas Gallery. *Niki de Saint Phalle*. 29 March – 23 April. Livre d'artiste. Nanas first exhibited in New York.

1967

Amsterdam, Stedelijk Museum. *Niki de Saint Phalle: Les Nanas au pouvoir*. 26 August – 15 October. Under the curatorship of Ad Petersen. Catalogue. First *Nana Dream House* created for this retrospective. An expanded version of the exhibition travels to the Dusseldorf Kunstverein as *Niki de Saint Phalle: Werke 1962-1968*. 19 November 1968 – 1 January 1969. Catalogue.
New York, Alexander Iolas Gallery. *Papier-Mâché Animals in a Zoo*. March.
Amsterdam, Galerie Espace. *Niki de Saint Phalle: Voir les mini-nanas en plâtre peint et aussi des dessins*. 26 August – 16 September.

1968

London, Hanover Gallery. *Niki de Saint Phalle*. 2 October – 1 November. Livre d'artiste.
Paris, Galerie Alexandre Iolas. *Flash Niki de Saint Phalle: Hier soir j'ai fait un rêve*. 24 October – 6 November.
Zurich, Gimpel & Hanover Galerie. *Niki de Saint Phalle*. 18 May – 6 July. Booklet.

1969

Hanover, Hanover Kunstverein, Künstlerhaus. *Niki de Saint Phalle: Werke 1962-1968*. 2 March – 2 April. Catalogue.
Munich, Galerie Stangl. *Plastiken, Zeichnungen und Graphiken von Niki de Saint Phalle*. 6 May – 21 June. Booklet.
Lucerne, Kunstmuseum. *Niki de Saint Phalle*. 27 July – 14 September.
Beverly Hills, California, Frank Perls Gallery. *New Lithographs and Sculptures*. July – August.
Geneva, Galerie Alexandre Iolas. *Niki de Saint Phalle: Nana fontaine*. September.
Amsterdam, Galerie Seriaal. *Niki de Saint Phalle: Grafieken en reliefs in Seriaal*. 20 – 29 September.

1969/1970

London, Hanover Gallery. *Niki de Saint Phalle*. 10 December – 10 January.

1970

Paris, Galerie Alexandre Iolas. *Niki de Saint Phalle: Le Rêve de Diane*. 5 – 28 February.
Milan, Galleria Alexandre Iolas. *The Dream Machine*. October. Livre d'artiste.
Paris, La Hune. *Niki de Saint Phalle: Nana Power*. 20 November – 4 December.
Basle, Galerie Felix Handschin. March.

1970/1971

Zurich, Gimpel & Hanover Galerie. *Niki de Saint Phalle zeigt neue Objekte und Serigraphien*. 3 December – 12 January.

1971

Berne, Kammerkunsthalle. *Niki de Saint Phalle: Serigraphien und kleine Skulpturen*. 27 February – 4 May.
Rome, La Galleria, Cavalieri Hilton. *Niki de Saint Phalle: Serigrafie – Sculture*. 26 March – 17 April. Booklet with reprint of essay by Pierre Descargues.
Stockholm, Svensk-Franska Konstgallerier. *Niki de Saint Phalle: Nana Power polykroma skulpturer*. Opened on 6 May.
Amsterdam, Galerie Espace. *Niki de Saint Phalle: 'the devouring mothers' and other sculptures*. 6 September – 16 October.
Amsterdam, Galerie Seriaal. *Niki de Saint Phalle: new multiples & graphics*. 4 – 25 September.

1972

Paris, Galerie Alexandre Iolas. *Niki de Saint Phalle: Les funérailles du père*. 23 February – 25 March.
Geneva, Galerie Bonnier. *Niki de Saint-Phalle: Niki avant les Nanas, œuvres de 1963 et 1964*. 19 October – 16 November.

1972/1973

London, Gimpel Fils. *Niki de Saint Phalle: The Devouring Mothers*. 4 December – 27 January. Livre d'artiste.

1973

New York, Gimpel & Weitzenhoffer Gallery. *Niki de Saint Phalle: The Devouring Mothers*. 10 April – 5 May.

1974

Paris, Galerie Alexandre Iolas. *Niki de Saint Phalle: Projets et réalisations d'architecture*. 5 February – 2 March. Livre d'artiste.
Baden-Baden, Galerie Dr. Ernst Hauswedell. *Niki de Saint Phalle: Skulpturen, Zeichnungen, Graphik, Ballon-Nanas*. 12 June – 14 July.

1975

Arles, exhibition organised in association with the 1975 Festival d'Arles in the Romanesque rooms at the Monastery of Saint-Trophime. *Niki de Saint-Phalle*. 9 July – 30 September. Booklet.
Brussels, Palais des Beaux-Arts. *Festival Europalia-France 1975*. The front of the Palais des Beaux-Arts is decorated with elements from *Last Night I Had a Dream*.

1976

Rotterdam, Museum Boymans-van Beuningen. *Beelden, modellen en maquettes van Niki de Saint Phalle*. 21 July – 5 September. Livre d'artiste.
Aalborg, Nordjyllands Kunstmuseum. *Niki de Saint-Phalles sculpturer*. 16 September – 24 October. Catalogue.
Geneva, Galerie Bonnier. *Niki de Saint Phalle*. Opened on 23 September.

1977/1978

New York, Gimpel & Weitzenhoffer Gallery. *Niki de Saint Phalle: Sculptures and Graphics*. 29 November – 21 January.

1979

Tokyo, Watari Gallery. *Niki de Saint Phalle*. 13 March – 4 April. Catalogue.
New York, Gimpel & Weitzenhoffer Gallery. *Niki de Saint Phalle: Monumental Projects, Maquettes and Photographs*. 3 April – 23 May. Booklet. Travels to Columbus Museum of Art, Columbus, Ohio, 17 May – 22 June 1980; Laumeier Sculpture Park, St Louis, Missouri, 25 February – 5 April 1981; Mandeville Art Gallery, University of California at San Diego, La Jolla, 16October – 25 November 1981; and Palm Springs Desert Museum, Palm Springs, California.

1980

Zurich, Galerie Bischofberger. *Niki de St. Phalle: Werke 1960-1980*. 22 March – 15 April.
Ulm, Ulm Museum. *Niki de Saint Phalle: Das graphische Werk 1968-1980. Figuren*. 18 May – 6 July. Catalogue.
Paris, Musée National d'Art Moderne, Centre Georges Pompidou. *L'Exposition retrospective de Niki de Saint Phalle*. 3 July – 1 September. Under the curatorship of Pontus Hulten and Jean-Yves Mock. Catalogue. Travels to Wilhelm-Lehmbruck-Museum, Duisburg, 19 October – 30 November 1980; Neue Galerie, Linz, 11 December 1980 – 31 January 1981; Nuremberg Kunsthalle, 20 February – 19 April 1981; Haus am Waldsee, Berlin, 3 May – 14 June 1981; Hanover Kunstmuseum with Sprengel Collection, 28 June – 23 August 1981; and Moderna Museet, Stockholm, 12 September – 25 October 1981.

1980/1981

Tokyo, Space Niki (inaugural exhibition). *Niki de Saint Phalle (Space Niki Collection), Part 1 – Prints Nana Power*, 13 December – 15 February; *Part 2 – Posters and Film 'Daddy'*, 21 March – 19 April. Catalogue. *Part 3 – Prints 'Ich' etc.*, 28 April – 28 June; *Part 4 – Newly Imported Prints*, 28 August – 18 October; *Part 5 – Portraits & Film 'Daddy'*, 23 October – 15 November; *Part 6 – Sculptures*, 20 November – 20 December.

1981

Paris, Galerie Samy Kinge. *Niki de Saint Phalle*. 19 February – 21 March.

1982

Tokyo, Watari Gallery. *Niki de Saint Phalle: Nana Object*. 28 January – 20 February.
New York, Gimpel & Weitzenhoffer Gallery. *Niki de Saint Phalle: New Works (My Skinnies)*. 11 May – 5 June. Catalogue.
London, Gimpel Fils. *My Skinnies*. 15 June – 31 July. Catalogue.

1982/1983

Tokyo, Space Niki. *Niki de Saint Phalle*. 11 December – 28 February.

1983. Montreal, Galerie Esperanza (inaugural exhibition). *Niki de Saint Phalle: Sculptures et lithographies*. 12 April – 14 May. Booklet.

1985

Basle, Galerie Klaus Littmann. *Niki de Saint Phalle 1962-1980: Retrospektive*. 30 May – 3 August. Catalogue.

Knokke-le-Zoute, Casino Knokke. *Niki de Saint Phalle*. 30 June – 1 September. Booklet with text by Pierre Restany.

London, Gimpel Fils. *Niki de Saint Phalle: The Tarot*. 2 July – 14 September. Livre d'artiste.

New York, Gimpel & Weitzenhoffer Gallery. *Niki de Saint Phalle: New Sculptures Based on 'The Tarot'*. 3 September – 5 October.

1986

Tokyo, Space Niki and Sagacho Exhibition Space. *Niki de Saint Phalle (Space Niki Collection): sculptures prints drawings films video performance talk-session*. 1 April – 28 June and 1 – 24 April respectively. Catalogues.

Tokyo, Space Niki. *Niki de Saint Phalle (Space Niki Collection): Prints*. 2 – 15 July.

Ohtsu, Japan, exhibition organised by Space Niki at Seibu Department Store. *Niki de Saint Phalle (Space Niki Collection)*. 30 October – 24 November. Booklet.

Paris, Galerie Colette Creuzevault. *Cinq Vases par Niki de St. Phalle*. 3 – 31 December. Catalogue.

1986/1987

Helsinki, Kaj Forsblom Gallery. *Niki de Saint Phalle: Veistoksja ja reliefejä / Sculptures et reliefs*. 27 November– 4 January. Booklet.

1987

Munich, Kunsthalle der Hypo-Kulturstiftung. *Niki de Saint Phalle: Bilder – Figuren – Phantastische Gärten*. 26 March – 5 July. Book.

Geneva, Galerie Bonnier. *Niki de Saint Phalle: Œuvres récentes*. 29 September – October. Catalogue.

1987/1988

Roslyn, New York, Nassau County Museum of Fine Art. *Fantastic Vision: Works by Niki de Saint Phalle*. 27 September – 3 January. Under the curatorship of Phyllis Stigliano and Janice Parente. Catalogue.

1988

London, Gimpel Fils. *Niki de Saint Phalle: The Wounded Animals*. 7 June – 10 September. Livre d'artiste.

Canterbury, The Blackfriars, presented by The Canterbury Theatre and Festival Trust. *Sculptures by Niki de Saint Phalle*. 2 – 22 October.

1989

Paris, Galerie de France and JGM. Galerie. *Niki de Saint Phalle: Œuvres des années 80*. 12 May – 17 June and 12 May – 24 June respectively. Organised by Jean Tinguely. Catalogue. Travels to Palais Bénédictine, Fécamp. 1 July – 10 September. Catalogue.

Athens, Zoumboulakis Galleries. *Niki de Saint Phalle*. Opened on 19 October.

1990

Paris, JGM. Galerie and Galerie de France. *Niki de Saint Phalle: Tirs ... et autres révoltes 1961-1964*. 26 June – 28 July. Text by Pierre Restany. Catalogue.

Knokke-le-Zoute, Guy Pieters Gallery. *Niki de Saint Phalle: Last Night I Had a Dream*. 8 September – 22 October. Booklet.

New York, Gimpel & Weitzenhoffer Gallery. *Niki de Saint Phalle: New Sculptures*. 3 October – 10 November. Booklet.

1990/1991

Paris, Musée des Arts Décoratifs. *Niki de Saint Phalle: Lutte contre le sida*. 30 November – 28 January. Livre d'artiste.

1991

Munich, Galerie Artcuriel. *Niki de Saint Phalle: Skulpturen und Grafik*. 29 May – 30 June.

Margaux, Château d'Arsac. *Niki de Saint Phalle au Château d'Arsac*. 7 June – 30 September.

London, Gimpel Fils. *Gods*. 19 June – 7 September. Catalogue.

Knokke-le-Zoute, Guy Pieters Gallery. *Niki de Saint Phalle: Œuvres récentes*. August. Catalogue.

Winterthur, Galerie Hochwacht. *Niki de Saint Phalle: Signierte Original-Serigraphien*. 9 September – 12 October.

1961

Paris, Musée d'Art Moderne de la Ville de Paris. *Comparaisons: Peinture Sculpture.* 6 February – 6 March. Catalogue.

Amsterdam, Stedelijk Museum. *Bewogen Beweging.* 10 March – 17 April. Organised by Willem Sandberg and Pontus Hulten. Catalogue. Travels to Moderna Museet, Stockholm, as *Rörelse i konsten,* 17 May – 3 September; and to Louisiana Museum of Modern Art, Humlebaek, as *Bevaegelse i kunsten,* 22 September – 22 October.

Stockholm, Galerie Samlaren. *Nouveaux Réalistes.* June. Organised by Daniel Spoerri. The exhibiting artists were Arman, César, Gérard Deschamps, François Dufrêne, Raymond Hains, Yves Klein, Nordenström, Martial Raysse, Pierre Restany, Daniel Spoerri, Jean Tinguely, Per Olof Ultvedt and Jacques de la Villeglé.

Paris, Galerie Rive Droite. *Le Nouveau Réalisme à Paris et à New York.* July – 15 September. Organised by Pierre Restany. Booklet, including essay by Pierre Restany. Artists: Arman, Lee Brontecou, César, John Chamberlain, Varden M. Chryssa, Raymond Hains, Jasper Johns, Yves Klein, Robert Rauschenberg, Richard Stankiewicz and Jean Tinguely.

Nice, Galerie Muratore. *Festival du Nouveau Réalisme 1961.* 13 July – 13 September. Organised by Pierre Restany. Booklet, with introduction by Pierre Restany. Opening action spectacles planned by Jean Larcade at the Abbaye Roseland, Nice.

Thun, Kunstsammlung der Stadt Thun (Thunerhof). *Der Surrealismus und verwandte Strömungen in der Schweiz.* 16 September – 22 October.

New York, The Museum of Modern Art. *The Art of Assemblage.* 2 October – 12 November. Curator: William C. Seitz. Catalogue. Travels to The Dallas Museum of Contemporary Arts, Dallas, Texas, 9 January – 11 February 1962; and San Francisco Museum of Modern Art, San Francisco, 5 March – 15 April 1962.

1962

Paris, Musée d'Art Moderne de la Ville de Paris. *Comparaisons: Peinture Sculpture.* 12 March – 2 April. Catalogue.

Rome, Galleria La Sallita. *Oggetto-Pittura.* Opened on 28 April. Booklet, including essay by Cesare Vivaldi.

Paris, Galerie Creuze. *Donner à voir no. 1.* 15 May – 8 June. Catalogue. Artists: Arman, Lee Bontecou, César, Gérard Deschamps, François Dufrêne, Raymond Hains, Yves Klein, Martial Raysse, Mimmo Rotella, Daniel Spoerri, Jean Tinguely and Jacques de la Villeglé.

Amsterdam, Stedelijk Museum. *DYLABY (Dynamic Labyrinth).* 30 August – 30 September. Organised by Pontus Hulten and Willem Sandberg. Catalogue. With the help of Daniel Spoerri, Per Olof Ultvedt, Martial Raysse, Robert Rauschenberg and Jean Tinguely, Niki de Saint Phalle creates a vast labyrinth of nine interconnecting rooms

1963

Munich, Neue Galerie im Künstlerhaus. *Les Nouveaux Réalistes.* 8 February – mid-March. Catalogue. Artists: Arman, César, Christo, Gérard Deschamps, François Dufrêne, Raymond Hains, Yves Klein, Jacques de la Villeglé, Mimmo Rotella, Daniel Spoerri and Jean Tinguely.

Houston, Texas, The Museum of Fine Arts. *Some Recent Accessions 1961-1963.* 4 May – 2 June.

Paris, Musée d'Art Moderne de la Ville de Paris. *Troisième Biennale de Paris: Manifestation biennale et internationale des jeunes artistes.* 28 September – 3 November. Catalogue.

1964

Paris, Musée d'Art Moderne de la Ville de Paris. *Mythologies quotidiennes.* July – October. Catalogue.

Basle, Galerie Felix Handschin. *Perspektiven.* 24 October – 30 November.

1965

Lund, Sweden, Lunds Konsthall. *Le merveilleux mode / Det underbara moderna / Det underbara idag.* 19 March – 25 April. Catalogue.

Paris, Musée d'Art Moderne de la Ville de Paris. *XXIe Salon de Mai.* 3 – 23 May. Catalogue.

Paris, Jean Larcade, Art Contemporain. *POP POR, POP CORN, CORNY.* 29 June – 14 August. Catalogue. Artists: Marcel Duchamp, Francis Picabia, Man Ray, Salvador Dalí, Max Ernst, Joan Miró, Lucio Fontana, Larry Rivers, Victor Brauner, Robert Rauschenberg, Arman, Jean Tinguely, Raynaud, Raymond Hains, Yves Klein, John Wesley, René Magritte and Camille Boyen.

Paris, Galerie Creuze (Salle Balzac). *La Figuration narrative: Dans l'art contemporain.* 1 – 29 October. Organised by Gérald Gassiot-Talabot. Catalogue.

1966

Chicago, The Art Institute of Chicago. *Four European Artists and the Figure.* 5 February – 6 March. Booklet. Artists: Niki de Saint Phalle, Karel Appel, Dado and Horst Antes.

Houston, Texas, The Museum of Fine Arts. *Contemporary Art from the Museum Collections with New Accessions.* 10 February – 26 March.

Boston, Massachusetts, War Memorial Auditorium. *Winterfest 1966.* 18 – 27 February.

Minneapolis, Minnesota, Walker Art Center. *Editions MAT 1964.* 17 March – 17 April.

Berne, Kunsthalle. *Weiss auf Weiss.* 25 May – 3 July. Catalogue.

Stockholm, Moderna Museet. *Hon – en katedral.* 3 June – 4 September. Organised by Pontus Hulten. Catalogue. Together with Jean Tinguely and Per Olof Ultvedt, Niki de Saint Phalle creates a giant recumbent Nana nearly twenty-nine metres in length. Visitors entered an inner labyrinth of rooms through the figure's sexual orifice.

Geneva, Galerie Bonnier. *MAT:EDITION.* 15 September – 15 October.

1967

Pittsburgh, Pennsylvania, Museum of Art, The Carnegie Institute. *Alcoa Collection of Contemporary Art: An Exhibition of Works Acquired from the G. David Thompson Collection.* 12 January – 5 February. Catalogue.

Paris, Animation Recherche Confrontation – Musée d'Art Moderne de la Ville de Paris. *La fureur poétique.* 15 March – 23 April. Organised by José Pierre. Catalogue. Artists: Eugenio Barbieri, Jorge Camacho, Augustin Lesage, Roberto Echauren, Matta, Jean-Claude Silbermann, Hervé Télémaque, Toyen, Ursula and Adolf Wölfli.

Montreal, Expo '67. 28 April – 27 October. Together with Jean Tinguely, Niki de Saint Phalle represents France and creates *Le paradis fantastique.* This collaborative sculpture, which is installed on the roof garden of the French Pavilion, consists of nine large polyester figures painted in neon colours by Niki de Saint Phalle and combined with six massive kinetic machines by Jean Tinguely. The exhibition travels to The Albright-Knox Art Gallery, Buffalo, New York, 21 November 1967 – 7 January 1968, and to The Conservatory Garden, Central Park, New York, where it opens on 1 May 1968 under the patronage of the city's Department of Cultural Affairs. It is now on permanent display at the Moderna Museet, Stockholm.

Hamburg, Kunsthaus. *Französische Malerei der Gegenwart / Tendances de la peinture française contemporaine.* 7 November – 10 December. Catalogue.

Paris, Galerie Henri Creuzevault. *Table d'orientation pour une sculpture d'aujourd'hui.* December. Catalogue.

1968

New York, The Museum of Modern Art. *Dada, Surrealism, and Their Heritage.* 27 March – 9 June. Curator: William S. Rubin. Catalogue. Travels to Los Angeles County Museum of Art, 16 July – 8 September, and Art Institute of Chicago, 19 October – 8 December.

London, Institute of Contemporary Arts. *The Obsessive Image 1960-1968.* 10 April – 29 May. Catalogue.

Paris, Musée Galliera. *Le Décor quotidien de la vie en 1968: Expansions et environments.* 10 April – May. Catalogue. Artists: François Arnal, César, Marc de Rosny, Jean-Michel Sandejouand, Jean Tinguely and Constantin Xenakis.

Saint-Paul-de-Vence, Fondation Maeght. *L'Art vivant 1965-1968.* 13 April – 30 June. Catalogue.

Chicago, Museum of Contemporary Art. *Selections from the Collection of Mr. and Mrs. Robert B. Mayer.* 13 July – 8 September.

1969

New York, Whitney Museum of American Art. *Contemporary American Sculpture Selection 2.* 14 April – 5 May.

Antwerp, Galerie Ad Libitum. *Niki de Saint Phalle & Jean Tinguely.* Opened on 6 June.

1969/1970

Chicago, Museum of Contemporary Art. *Selections from the Joseph Randall Shapiro Collection.* 20 December – 1 February. Catalogue.

Frankfurt am Main, Kunstverein. *Figuren Gestalten Personen / Personen Gestalten Figuren.* 30 December – 1 February. Catalogue.

1970

Syon Park, Middlesex. *Open Air Sculpture II: Syon Park Summer 1970.* May – September. Catalogue. Exhibition organised by Gimpel Fils, London.

Knokke-le-Zoute, Casino Knokke. *Pop Art.* 27 June – 9 September.

Paris, Galerie Mathias Fels. *Nouveau Réalisme 1960-1970.* 27 October – 27 November. Catalogue. Artists: Arman, César, Christo, Gérard Deschamps, François Dufrêne, Raymond Hains, Yves Klein, Martial Raysse, Mimmo Rotella, Daniel Spoerri, Jean Tinguely and Jacques de la Villeglé.

1970/1971

Milan, Rotonda della Besana. *10th Anniversary of the Nouveaux Réalistes.* 27 November – 25 January. Organised by Pierre Restany and Guido Le Noci. Catalogue. An open-air shooting session is held on the evening of 29 November, when Niki de Saint Phalle fires shots at an altar assemblage.

London, Whitechapel Gallery. *3 — ∞ : new multiple art.* Sponsored by the Arts Council of Great Britain. 19 November – 2 January. Catalogue.

1971

Södertälje, Sweden. Södertälje Konsthall. *Multiplication.* 18 February – 14 March. Catalogue.

Dublin, Royal Dublin Society. *ROSC '71: The Poetry of Vision.* 24 October – 29 December. Catalogue.

1972

Houston, The Museum of Fine Arts. *A Salute to the Contemporary Arts Museum: Twentieth-Century Art from The Museum of Fine Arts.* 17 March – 16 April.

Paris, Galerie Henri Creuzevault. *Etudes et épures.* 17 May – 30 June. Catalogue. Artists: Arman, Enrico Baj, César, Christo, Dado, Jean Dewasne, Fred Deux, Lalanne, Georges Mathieu, Roberto Echauren, Matta, Pons and Jean Tinguely.

1973

Hanover, Kunstverein. *Jahresgaben 1973.* 25 September – 14 October. Catalogue.

1977

Marseilles, Musée Cantini. *3 Villes, 3 collections: Grenoble – Marseille – Saint-Étienne. L'Avant-Garde 1960-1976*. February – March. Organised by Marie-Claude Beaud, Jacques Beauffet, Marie-Christine Bouille, Bernard Ceysson and Marielle Latour. Catalogue. Travels to Musée de Peinture et de Sculpture, Grenoble, April – May; Musée d'Art et d'Industrie, Saint-Etienne, summer 1977; and Musée National d'Art Moderne, Centre Georges Pompidou, autumn 1977.

Rotterdam, Museum Boymans-van Beuningen. *De Fiets*. 7 April – 12 June. Catalogue.

Paris, Musée National d'Art Moderne, Centre Georges Pompidou. *Paris – New York: Un Album*. 1 June – 19 September. Catalogue.

1978

Athens, Zoumboulakis Galleries. *Nouveaux Réalistes*. Opened on 19 January. Organised by Pierre Restany. Catalogue.

Tokyo, The Seibu Museum of Art. *Biennale de Paris '59 – '73*. 3 – 29 March. Catalogue.

Beaulieu-en-Rouergue, Abbaye de Beaulieu-en-Rouergue, Centre d'Art Contemporain. *Réel? Réalisme? Réalité? Du Pop-art au Néo-réalisme 1958-1978*. 25 June – 13 September. Catalogue.

Basle, Hammerstraße 158. *Hammer Ausstellung*. 23 September – 29 October. Catalogue.

1980

New York, Whitney Museum of American Art. *American Sculpture: Gifts of Howard and Jean Lipman*. 15 April – 15 June.

Basle, Wenkenpark. *Skulptur im 20. Jahrhundert*. 10 May – 14 September. Catalogue.

New York, Whitney Museum of American Art. *The Figurative Tradition and the Whitney Museum of American Art*. 25 June – 28 September.

Ulm, Hochbauamt der Stadt Ulm and Ulm Museum. *Skulpturen zur Landesgartenschau*. Catalogue.

1981

Amsterdam, Stedelijk Museum. *Fantastic Architecture*. 26 February – 12 April. Organised by Joost Eiffers and Michael Schuyt.

1982

Geneva, Galerie Bonnier. *L'Empreinte du Nouveau Réalisme*. Opened on 20 April.

Hanover, Kestner Museum. *Rosenthal: Hundert Jahre Porzellan*. 29 April – 13 June. Catalogue. Travels to Focke Museum, Bremen, 20 June – 15 August; Kunstgewerbemuseum, Cologne, 10 September – 31 October; Germanisches Nationalmuseum, Nuremberg; and Stadtmuseum, Munich.

Zurich, Museum Bellerive. *heiter bis aggressiv*. 26 May – 15 August. Catalogue.

1983

Paris, Musée d'Art Moderne de la Ville de Paris. *Autour de la Fontaine Stravinsky de Niki de Saint Phalle et Jean Tinguely*. 25 June – 25 September.

1984

Washington, D.C., Hirshhorn Museum and Sculpture Garden, Smithsonian Institution. *Artistic Collaboration in the Twentieth Century* 9 June – 19 August. Curator: Cynthia Jaffee McCabe. Catalogue. Travels to Milwaukee Art Museum, Wisconsin, 18 November 1984 – 13 January 1985; and J.B. Speed Art Museum, Louisville, Kentucky, 21 February – 21 April 1985.

St Louis, Missouri, Laumeier Sculpture Park. *Olga Hirshhorn Collection: A Collector's Eye*. 19 August – September.

1985

Chicago, Museum of Contemporary Art. *Permanent Collection: Selected Gifts from The Joseph and Jory Shapiro Collection*. 30 January – April. Catalogue.

New York, Gimpel & Weitzenhoffer Gallery. *Sixteen Sculptors*. 14 February – 9 March.

Chicago, The Art Institute of Chicago. *Mr. and Mrs. Joseph Randall Shapiro Collection*. 23 February – 14 April.

Huntington, New York, Heckscher Museum. *Sights for Small Eyes*. 28 April – 16 June.

Chicago, Museum of Contemporary Art. *Nouveau Réalisme and Pop Art: Selections from the Permanent Collection*. 6 September – 12 November. Booklet.

Paris, Galerie Colette Creuzevault. *Œuvre unique*. 2 October – 15 November.

1985/1986

Birmingham, Michigan, Robert L. Kidd Associates Gallery. *Animals: Contemporary Visions*. 6 December – 31 January.

1986

Fitchburg, Massachusetts, Fitchburg Art Museum. *New Works in Plastic*. 26 January – 30 March. Curator: Ursula Pitman.

Paris, Musée d'Art Moderne de la Ville de Paris. *1960: Les Nouveaux Réalistes*. 15 May – 7 September. Curator: Sylvain Lecombre. Catalogue.

1987

Syracuse, New York, Everson Museum of Art. *Sacred Spaces*. 22 January – 23 March. Curator: Dominique Nahas. Catalogue.

Winterthur, Kunstmuseum. *1960: Les Nouveaux Réalistes*. 25 January – 22 March. Catalogue.

New York, Urban Gallery. *The World Through 'Naive' Eyes*. 10 March – 11 April. Catalogue.

Paris, Galerie Colette Creuzevault. *Trois Femmes sculpteurs: Germaine Richier, Niki de Saint Phalle, Alicia Panalba*. 21 May – 28 June. Booklet.

1988

New York, Zabriskie Gallery. *Nouveaux Réalistes: Works from 1957 to 1963*. 17 May – 8 June. Catalogue.

Paris, JGM. Galerie. *Sculptures du XXe siècle: De Rodin aux années soixantes*. 16 June – 24 September. Catalogue.

Venice, XLIII Esposizione Internazionale d'Arte: La Biennale di Venezia. *Ambiente Italia*. 26 June – 25 September. Catalogue.

Prague, Central Library. *Présence de l'art contemporain français*. 5 July – 25 September.

1988/1989

New York, The Jewish Museum. *Golem! Danger, Deliverance and Art*. 20 November – 2 April. Curator: Emily D. Bilski. Catalogue.

1988/1992

Osaka, *Art Kites*, organised by Goethe-Institut. Artists are invited to design a kite in one of Japan's eight traditional regional styles. Catalogue. Travels to seven museums in Japan and thereafter to numerous galleries and museums in Europe and North America.

1989

Paris, Artcurial. *Corps-Figures: La Figuration humaine dans la sculpture du XXe siècle*. April – June. Catalogue.

London, Gimpel Fils. *Sculpture Reliefs & Drawings*. 8 June – 9 September. Catalogue.

Paris, Galerie Colette Creuzevault. *Sculptures dessins reliefs*. 3 October – 30 November.

Lausanne, Musée Cantonal des Beaux-Arts. *Dimension: Petit, l'art suisse entre petite sculpture et objet d'Alberto Giacometti à nos jours*. 7 October – 24 December. Catalogue.

1990

Columbus, Ohio, Wexner Center for the Visual Arts, The Ohio State University. *Art in Europe and America: The 1950s and 1960s*. 17 February – 22 April. Catalogue. Artists: Willem de Kooning, Lucio Fontana, Eva Hesse, Jasper Johns, Yves Klein, Piero Manzoni, Louise Nevelson, Claes Oldenburg, Robert Rauschenberg, Frank Stella, Jean Tinguely and Andy Warhol.

Paris, JGM. Galerie. *Années 60: L'Objet-sculpture*. May – June. Catalogue.

St Petersburg, Russian Museum. *Le Territoire de l'art*. 31 May – 16 July. Organised in association with the Institut des Hautes Etudes en Arts Plastiques, Paris. Catalogue.

Albi, Moulins Albigeois. *Vénus: Prénom d'un rendez-vous artistique et archéologique*. 6 July – 31 August. Catalogue. Travels to Musée d'Art et d'Histoire, Saint-Denis, 26 October – 31 December; Musée de l'Evêché-Evreux-Eure, 15 January – 30 March 1991; and Galerie Enrico Navarra, Paris, 27 September – 19 November 1991.

Florence, Galleria Vivita 1. *Eva Aeppli – Guillaume Bijl – Bernhard Johannes Blume – Katharina Duwen – Niki de Saint Phalle – Meret Oppenheim – Dieter Roth – Daniel Spoerri – Jean Tinguely*. 13 October – 1 December.

Paris, Galerie Montaigne. *Virginia Dwan et les Nouveaux Réalistes: Los Angeles, les années 60 – Arman, Klein, Raysse, Niki de Saint-Phalle, Tinguely*. 23 October – 29 December. Catalogue.

Rijeka, Museum of Modern Art. *12th International Biennale of Drawings*. 20 December – 17 February. Curator: Pontus Hulten. Catalogue.

1991

Geneva, Galerie Bonnier au Pont de la Machine. *Une touche suisse: Trente ans d'activité*. 27 April – 1 June. Catalogue.

Paris, JGM. Galerie. *Choix d'atelier*. 4 September – 12 October.

Morlaix, Musée des Jacobines. *Pierre Restany: Le cœur et la raison*. 12 July – 10 November. Catalogue.

London, The Royal Academy of Arts. *The Pop Art Show*. 13 September – 15 October. Catalogue. Travels to Museum Ludwig, Cologne and Reina Sofia, Madrid.

Solo Exhibition Catalogues

See *Livres d'artiste* for additional volumes published to coincide with solo exhibitions

Niki de Saint Phalle. Galerie Rive Droite, Paris 1962. Texts by John Ashbery and Pierre Restany.

Les Nanas au pouvoir. Stedelijk Museum, Amsterdam 1967. Text by Pierre Descargues.

Niki de Saint Phalle: Werke 1962-1968. Kunstverein für die Rheinlande und Westfalen, Düsseldorf 1968. Texts by Karl-Heinz Hering, Pierre Restany and Hans Strelow.

Niki avant les Nanas: Œuvres de 1963 et 1964. Galerie Bonnier, Geneva 1972.

Niki de Saint-Phalles sculpturer. Nordjyllands Kunstmuseum, Aalborg 1976. Texts by Lars Rostrup Bøyesen, Jørn Otto Hansen and Pierre Restany.

Niki de Saint Phalle. Watari Gallery, Tokyo 1979. Texts by K. Michishita and Yoshiaki Tono.

Niki de Saint Phalle: Das graphische Werk 1968-1980. Figuren, Ulm Museum, Ulm 1980. Texts by Karl Heinz Reisert, Hans Strelow and Erwin Treu.

Niki de Saint Phalle: Exposition retrospective. Musée National d'Art Moderne, Centre Georges Pompidou, Paris 1980. Texts by John Ashbery, Pontus Hulten, Jean-Yves Mock, Pierre Restany, Larry Rivers and Niki de Saint Phalle.

Niki de Saint Phalle: Retrospektive 1954-1980. Wilhelm-Lehmbruck-Museum der Stadt Duisburg, Duisburg 1980. Texts by Michael Hesse, Pontus Hulten, Siegfried Salzmann and others.

Niki de Saint Phalle in DADDY. Space Niki, Tokyo 1981.

Niki de Saint Phalle 1962-1980. Galerie Klaus Littmann, Basle 1985. Text by Jean-Christophe Ammann.

Space Niki Collection: Niki de Saint Phalle Exhibition. Space Niki, Tokyo 1986. Texts by Yoko Shizue Masuda, Pierre Restany, Yoshiaki Tono and others.

Cinq Vases par Niki de St.-Phalle. Galerie Colette Creuzevault, Paris 1986.

Niki de Saint Phalle: Bilder – Figuren – Phantastische Gärten. Kunsthalle der Hypo-Kulturstiftung, Munich. Prestel-Verlag, Munich 1987. Texts by Pierre Descargues, Pontus Hulten, Pierre Restany, Carla Schulz-Hoffmann, Daniel Spoerri, Jean Tinguely and Niki de Saint Phalle.

Niki de Saint Phalle: Œuvres récentes. Galerie Bonnier, Geneva 1987.

Fantastic Vision: Works by Niki de Saint Phalle. Nassau County Museum of Fine Art, Roslyn, New York 1987. Texts by David Bourdon, John Cage, Harry Mathews, Janice Parente and Phyllis Stigliano.

Niki de Saint Phalle: Œuvres des années 80. Galerie de France and JGM. Galerie, Paris 1989. Texts by Pontus Hulten, Pierre Restany, Jean Tinguely and Niki de Saint Phalle. (This same catalogue was published by the Palais Bénédictine, Fécamp, in 1989 but with a different cover.)

Niki de Saint Phalle: Tirs ... et autres révoltes 1961-1964. Galerie de France, Paris 1990 (for exhibition presented by Galerie de France and JGM. Galerie, Paris). Photographs by Laurent Condominas.

Gods. Gimpel Fils, London 1991.

Niki de Saint Phalle: Œuvres récentes. Guy Pieters Gallery, Knokke-le-Zoute 1991.

Group Exhibition Catalogues

Comparaisons: Peinture Sculpture. Musée d'Art Moderne de la Ville de Paris, Paris 1961. Texts by Hubert Deschamps and Waldemar George.

Bewogen Beweging. Stedelijk Museum, Amsterdam 1961. Texts by Pontus Hulten and Willem Sandberg.

Rörelse i konsten. Moderna Museet, Stockholm 1961. Texts by Pontus Hulten, Daniel Spoerri and others.

Louisiana Revy, (Bevaegelse i Kunsten), Vol. 2, No. 1, Louisiana Museum of Modern Art, Humlebaek, Denmark, September 1961. Texts by Pontus Hulten, Ulf Linde, George Rickey and others.

Nouveaux Réalistes. Galerie Samlaren, Stockholm 1961. Text by Pierre Restany.

The Art of Assemblage. The Museum of Modern Art, New York 1961. Text by William C. Seitz.

Comparaisons: Peinture Sculpture. Musée d'Art Moderne de la Ville de Paris, Paris 1962. Texts by Denys Chevalier and Raymond Cogniat.

Donner à voir no. 1. Galerie Creuze, Paris 1962. Texts by Pierre Restany and others.

DYLABY (Dynamic Labyrinth). Stedelijk Museum, Amsterdam 1962. Photographs by Ed van der Elsken.

Les Nouveaux Réalistes. Neue Galerie im Künstlerhaus, Munich 1962. Text by Pierre Restany.

Troisième Biennale de Paris: Manifestation biennale et internationale des jeunes artistes. Musée d'Art Moderne de la Ville de Paris, Paris 1963. Texts by Raymond Cogniat and others.

XXe Salon de Mai. Musée d'Art Moderne de la Ville de Paris, Paris 1963. Texts by Gaston Diehl, Yvon Taillandier and others.

Mythologies quotidiennes. Musée d'Art Moderne de la Ville de Paris, Paris 1964. Text by Gérald Gassiot-Talabot.

Perspektiven. Galerie Felix Handschin, Basle 1964.

Le merveilleux moderne / Det underbara moderna / Det underbara idag. Lunds Konsthall, Lund 1965. Texts by Eje Högestätt and Jean-Jacques Lévêque.

XXIe Salon de Mai. Musée d'Art Moderne de la Ville de Paris, Paris 1965. Text by Gaston Diehl.

La Figuration narrative dans l'art contemporain. Galerie Creuze, Paris 1965. Text by Gérald Gassiot-Talabot.

Weiss auf Weiss. Kunsthalle, Berne 1966. Text by Udo Kultermann.

Hon – en katedral. Moderna Museet, Stockholm 1966. Texts by Pontus Hulten, Ulf Linde, Niki de Saint Phalle, Jean Tinguely, Per Olof Ultvedt and others.

Alcoa Collection of Contemporary Art: An Exhibition of Works Acquired from the G. David Thompson Collection. The Alcoa Collection, Museum of Art, Carnegie Institute, Pittsburgh 1967. Texts by David Rockefeller and others.

La fureur poétique. Musée d'Art Moderne de la Ville de Paris, Paris 1967. Texts by Pierre Descargues, José Pierre and others.

Französische Malerei der Gegenwart / Tendances de la peinture française contemporaine. Kunsthaus, Hamburg 1967. Text by Bernard Dorivae.

Table d'orientation pour une sculpture d'aujourd'hui. Galerie Henri Creuzevault, Paris 1967. Text by Jean-Jacques Lévêque.

Dada, Surrealism, and Their Heritage. The Museum of Modern Art, New York 1968. Text by William S. Rubin.

The Obsessive Image 1960-1968. Institute of Contemporary Art, London 1968. Texts by Mario Amaya, Robert Melville and Roland Penrose.

Le Décor quotidien de la vie en 1968: Expansions etenvironments. Musée Galliera, Paris 1968. Text by Pierre Restany.

L'Art vivant 1965-1968. Fondation Maeght, Saint-Paul-de-Vence 1968. Text by François Wehrlin.

Selections from the Collection of Mr. and Mrs. Robert B. Mayer. Museum of Contemporary Art, Chicago 1968. Texts by David H. Katzive and Jan van der Marck.

Selections from the Joseph Randall Shapiro Collection. Museum of Contemporary Art, Chicago 1961. Text by Jan van der Marck.

Figuren Gestalten Personen / Personen Gestalten Figuren. Kunstverein, Frankfurt am Main 1969. Text by Ewald Rathke.

Open Air Sculpture II: Syon Park Summer 1970. Gimpel Fils, London 1970.

Pop Art: Nieuwe Figuratie / Nouveau Realistie. Knokke Casino, Knokke-le-Zoute 1970. Texts by Gert Bekaert, Pierre Restany and John Russell.

Nouveau Réalisme 1960-1970. Galerie Mathias Fels, Paris 1970. Text by Pierre Restany.

3 — ∞: new multiple art. Arts Council of Great Britain, London 1970. Texts by Janet Daley, Karl Gerstner and others.

Multiplication. Södertälje Konsthall, Södertälje 1971. Text by Eje Högestätt.

ROSC '71: The Poetry of Vision. Royal Dublin Society, Dublin 1971. Texts by Pontus Hulten, Werner Schmalenbach and James Johnson Sweeney.

Douze ans d'art contemporain en France. Grand Palais, Paris 1972. Texts by Daniel Cordier, Maurice Eschapasse, François Mathey and others.

Etudes et épures. Galerie Henri Creuzevault, Paris 1972. Text by Colette Creuzevault.

100 Acquisitions récentes Cantini 1969-1972. Musée Cantini, Marseilles 1972.

Jahresgaben 1973. Kunstverein, Hanover 1973.

3 villes, 3 collections: Grenoble – Marseille – Saint-Etienne: L'Avant-Garde 1960-1976. Musée Cantini, Marseilles 1977. Texts by Marie-Claude Beaud, Bernard Ceysson and Marielle Latour.

De Fiets. Museum Bomans-van Beuningen, Rotterdam 1977. Texts by J.M. Fuchs and W.J. Simons, E. Langui and Bob den Uyl.

Paris – New York: Un Album. Musée National d'ArtModerne, Centre Georges Pompidou, Paris 1977. Text by Pontus Hulten.

Nouveaux Réalistes. Zoumboulakis Galleries, Athens 1978. Texts by Pierre Restany.

Biennale de Paris '59 – '73. The Seibu Museum of Art and Yomiuri Shimbun Sha, Tokyo 1978. Texts by Georges Boudaille and others.

Réel? Réalisme? Réalité? Du Pop-art au Néo-réalisme 1958-1978. Association Culturelle de l'Abbaye de Beaulieu, Beaulieu-en-Rouerque 1978. Text by Geneviève Bonnefoi.

Hammer Ausstellung. Hammerstraße 158, Basle 1978. Texts by Felix Handschin and Werner Jehle.

Skulptur im 20. Jahrhundert. Wenkenpark, Basle 1980.

Skulpturen zur Landesgartenschau. Hochbauamt der Stadt Ulm and Ulm Museum, Ulm 1980. Texts by Jürgen Morschel and Norbert Nobis.

Rosenthal: Hundert Jahre Porzellan. Kestner Museum, Hanover 1982.

Heiter bis aggressiv. Museum Bellerive, Zurich 1982. Text by Sigrid Barten.

Artistic Collaboration in the Twentieth Century. Hirshhorn Museum and Sculpture Garden, Smithsonian Institution Press, Washington, D.C., 1984. Texts by Robert C. Hobbs, Cynthia Jaffee McCabe and David Shapiro.

Permanent Collection: Selected Gifts from The Joseph and Jory Shapiro Collection. Museum of Contemporary Art, Chicago 1985.

The Mr. and Mrs. Randall Shapiro Collection. The Art Institute of Chicago, Chicago 1985. Texts by Dennis Adrian, Katharine Kuh, Joseph Randall Shapiro and James N. Wood.

1960: Les Nouveaux Réalistes. Musée d'Art Moderne de la Ville de Paris, Paris 1986. Texts by Aude Bodet and Sylvain Lecombre, Bernadette Contensou and Pierre Restany.

1960: Les Nouveaux Réalistes. Mannheim Kunsthalle and Winterthur Kunstmuseum, 1986.

Sacred Spaces. Everson Museum of Art, Syracuse, NY, 1987. Texts by David L. Miller and Dominique Nahas.

The World Through 'Naive' Eyes. Urban Gallery, New York 1987.

Nouveaux Réalistes. Zabriskie Gallery, New York 1988. Texts by Allan Kaprow and Pierre Restany.

XLIII Esposizione Internazionale d'Arte: La Biennale di Venezia. Venice 1988. Texts by Pontus Hulten and others.

Golem! Danger, Deliverance and Art. The Jewish Museum, New York 1988. Texts by Emily D. Bilski, Moshe Idel, Elfi Ledig and Isaac Bashevis Singer.

Bilder für den Himmel: Kunstdrachen. Goethe-Institut, Osaka 1988. Texts by Paul Eubel and others.

Corps-Figures: La Figuration humaine dans la sculpture du XXe siècle. Artcurial, Paris 1989. Text by Dominique Le Buhan.

Sculptures, Reliefs & Drawings. Gimpel Fils, London 1989.

Dimension: Petit, l'art suisse entre petite sculpture et objet d'Alberto Giacometti à nos jours. Musée Cantonal des Beaux-Arts, Lausanne 1989. Texts by Erika Billeter, Reinhold Hohl, Dieter Honisch and others.

The Evidence of Magic. Seoul Gallery, Seoul 1989. Text by Pontus Hulten.

Art in Europe and America: The 1950s and 1960s. Wexner Center for the Visual Arts, The Ohio State University, Columbus, Ohio, 1990. Texts by Dore Ashton, David Bourdon, Pierre Restany and others.

Europäische Skulptur der 2. Moderne. Wilhelm-Lehmbruck-Museum, Duisburg 1990. Texts by Christoph Brockhaus, Gottlieb Leinz and Dieter Ronte.

Années 60: L'Objet-Sculpture. JGM. Galerie, Paris 1990. Text by Pierre Restany.

Le Territoire de l'art. Russian Museum, St Petersburg 1990. Text by Pontus Hulten.

L'Art en France 1945-1990. Fondation Daniel Templon, Paris 1990. Texts by Jean-Louis Andral, Michel Ragon, Daniel Templon and others.

Vénus. Moulins Albigeois, Albi, 1990. Texts by Daniel Dobbels, Gilbert Lascault and others.

Virginia Dwan et les Nouveaux Réalistes: Los Angeles, les années 60. Galerie Montaigne, Paris 1990. Texts by Virginia Dwan and Pierre Restany.

Au rendez-vous des amis. Galerie Enrico Navarra, Paris 1990. Texts by Pierre Alechinski, Pierre Hebey, Jorge Semprun and Werner Spies.

12th International Biennale of Drawings. Museum of Modern Art, Rijeka 1990/1991. Texts by Jerko Denegri, Pontus Hulten, Želimir Koščevic, Željko Lužavec and others.

Une touche suisse: trente Ans d'activité 1961-1991. Galerie Bonnier, Geneva 1991. Texts by Dagny and Jan Runnquist.

Pierre Restany: Le Cœur et la raison. Musée de Morlaix, Morlaix 1991. Texts by José Arthur, César, Maria Eugenia Le Noci, Thomas M. Messer, Pierre Restany and others.

The Pop Art Show. The Royal Academy of Arts, London 1991. Texts by Marco Livingstone, Sarah Maharaj, Alfred Pacquement and others.

1961

Together with Jean Tinguely, Robert Rauschenberg and Jasper Johns, Niki de Saint Phalle takes part in a concert/performance of John Cage's *Variations II* at the United States Embassy in Paris on Tuesday 20 June 1961 at 9:00 pm. The soloist is David Tudor. Works by the above-named artists, including a shooting event by Niki de Saint Phalle, serve as a changing backdrop.

Jean Tinguely and Niki de Saint Phalle are invited by Marcel Duchamp to take part in celebrations in honour of Salvador Dalí. For this *Homenaje a Salvador Dalí* they construct a bull, *Toro de fuego*, 2.80 metres in height. Made of plaster and paper, it explodes in the Arena at Figueras during the performance on 12 August.

1962

On 21 March Niki de Saint Phalle assists Jean Tinguely in building his third auto-destructive machine, *Study for the End of the World Number 2*, in the Nevada Desert. The event is filmed for David Brinkley's *Journal* and telecast by NBC.

Takes part in Kenneth Koch's play, *The Construction of Boston*, directed by Merce Cunningham. Her part is to bring art to the city of Boston by firing a .22 rifle at her on-stage plaster sculpture, *Vénus de Milo*. The single performance is given at New York's Maidman Playhouse, 416 West 42nd Street, on the evening of Friday 4 May. Other participants include Jean Tinguely, Robert Rauschenberg, Henry Geldzahler, Öyvind Fahlström and Billy Klüver.

1965

Takes part in lottery sponsored by The American Theater for Poets and organised by the Artists' Key Club of New York on 13 March. For a ten-dollar bet participants could win an artwork by one of thirteen artists – Arman, Ayo, George Brecht, Christo, William Copley, Niki de Saint Phalle, Robert Filliou, Greko, Allan Kaprow, Roy Lichtenstein, Diter Rot, Daniel Spoerri and Andy Warhol. Entrants had to buy a key to a locker at Penn Station, locate the corresponding locker and find either a signed work of art or a small gift.

Plays role of 'Spirit of the Night' in a performance of Kenneth Koch's *The Tinguely Machine Mystery or The Love Suicides at Kaluka* at The Jewish Museum, New York, on 22 December. Directed by Remy Charlip and Kenneth Koch, with music by Morton Feldman, and performed by Michael Zwerin, Richard Davis, Larry Rivers and Howard Kanovitz. The machines are by Jean Tinguely and the cast also includes Clarice Rivers, Syd Solomon, Jane Freilicher, Larry Rivers, Alexander Iolas, John Ashbery and others.

1966

Together with Jean Tinguely and Martial Raysse designs sets for Roland Petit's ballet, *Eloge de la folie*, performed during March at the Théâtre des Champs-Elysées, Paris.

Papier-mâché Nanas used to model clothes at the opening of Yves Saint Laurent's first boutique on Paris's Left Bank.

Designs sets and costumes for Aristophanes's comedy, *Lysistrata*, in a production by Rainer von Diez at the Kassel Staatstheater in October. For the sets, she creates a variant of *Hon*, a ten-metre-long, painted plaster version of a recumbent Nana. The entrance is through the sexual orifice.

1967

Contributes a series of drawings to *Frank O'Hara: In Memory of My Feelings*, a commemorative volume published in a limited edition by The Museum of Modern Art, New York, and containing poems by Frank O'Hara and drawings by his artist friends, including Willem de Kooning, Helen Frankenthaler, Jasper Johns, Lee Krasner, Larry Rivers, Robert Rauschenberg and Claes Oldenburg.

1967/1968

Writes story, *MOI* (1967), and, in collaboration with Rainer von Diez, turns it into a stage play, *ICH (All About ME)*, which is premièred at the Kassel Staatstheater on 28 June 1968 as part of *documenta 4*. The sets are designed by the artist.

1968

Designs inflatable plastic Nana sculptures distributed by Elizabeth de Saint Phalle, New York. The inflatables are made in three sizes and three colours – yellow, blue and pink. From 1968 to 1970 they are also marketed by Multiples of New York.

Designs a Nana Christmas card for The Museum of Modern Art, New York.

1970

Creates a portfolio of seventeen colour serigraphs, *Nana Power*, which is published by Editions Essellier, Paris. Each print is numbered and signed by the artist. Handprinted on handmade paper, 56 x 76 cm., 115 numbered examples and fifteen artist's examples numbered I to XV.

Designs poster with dancing Nana for Théâtre de France, Place de l'Odéon, publicising Merce Cunningham Dance Company (3 – 16 June) and Paul Taylor Dance Company (17 – 30 June).

1971 to the present

Designs limited edition jewelry including Nana brooches, 'serpent' pins and cufflinks, 'bird' necklaces and so on.

1973

Designs programme cover for *11th New York Film Festival* presented by The Film Society of Lincoln Center, New York, 28 September – 13 October. Among the films premièred under the category of 'New Directions/New Films 1973' is *Daddy* by Niki de Saint Phalle and Peter Whitehead.

1981

Designs exterior of new twin-motor aeroplane, *Le Piper aérostar 602 P* (1909) for The Peter Stuyvesant Foundation, Amsterdam. The plane takes part in the first transatlantic race from Paris to New York and back. Organised under the auspices of The Peter Stuyvesant Foundation, the race begins at Paris's Le Bourget Airport on the night of 8/9 June.

1983

In September designs unique perfume bottles of entwined serpents, together with packaging for perfume, *Niki de Saint Phalle*, marketed by Jacqueline Cochran, New York. The perfume is launched in Paris in April 1984.

1980 to the present

Active involvement in the fight against Aids through numerous international projects:

Designs booklet, *Aids: You Can't Catch It Holding Hands*, 1987; revised edition, *Le sida: Tu ne l'attraperas pas ...*, 1990 (see Livres d'artiste)

Designs limited edition serigraph, *Le sida est là, préservons-nous*, 1987.

Designs inflatable condom, *Stop Aids*, 1987.

Designs limited edition serigraph, *Attention Dragueurs!*, 1990, with all proceeds going to the Agence française de lutte contre le sida.

Designs enamel pin of a decorated condom, 1990, with all proceeds going to the Agence française de lutte contre le sida.

1966

Hon, in collaboration with Jean Tinguely and Per Olof Ultvedt. A giant Nana lying on her back with her legs apart; visitors entered through the sexual orifice. The interior was a giant 'environment' comprising a labyrinth of playrooms, including cinema, microphoned 'Lovers' Seat', milk bar and bottle- crushing machine, 'Gallery of Fakes', a postcard 'Piennale' of paintings from the Moderna Museet, roof terrace on the stomach. For exhibition in Main Hall of Moderna Museet. 28.70 metres long, 6.10 metres high and 9.15 metres wide. Weight: 6 tons. Destroyed. Only the head has been preserved.

Le paradis fantastique, in collaboration with Jean Tinguely. Nine large polyester figures by Niki de Saint Phalle and six massive kinetic structures by Jean Tinguely, originally built for Expo '67 in Montreal, since 1971 on permanent exhibition at Moderna Museet, Stockholm.

1967

Nana Dream House, the first Nana house, an 'adult doll's house' for exhibition at the Stedelijk Museum, Amsterdam. A second Nana house, *Nana-Maison*, was created in 1968 for exhibition at Fondation Maeght, Saint-Paul-de-Vence. Each house measures 4 x 3.75 x 3 metres. Both are extant.

1969/1971

First full-scale architectural project in the form of three houses for Rainer von Diez in a mountain range in the South of France. Each house functions as a separate room – *Le rêve de l'oiseau* (kitchen), *Big Clarice* (living room) and *La sorcière* (bathroom). Permanent installation.

1970 to the present

One of many collaborators on Jean Tinguely's monumental sculpture *La tête* (Le cyclope) or *Le monstre dans la forêt* at Milly-la- Forêt. Uses mirror mosaics for the façade. The sculpture was declared a French monument. 22.50 metres high. In progress.

Scheduled opening: September 1992.

1972

Golem, first architectural project for children in the form of a large black-and-white head with three red tongues as slides; the interior functions as a children's playhouse. Technical assistance and subframe by Jean Tinguely, assisted by Rico Weber and Paul Wiedemer. District of Kiryat Hayovel, Jerusalem. Height 6 metres. Permanent installation.

1975

Dragon (of Knokke), a fully equipped 'house for children' with a tongue as slide; built for the children of Roger and Fabienne Nellens. Technical assistance and subframe by Jean Tinguely, assisted by Rico Weber. Knokke-le-Zoute, Belgium. Height 6.40 metres, length 33.40 metres. Permanent installation.

1975/1976

Nana-Piscine, indoor swimming pool for private residence in Saint-Tropez. Permanent installation.

1974

Caroline, Charlotte, Sophie, three giant outdoor Nanas for the city of Hanover. Permanent installation.

Le poète et sa muse, outdoor sculpture for the 'Art Way' at Ulm University. Height 5.50 metres. Permanent installation.

1979 to the present

The Tarot Garden or *Giardino dei Tarocchi*, a fantasy garden based on the twenty-two cards in the Major Arcana. Uses mirrors, ceramic and glass mosaics. The garden represents the realisation of the artist's life's dream. *The Falling Tower* and *La Maison-Dien* are created in collaboration with Jean Tinguely; *The Wheel of Fortune* is a fountain by Tinguely. Niki de Saint Phalle regards the project as a collaborative effort on the part of all who have worked on it. Garavicchio, Tuscany. In progress.

1983

La fontaine Stravinsky, fifteen combined sculptures created in collaboration with Jean Tinguely. Place Igor Stravinsky, Centre Georges Pompidou, Paris. Fountain basin: 0.35 x 16.5 x 36 metres. Permanent installation.

Sun God, first work commissioned by The Stuart Foundation, California, for the grounds of The University of California, San Diego. First major commission in the USA. Height 10.50 metres. Permanent installation.

1988

La fontaine Château-Chinon, eight combined sculptures created in collaboration with Jean Tinguely. Place de la Mairie, Château-Chinon. Diameter of fountain basin: 5 metres. Permanent installation.

1988/1989

La fontaine à têtes de serpent, outdoor sculpture for Schneider Children's Hospital, Long Island Jewish Medical Center, New Hyde Park, Long Island, New York. Height: 5.50 metres. Permanent installation.

1990

Tombstone monument in the form of a cat for the grave of Ricardo Menon, a friend, assistant and fellow-artist, at Montparnasse Cemetery, Paris.

Le temple idéal, Nîmes, France. A house of worship for all denominations, still at the preliminary planning stage.

1991

Proposed Niki Art Museum, a Nana sphinx which will house artwork by Niki de Saint Phalle, suggested by Yoko Shizue Masuda of Space Niki, Tokyo, and intended to be built at Nasu in the Tochigi district of the city.

1965
Niki de Saint Phalle
Published by Delpire, Paris
22 pages + four loose leaves
21 x 17 cm
8 black-and-white photographs, 4 coloured drawings by Niki de Saint Phalle on loose leaves. French commentaries on the illustrations by the artist. French text by Pierre Descargues, 'les nanas, c'est mieux que les gonzesses, les pépées ...' (in French). Biography of the artist. Published on the occasion of the first showing of Nanas at the Galerie Alexandre Iolas, Paris (30 September – 30 October 1965).

1966
Niki nanas
Published by Galerie Alexandre Iolas
Printed by Mourlot, France
6 pages + 4 coloured drawings on loose leaves (*Jane*, *Samuela*, *Black Clarice* and *My Heart Belongs to Rosy*)
21 x 16.5 cm
Text by Pierre Descargues, translated into English by France Frank. Published on the occasion of the first showing of Nanas at the Alexander Iolas Gallery, New York (29 March – 23 April 1966).

1968
Niki de Saint Phalle
Printed by Sergio Tosi, Milan, under licence to Alexandre Iolas
16 pages
20.5 x 16.5 cm
11 coloured drawings on black background by Niki de Saint Phalle. No accompanying text. Published on the occasion of an exhibition by the artist at the Hanover Gallery, London (2 October – 1 November 1968).

1970
Please, Give Me a Few Minutes of Your Eternity
Published by Galerie Alexandre Iolas
Printed by Sergio Tosi, Milan
800 copies printed, of which 100 include 4 original lithographs numbered and signed by the artist
38 folios, thread-stitching
Bound in plastic-covered boards
15 x 21 cm
22 coloured drawings by the artist
Handwritten English text by Niki de Saint Phalle
Published on the occasion of an exhibition by the artist at the Galleria Alexandre Iolas, Milan (October 1970).

1971
My Love
Published by Moderna Museet, Stockholm, under the supervision of Pontus Hulten
Lithographs by Litografisk AB
Printed by Skaneoffset AB, Malmö, Sweden
50 pages, folder
18 x 18 cm
50 coloured and black-and-white drawings by Niki de Saint Phalle. English text by the artist
My Love was the first collection of drawings to be completed by Niki de Saint Phalle. It dates from 1964 but was not published until around 1971.

1972
The Devouring Mothers: Story Book by Niki de Saint Phalle
Published by Gimpel Fils Gallery, London
Printed by Sergio Tosi, Milan
28 folios bound in boards with thread-stitching
14 x 16.5 cm
28 coloured drawings by Niki de Saint Phalle with handwritten English captions by the artist. Published on the occasion of an exhibition by Niki de Saint Phalle at Gimpel Fils Gallery, London (5 December 1972 – 27 January 1973).

1974
Réalisations et projets d'architecture de Niki de Saint Phalle
Published by Galerie Alexandre Iolas, Paris
Printed by Graphic Olympia, Milan
24 pages
Bound in boards
16 x 24 cm
5 coloured and black-and-white drawings by Niki de Saint Phalle; 19 black-and-white and 6 colour photographs
Handwritten English captions to illustrations by the artist. Published on the occasion of an exhibition by the artist at the Galerie Alexandre Iolas, Paris (5 February – 2 March 1974).
The book deals with *Hon*, *Le paradis fantastique*, the set designs for *Lysistrata*, the three 'environments' for Rainer von Diez, *Golem* in Jerusalem, the *Dragon* at Knokke-le-Zoute, *La tête* at Milly-la-Forêt, a Nana swimming pool, a chapel for Alexandre Iolas and a projected kindergarten in the form of a snake.

1976
Niki de Saint Phalle ... (two architectures for children)
Published by Museum Boymans-van Beuningen, Rotterdam
Printed by Gemeentedrukkerij, Rotterdam
35 pages, folder
15 x 10.5 cm
17 black-and-white and 3 colour photographs by Leonardo Bezzola. Handwritten English text by Niki de Saint Phalle, with Dutch translation at end. List of 33 exhibited works. Dutch text by R. Hammacher-van den Brande. Biography of the artist. The book deals with the Knokke-le-Zoute *Dragon* and the Jerusalem *Golem*.
Published on the occasion of an exhibition by the artist at the Boymans-van Beuningen Museum, Rotterdam (22 July – 5 September 1976).

1985
Tarot Cards in Sculpture by Niki de Saint Phalle
Printed by Giuseppe Ponsio, Milan
Designed by Fausta Squatritti
9500 copies, with an additional 1000 inspection copies produced for the Niki de Saint Phalle Foundation in Capalbio, Italy
40 pages
Jacketed boards
22 x 24 cm
12 coloured drawings by Niki de Saint Phalle. 24 colour and 5 black-and-white photographs by Leonardo Bezzola, Laurent Condominas, François Hatte and Giulio Pietromarchi
Handwritten English captions to the illustrations by Niki de Saint Phalle
Published on the occasion of Niki de Saint Phalle's first exhibition of work inspired by Tarot cards at Gimpel Fils Gallery, London, and subsequently at Gimpel & Weitzenhoffer Gallery, New York (3 September – 5 October 1985).

1986
Portrait of Niki de Saint Phalle
Bilingual edition (French/Japanese)
Published by Parco Co., Ltd., Tokyo
Produced in association with Yoko Shizue Masuda of Space Niki
Designed by Fausta Squatritti
60 pages
Transparent plastic jacket
25.5 x 21 cm
10 coloured and black-and-white drawings by Niki de Saint Phalle. 33 black-and-white and 16 colour photographs by Michiko Matsumo. Text by Pierre Restany (February 1986). Translated into Japanese by Kasuko Shiraishi.

1986/1987
AIDS: You Can't Catch It Holding Hands / Aids: Vom Händchenhalten kriegt man's nicht
English and German editions published by C.J. Bucher GmbH, Munich and Lucerne, 1986
Reissued by Franco Muzzio and c. editore spa, Milan, 1987; Flammarion, Paris, 1987; The Lapis Press, San Francisco and Santa Monica, 1987
52 pages
25 x 20 cm
39 coloured drawings by Niki de Saint Phalle. The accompanying handwritten text was written by the artist in consultation with Dr Silvio Barandun, Professor of Immunology at Berne.

1988
The Wounded Animals
Printed by Giuseppe Ponsio, Milan
Photolithography: Domino, Milan
Designed by Fausta Squatritti
5000 copies
40 pages
Jacketed boards
22 x 23 cm
5 coloured drawings by Niki de Saint Phalle. 30 colour photographs by Laurent Condominas and Piero Orsi. The English text was written by the artist. Biography of Niki de Saint Phalle by Harry Mathews
Published on the occasion of an exhibition by Niki de Saint Phalle at Gimpel Fils Gallery, London (7 June – 10 September 1988) and subsequently at Gimpel & Weitzenhoffer Gallery, New York.

1989
Meany Meany and the Stolen Toys
Published by Niki de Saint Phalle and Laurent Condominas
Limited edition, not intended for the trade, financed by Jean Tinguely
1500 copies
32 pages
Glazed board covers
26.5 x 21.5 cm
Children's book. 24 coloured drawings and text by Niki de Saint Phalle and Laurent Condominas. Handwritten English text.

1990
Le sida: Tu ne l'attraperas pas ...
Realised by Niki de Saint Phalle in collaboration with Philip Mathews
Published by Agence française de lutte contre le sida
Printed by UFI, Pressac, Gironde
25,000 copies
54 pages
22 x 16 cm
Published to coincide with the first World Aids Day, 1 December 1990. Proceeds from the sale of the book and from a sticker designed by Niki de Saint Phalle went to an organisation to help Aids sufferers
At the same time an exhibition of the original drawings from the book and a number of sculptures (*Obélisques*) was held in the foyer of the Musée des Arts Décoratifs in Paris (30 November 1990 – 28 January 1991).
Philip Mathews used the drawings as the basis for a cartoon film.

Select bibliography

Agnelli, Marella. *Gardens of the Italian Villas*. Weidenfeld and Nicolson, London 1987.
Arthaud, Claude. *Les palais de rêve*. B. Arthaud et Paris-Match, Paris 1970.
Ashbery, John. *Reported Sightings: Art Chronicles 1957-1987*. Harvard University Press, Cambridge, Massachusetts, 1991.
Bablet, Denis. *Les révolutions scéniques du XXe siècle*. Société internationale d'art du XXe siècle, Paris 1975.
Baker, Elizabeth C. and Hess, Thomas B. *Art and Sexual Politics*. Collier Books, New York 1971.
Bernard, Edina. *Les hauts lieux de l'art moderne en France*. Bordas, Paris 1991.
Bezzola, Leonard and de Saint Phalle, Niki. *The Birth of a Monster*. Niki de Saint Phalle, Leonard Bezzola and others, Zurich 1991.
Bony, Anne. *Les années 60*. Editions du Regard, Paris 1983.
Bordaz, Jean-Pierre. *Les nouveaux réalistes et leur temps*. Dissertation supervised by Mme M. Perrot, Université de Paris VII, Paris 1976.
Boulez, Pierre; Hulten, Pontus; Meyer, Franz, and Poley, Stephanie. *Jean Tinguely, Niki de Saint Phalle, Stravinsky Brunnen*. Benteli Verlag, Berne 1985.
Breteau, Gisèle. *Abécédaire des films sur l'art moderne et contemporain 1905-1984*. Musée National d'Art Moderne, Centre Georges Pompidou, Paris 1985.
Burnham, Jack. *Beyond Modern Sculpture*. George Braziller, New York 1969.
Cabanne, Pierre and Restany, Pierre. *L'Avant-Garde au XXe siècle*. André Balland, Paris 1969.
Castelman, Riva. *Prints of the Twentieth Century: A History*. Thames and Hudson, London 1976. Revised edition 1988.
Celant, Germano. *Ambiante: Arte del Futurismo alla Body Art*. Edizione Biennale di Venezia, Venice 1977.
Ceysson, Bernard; Lemoine, Serge; Abadie, Daniel; Pradel, Jean-Louis; Pacquement, Alfred; Gintz, Claude; Tronche, Anne; Bernard, Christian; Strasser, Catherine and Bloch, Dany. *Vingt-cinq ans d'art vivant en France 1960-1985*. Jacques Legrand S.A., Paris 1986.
Chadwick, Whitney. *Women, Art and Society*. Thames and Hudson, London 1990.
Chalumeau, Jean-Luc. *Lectures de l'art: Reflexion esthétique et création plastique en France aujourd'hui*. Société nouvelle des Editions du Chêne, Paris 1981.
Collection du Musée National d'Art Moderne. Catalogue compiled under the supervision of Agnès de la Beaumelle and Nadine Pouillon, with an Introduction by Dominique Bozo. Editions du Centre Georges Pompidou, Paris 1986.
Contemporary Artists. Macmillan, London 1977, 2nd edn., 1983.
Depuis 45. Volume II: L'art de notre temps. LaConnaissance, Exclusivité Weber, Brussels 1970.
Dictionary of Contemporary Artists. Clio Press, Santa Barbara 1981.
Dictionary of Twentieth-Century Art. Phaidon Press, Oxford 1973.
Dictionnaire de peinture et de sculpture: L'art du XXe siècle. General Editor: Jean-Philippe Breuille. Larousse, Paris 1991.
Dunford, Perry. *A Biographical Dictionary of Women Artists in Europe and America since 1850*. University of Pennsylvania Press, Philadelphia 1989.
Elffers, Joost and Schuut, Michael (eds.). *Fantastische architectuur*. Meulenhoff/Landshoff, Amsterdam 1980.
Evren, Robert; Krane, Susan and Raye, Helen. *The Painting and Sculpture Collection: Acquisitions since 1972*. Hudson Hills Press in association with Albright-Knox Art Gallery, New York 1987.
Glozer, Laszlo. *Westkunst: Zeitgenössische Kunst seit 1939*. DuMont Buchverlag, Cologne 1981.
Gottlieb, Carla. *Beyond Modern Art*. E.P. Dutton and Co., New York 1976.
Hammacher, A.M. *La sculpture*. Cercle d'art, Paris 1988.
Hammann, Barbara. *Künstler: Kritisches Lexikon der Gegenwartskunst*. Special number devoted to Niki de Saint Phalle. Weltkunst Bruckmann Verlag, Munich 1989.
Happenings – Fluxus – Pop Art – Nouveaux Réalisme: Eine Dokumentation. With an Introduction by Jürgen Becker and Wolf Vostell. Rowohlt Verlag, Hamburg 1965.
Harrison, Helen A. *Larry Rivers*. Harper & Row, New York 1984.
Hartford, Huntington. *Art or Anarchy? How Extremists and Exploiters Have Reduced the Fine Arts to Chaos and Commercialism*. Doubleday & Co., Garden City, New York 1984.
Heller, Nancy G. *Women Artists: An Illustrated History*. Abbeville Press, New York 1987.
Henri, Adrian. Environments and Happenings. Thames and Hudson, London 1974.
Hermand, Jost. *Pop International: Eine kritische Analyse*. Athenäum Verlag, Frankfurt am Main 1971.
Hulten, Pontus. *Jean Tinguely: A Magic Stronger Than Death*. Abbeville Press, New York 1987.
Jencks, Charles and Silver, Nathan. *Adhocism: The Case for Improvisation*. Doubleday & Co., Garden City, New York 1972.
Joray, Marcel. *Le béton dans l'art contemporain*. Editions du Griffon, Neuchâtel 1977.
Jouffroy, Alain and others. *New Art Around the World: Painting and Sculpture*, Harry N. Abrams, New York.
Kultermann, Udo. *Histoire mondiale de la sculpture: Art contemporain*. Hachette Réalités, Paris 1980.
Kultermann, Udo. *The New Sculpture: Environments and Assemblages*. Frederick A. Praeger Publishers, New York and Washington 1968.
Lawless, Catherine. *Artistes et ateliers*. Editions Jacqueline Chambon, Nîmes 1990.
Le Normand-Romain, Antoinette; Pingeot, Anne; Hohl, Reinhold; Rose, Barbara and Daval, Jean-Luc. *L'Aventure de la sculpture moderne: XIXe et XXe siècles*. Editions d'Art Albert Skira, Geneva 1986.
Lippard, Lucy R. *Pop Art*. Thames and Hudson, London 1966.
Livingstone, Marco. *Pop Art: A Continuing History*. Harry N. Abrams, New York 1990.
Lobenthal, Joel. *Radical Rags: Fashions of the Sixties*. Abbeville Press, New York 1990.
Lucie-Smith, Edward. *Art Now: From Abstract Expressionism to Surrealism*. William Morrow and Company, New York 1977.
Mannoni, Gérard. *Roland Petit: Un Chorégraphe et ses peintres*. Hatier, Paris 1990.
Mathews, Harry. *The Way Home: Collected Longer Prose*. Atlas Press, London 1989.
Mashun, Carol Anne. *Pop Art and the Critics*. UMI Research Press, Ann Arbor, Michigan 1987.
Montreynaud, Florence. *Le XXe siècle des femmes*. Nathan, Paris 1989.
Millet, Catherine. *L'Art contemporain en France*. Flammarion, Paris 1987.
Munsterberg, Hugo. *A History of Women Artists*. Clarkson N. Potter, New York 1975.
Naylor, Colin and Orridge, Genesis. *Contemporary Artists*. St James Press, London and St Martin's Press, New York 1977.
Neret, Gilles. *Trente ans d'art moderne*. Fribourg 1988.
Nouveau Dictionnaire de la sculpture moderne. Fernard Hazan, Paris 1970.
Nuridsany, Michel. *La Commande publique*. Edition de la Réunion des Musées Nationaux (Collection 'Enjeux-Culture'), Paris 1991.
Osterwold, Tilman. *Pop Art*. Benedikt Taschen Verlag, Cologne 1989.
Pellegrini, Aldo. *New Tendencies in Art*. Crown Publishers, New York 1966.
Pierre, José. *Le premier livre de peinture: L'abécédaire, précédé par le dialogue monotone, et suivi de le gouvernement de l'écume*. Le Terrain Vague, Paris 1971.
Pierre, José. *Dictionnaire de poche: Le pop art*. Fernand Hazan, Paris 1975.
Pluchart, François. *1960-1070: Pop Art and cie*. Editions Martin-Malbur, Paris 1971.
Popper, Franck. *Art Action Participation 1: Le déclin de l'objet*. Editions du Chêne, Paris 1975.
Ragon, Michel. *Naissance d'un art nouveau*. Albin Michel, Paris 1963.
Ragon, Michel. *Vingt-cinq ans d'art vivant: Chronique vécue de l'art contemporain, de l'abstraction au pop art 1944-1969*. Editions Galilée, Paris 1966. Revised and expanded edition, 1986.
Rellecke, Horst. *Der Glaselefant*. Bauverlag, Wiesbaden and Berlin 1986.
Restany, Pierre. *Les Nouveaux Réalistes*. Editions Planète, Paris 1968.
Restany, Pierre. *L'autre face de l'art*. Editions Galilée. Paris 1975.
Restany, Pierre. *Une vie dans l'art*. Conversations with Jean-François Bory. Editions Ides et Calendes, Neuchâtel 1983.
Restany, Pierre. *60/90: Trente ans du Nouveau Réalisme*. Editions de la Différence, Paris 1990.
Rischbieter, Henning (ed.). *Art and the Stage in the 20th Century: Painters and Sculptors Work for the Theater*. New York Graphic Society, Greenwich, Connecticut, 1968.
Rotzler, Willy. *Objekt-Kunst: Von Duchamp bis Kienholz*. Verlag M. DuMont Schauberg, Cologne 1972.
Rubin, William S. and Pleynet, Marcelin. *Paris – New York: Situation de l'art*. Editions du Chêne, Paris 1978.
Rubinstein Streifer, Charlotte. *American Women Artists from Early Indian Times to the Present*. G.K. Hall & Co., Boston and Avon Books, New York 1982.
Rubinstein Streifer, Charlotte. *American Women Sculptors*. G.K. Hall & Co., Boston 1990.

Sandler, Irving. *American Art of the 60s*. Icon Editions, Harper & Row, New York 1961.
Seitz, William C. *The Art of Assemblage*. The Museum of Modern Art, New York 1961.
Selz, Peter. *Art in Our Times: A Pictorial History 1890-1980*. Harry N. Abrams, New York 1981.
Takashina, Shuji (ed.). *Assemblage and Accumulation*. Kodansha (*Art Now*, 7), Tokyo 1971.
Thomas, Karin and De Vries, Gerd. *DuMont's Künstler Lexikon von 1945 bis zur Gegenwart*. DuMont Buchverlag, Cologne 1977.
Thorn-Petit, Liliane. *Portraits d'artistes*. RTL Edition, Paris and Luxembourg 1987.
Tomkins, Calvin. *Off the Wall: Robert Rauschenberg and the Art World of Our Time*. Doubleday & Co., Garden City, New York 1980.
Tono, Yoshiaki (ed.). *The Pop Image of Man*. Kodansha (*Art Now*, 4), Tokyo 1971.
Trente ans de ballets français. Photographs by Serge Lido. Preface by Pierre Gaxotte. Edition Vilo, Paris 1969.
Trichon-Milsani, Eurydice; Makarius, Michel and Marcheschi, Jean-Paul. *Au Musée National d'Art Moderne*. Fernard Hazan, Paris 1983.
Tronche, Anne and Gloagen, Hervé. *L'art actuel en France: Du cinétisme à l'hyperréalisme*. André Balland, Paris 1973.
Turner, Ralph. *Contemporary Jewelry*. Macmillan (Studio Vista Book), London 1976.
Wheeler, Daniel. *Art Since Mid-Century: 1945 to the Present*. The Vendome Press, New York 1991.
Wolfram, Eddie. *History of Collage*. MacMillan Publishing Co., New York 1969.

Newspapers/Periodicals

1961

Ashbery, John. "'Comparaisons', at Musee d'Art Moderne". *New York Herald Tribune,* Paris, 8 February. (illus.)

Ashbery, John. "Midsummer Madness Fills Void in Paris Art Calendar". *New York Herald Tribune,* Paris, 25 July.

Ashbery, John. "Paris Art Season Ending With Bangs, Not Whimpers". *New York Herald Tribune,* Paris, 1–2 July. (illus.)

"'Bewogen Beweging': Bizarre Expositie". *Brabants Nieuwsblad,* Roosendaal, 11 March.

Coruzzi, Giovanni. "Dipinge a colpi di fucile". *Libertá-Piacenza,* 21 July.

Descargues, Pierre. "Tirez, nous ferons le reste!". *Feuille d'Avis de Lausanne,* No. 139, 19 July, Magazine p. 2. (illus.)

Devay, Jean-Françoise. "Un scandale nommé Niki ...". *Paris-presse-l'Intransigeant,* 29 June, p. 3D. (illus.)

"Fyrvaerkeri med farver". *Politiken,* No. 347, 16 September, p. l. (illus.)

Kühn, Siegfried. "Gräfin Niki malt mit dem Karabiner". *Offenburger Tageblatt,* 1 September.

"Kunsten". *Billed Bladet,* No. 38, 22 September, p. 37. (illus.)

Lewino, Walter. "Le maître, la lumiste, le modeste". *Démocratie 61,* 13 July.

London, John. "The girl who paints with a gun". *The Evening News and the Star,* 7 July, p. 8.

Quain, Anthony. "Stoep Talk". *Johannesburg Star,* 13 July.

Restany, Pierre: "Die Beseelung des Objektes". *Das Kunstwerk,* Vol. XV, No. 1–2, July/August, pp. 37–56. (illus.)

Rohde, H. P. "Hvor Dan Ramme Kunsten?" *Berlingske Aftenavis,* 20 September. (illus.)

Schilling Tonia. "Shotgun Painter Does Brisk Trade". *Montreal Star,* 19 July.

Schöffer, N. "Parisungrare visar dynamisk konst". *Svenska Dagbladet,* 14 May. (illus.)

"Seltene 'Kunst' Ausstellung in Paris". *Hohenloher Tagblatt,* 15 July.

"Skjut inte på konstnärinnan...". *Idun,* No. 30, 24–30 July, p. 4. (illus.)

Thomaeus, Jan. "Bödlar och martyrer". *Dagens Nyheter,* May. (illus.)

Vincent, Paul. "Art et Sport". *Le Petit Marocain,* Casablanca, 9 July.

1962

Ashbery, John. "Paris Letter". *Art International,* Vol. VI, No. 7, September, p. 64. (illus.)

Ashbery, John. "Old and New Art in Holland: Hals Show in Haarlem; Moderns Have Fun". *New York Herald Tribune,* Paris, 19 September.

"Beeldende Kunst: What's Happening?". *Haagse Post,* 8 September, p. 15. (illus.)

Buzzati, Dino. "La bellissima Niki chiude il vampiro in 'frigidaire'". *Corriere d'Informazione,* 10–11 February, p. 3. (illus.)

"Cannon Field?". *Newsweek,* 12 February. (illus.)

"Dipinge sparando". *Roma-Napoli,* 7 January.

"Dylaby-Dynamisch Labyrinth". *Het Parool,* 31 August.

Gray, Beverly. "Closeup: Avant-Garde Artist". *The New York Post,* 5 December, Magazine p. 3. (illus.)

Johnston, Jill. "Niki de Saint-Phalle (Iolas)". *Art News,* Vol. 61, No. 8, December, p. 16. (illus.)

Johnston, Jill. "Robert Rauschenberg, Jean Tinguely, Niki de Saint-Phalle (Maidman Theater)". *Art News,* Vol. 61, No. 4, Summer, pp. 53–54.

Judd, Donald. "Exhibition at Iolas Gallery". *Arts Magazine,* Vol. 37, December, p. 44. (illus.)

Kouwenaar, Gerritt. "Publiek is meemaker aan Dylaby in het Stedelijk Museum". *Het Vrije Volk,* 8 September.

"Le Coin du Bricoleur". *Spirou,* No. 1240, 18 January, pp. 30–31. (illus.)

"Mit Ochsenblut und Dynamit". *Frankfurter Illustrierte,* 18 February. (illus.)

Secunda, Arthur. "Sunset Whammy: Art? – Maybe; Fun? – Definitely". *Beverly Hills Times,* 8 March, p. 9. (illus.)

Spierdijk, Jan. "Dylaby, Het Stedelijk als wondertent". *De Telegraaf,* 4 September.

Tallmer, Jerry. "Entertainment?: The Building of Boston". *The Village Voice.* 10 May, pp. 9–10.

1963

Ashton, Dore. "New York Commentary: High Tide for Assemblage". Studio International, Vol. 165, January, pp. 24–25. (illus.)

Restany, Pierre. "Le nouveau réalisme und was darunter zu verstehen ist" (with French text). *Das Kunstwerk,* Vol. XVI, No. 7, January, pp. 1–18.

Restany, Pierre. "Paris Letter: The New Realism". *Art in America,* Vol. 51, No. 1, February, pp. 102–104. (illus.)

Seckler, Dorothy G. "The Artist In America: The Audience Is His Medium!" *Art In America,* Vol. 51, No. 2, April, pp. 62–67. (illus.)

"Sweeney's Way". *Time,* 14 June, p. 74. (illus.)

Wholden, Rosalind G. "Puerealism: 'The End' With Innocence". *Artforum,* Vol. 2, No. 3, September, pp. 30–33. (illus.)

Wulp, John. "Happening: A timely exercise in the pursuit of happiness". *Esquire,* November, pp. 134–138.

1964

Brumagne, M. M. "Niki de Saint-Phalle expose ses tableaux-objets à Genève". *Tribune de Lausanne,* 16 April. (illus.)

Deroudille, René. "Niki de Saint-Phalle (Galerie Iolas) vedette des quelques expositions Genèvois". *Le Daupiné Libéré,* 20 April. (illus.)

Descargues, Pierre. "Niki de Saint-Phalle construit... des monstres!". *Tribune de Lausanne,* 2 August. (illus.)

Glueck, Grace. "Art Notes: Growing Pains". *The New York Times,* 7 June. (illus.)

Peillex, G. "Exposition à Genève". *Das Werk,* Vol. 54, June p. 135.

Perkins, Constance. "The Galleries: St. Phalle Doubles Paradox". *Los Angeles Times,* 17 January, Part IV.

"Pop-art Diskussion". *Das Kunstwerk,* Vol. XVII, April, p. 24.

Russell, John. "Niki de Saint-Phalle". *The Sunday Times,* 27 September.

Wholden, Rosalind G. "Paint and Fable in Los Angeles". *Arts Magazine,* Vol. 38, March, p. 40.

Williams, Sheldon. "Pale Pink and Monsters". *New York Herald Tribune,* Paris, October 13.

1965

"Art/Galleries: The Box, Glue & Nail Set". *Time,* Vol. 86, 14 May, p. 70. (illus.)

Ashbery, John. "Paris: Pop, Nanas". *Art News,* Vol. 64, No. 8, December, pp. 37, 54. (illus.)

Ashbery, John. "What's New In Paris Art? Murder, That's What". *New York Herald Tribune,* Paris, 12 October. (illus.)

Barotte, René. "Les 'Grosses Nanas' de Niki". *France-Soir,* 5 October, p. 5. (illus.)

Berkson, W. "Exhibition at Iolas Gallery". *Arts Magazine,* Vol. 39, May, p. 56. (illus.)

Constable, Rosalind. "The Mid 60s/Art: Is It Painting or Is It Sculpture?". *Life,* Vol. 59, 20 December. (illus.)

Crespelle, Jean-Paul. "L'Exposition: le temps des Nanas". *Le Journal du Dimanche,* 3 October.

Descargues, Pierre. "Niki de Saint-Phalle expose de redoutables ouvrages de dame les Nanas". *Tribune de Lausanne,* 26 September. (illus.)

Douillard, Imy. "Vad är en Nana?". *Göteborgs-Tidningen,* 6 November. (illus.)

Emerson, Gloria. "Jean Shrimpton Beware! 'Nanas' of Paris Are After You". *The New York Times,* 25 October, p. 39. (illus.)

Gablik, Suzi. "Niki de Saint-Phalle (Iolas)". *Art News,* Vol. 64, No. 5, September, p. 10. (illus.)

Gassiot-Talabot, Gérald. "La figuration narrative dans la peinture contemporaine". *Quadrum,* No. 18, pp. 31–32. (illus.)

Gassiot-Talabot, Gérald. "Lettre de Paris". *Art International,* Vol. IX, No. 8, November, pp. 48–50 (illus.)

Gertz, Gerda. "Konkurrenz für Gartenzwerge". *Hamburger Abendblatt,* 6 November. (illus.)

Kousbroek, Rudy. "De Vrouwen van Niki de Saint-Phalle". *Algemeen Handelsblad,* 13 November, p. 27. (illus.)

Lacoste Conil, Michel. "Niki Hottentote". *Le Monde,* 5 November.

Lescaut, Sonia. "Profil: Niki de Saint-Phalle invente les 'nanas' en couleur". *Arts,* 6–12 October, p. 33. (illus.)

"Les Nanas de Niki de Saint-Phalle". *Beaux-Arts,* 21 October. (illus.)

"Niki de Saint-Phalle". *Town & Country,* June, p. 79. (illus.)

"Om dat zij vrij zijn (De 'Nanas' van Niki de Saint-Phalle)". *Haagse Post,* 20 November, p. 27. (illus.)

"Paris par express: Les dames de Niki de Saint-Phalle". *L'Express,* 4–10 October, p. 61. (illus.)

Patterson, Suzy. "Artist Expresses Feminine Revolt". *Journal Herald,* Dayton, Ohio, 9 October, pp. 1, 26. (illus.)

Rheims, Maurice. "Niki de Saint-Phalle: L'art et les mecs." *Vogue,* February, pp. 58–61. (illus.)

Roditi, Edouard. "Niki de Saint-Phalle". *Du,* No. 295, August, pp. 599–611. (illus.)

Sheppard, Eugenia. "Inside Fashion: Fashion Is Art, Honestly". *New York Herald Tribune,* 19 March. (illus.)

Sweetinburgh, Thelma. "Niki's Nanas". *Women's Wear Daily,* 15 October, pp. 4–5. (illus.)

Vilaine, Anne-Marie de. "Confession: Mieux que les hommes". *Le Nouvel Observateur,* No. 48, 13 October. (illus.)

Watt, Alexander. "Exhibition at Galerie Iolas". *Studio International,* Vol. 127, December, p. 247.

Watt, Alexander. "Paris Commentary: Kinetics Closes the Gap". *Studio International,* Vol. 170, September, p. 128. (illus.)

1966

"Art: Calico Dames in a Frolic of Art". *Life,* Vol. 60, No. 13, 1 April, pp. 58–60, 64. (illus.)

"Art/Sculpture: The Ultimate She". *Time,* Vol. 87, No. 24, 17 June, pp. 92, 93. (illus.)

"Ausstellung in der Galerie Alexander Iolas". Das Kunstwerk, Vol. XIX, April, p. 86. (illus.)

"Ballet: Petit Lob des Irrsinns". *Der Spiegel,* No. 13, March. (illus.)

Bourgeois, Jacques. "Une énorme réussite de Roland Petit: Eloge de la folie". *Arts,* 16–22 March p. 18. (illus.)

Brunius, Clas. "Moderna museets senaste: Jättekvinna på rygg". *Expressen,* 3 June.

Burton, Scott. "Niki de St.-Phalle (Iolas)". *Art News,* Vol. 65, No. 3, May. pp. 14, 20. (illus.)

Canaday, John. "Five Shows Blossom Among Current Fare". *The New York Times,* 2 April.

Colberg, Klaus. "Pox durch Sex in Pop und Op". *Mannheimer Morgen,* 4 October, p. 24.

Cournand, Gilberte. "La danse". *Opéra,* 15 April, p. 33.

Cullberg, Staffan. "Suggestiv Urmoder". *Svenska Dagbladet,* 5 June. (illus.)

Curtiss, Thomas Quinn. "Petit's Ballet in Paris". *The New York Times,* 13 March.

Cutler, Carol. "Paris not so French". *Art in*

America, Vol. 54, March, p. 109. (illus.)
"Deçà, Delà". *Les Annales,* May. (illus.)
"De quoi devenir fou". *France-Soir,* 8 March. (illus.)
Descargues, Pierre. "Niki de Saint-Phalle 'Nanas'" (with English text). *Quadrum,* No. 20, pp. 67–74, 178. (illus.)
Drommert, René. "Hier die Königin – dort 'Sie'". *Die Zeit,* No. 29, 15 July, p. 16. (illus.)
Emerson, Gloria. "Ballet Throbs With Odd Props Designed by 3 Artists in Paris". *The New York Times, 27 March.*
Fleuret, Maurice. "Ce qu'il en coûte d'être fou par Roland Petit". *Le Nouvel Observateur,* 16 March. (illus.)
Friedrich, Heinz. "Das Monstrum von Stockholm". *Die Welt,* No. 169, p. 1. (illus.)
Gassiot-Talabot, Gérald. "Lettre de Paris et de Saint-Paul-de-Vence". *Art International,* Vol. X, No. 7, September.
Hahn, Otto. "The Death of Paris". *Art & Artists,* Vol. 1, No. 2, May.
Hensel, Georg. "Die Comic Strippers von Kassel". *Darmstädter Echo,* 9 October.
Iden, Peter. "Oh, Lysistrata, meine Knie werden weich". *Frankfurter Rundschau,* 5 October, p. 6.
"Jeunes artistes français". *Aujourd'hui,* Vol. 10, September, p. 86.
Kersting, Claus. "Lysistrata". *Waldeckische Landeszeitung,* 4 October. (illus.)
Kramer, Hilton. "Stockholm: Like Reading Keats in Rush Hour". *The New York Times,* 9 July. (illus.)
"Kunst: Niki de Saint Phalle – Dame: Ohne Unterschenkel". *Der Spiegel,* No. 41, 3 October. (illus.)
"Le 'Nanas' e i capelloni". *Specchio,* 24 April.
Linde, Ulf. "En valdig varelse". *Dagens Nyheter,* 4 June. (illus.)
"Lysistrata à la mode-pop". *La Tribune D'Allemagne,* 5 November. (illus.)
Martin, Gregory. "A female Gulliver in Stockholm". *The Times,* 27 June. (illus.)
Mayer, Tony. "The Petit Romance". *Financial Times,* 26 April.
Mellow, James. "New York Letter". *Art International,* Vol. X, No. 7, September, p. 57.
Olvång, Bengt. "Hon". *Aftonbladet,* 9 June.
Pluchart, François. "Fire Sermons" (translated by Suzi Gablik). *Art & Artists,* Vol. 1, No. 5, August, pp. 24–27. (illus.)
Restany, Pierre. "'Hon' a Stoccolma" (with English and French texts). *Domus,* No. 442, September, p. 49.
Restany, Pierre. "Qu'est-ce qui fait fuir nos peintures en Amérique?". *Arts-Loisirs,* No. 64, 14 December, pp. 34–40. (illus.)
Reuther, Hanno. "Wenn man will, geht es auch anders". *Westfälische Rundschau,* No. 239, 14 October. (illus.)
"Roland Petit: Eloge de la folie". *Parisien Libéré,* 3 March, (illus.)
Rühle, Günther. "Die gepopte Lysistrata". *Frankfurter Allgemeine Zeitung,* No. 232, 6 October, p. 24.
Runge, Gertrud. "Lysistrata als Pop-Figur". *Die Welt,* No. 233, 6 October, p. 13. (illus.)
"Saint-Phalle (Niki) (de)". *Nouveau Candide,* 15 August.
Scheidegger, A. "Riesenweib von Stockholm". *Der Bund,* 7 July.
Schyle, Hans-Joachim. "Das Blut der Venus von Milo". *Saarbrücker Zeitung,* 29 March.
Scott, Lael. "Woman in the news: Niki de Saint-Phalle". *The New York Post,* 10 April, Magazine, section II, cover and p. 27. (illus.)
Secunda, Arthur and Thunholm, Jan. "Everyman's Girl". *Ramparts,* November, pp. 66–68. (illus.)
Stimson, Ermina and Weir, June. "Niki's Nanas". *Women's Wear Daily,* Vol. 112, No. 61, 28 March, p. 1, 10. (illus.)
"Stockholm: Dame über alles". *Der Spiegel,* No. 27, June. (illus.)
"They're Stealing the Show from Correggio". *Chicago Daily News,* 23 February. (illus.)
Trenet, Charles. "Entretien avec Roland Petit". *Le Monde,* 3 March.
Valogne, Catherine. "La 'Hon-Cathédrale' et le musée de Stockholm". *Les Lettres Françaises,* 1 September. (illus.)
V. J. "Anatomie – La super-nana de Stockholm". *Arts-Loisirs,* No. 40, 29 June, pp. 4–5. (illus.)
W. B. "hon = she = zig, een kathedraal". *Museumjournaal,* Series XI, No. 7, pp. 199–203. (illus.)
Willard, Charlotte. "The Nanas of Niki de Saint Phalle". *The New York Post,* 10 April, Magazine, section II, p. 48.
Zimmermann, Sidney. "In the Galleries: Niki de Saint Phalle". *Arts Magazine,* Vol. 40, No. 8, June, p. 52. (illus.)

1967

Albert-Levin, Marc. "Les Arts: La fureur poétique". *Les Lettres Françaises,* 20 April.
"Amsterdam: La Nana à habiter". *Tribune de Lausanne,* 17 September. (illus.)
"Around Paris Galleries". *New York Herald Tribune,* Paris, 5 December.
"Art: Sculpture at Expo". *Time,* Vol. 90, No. 5, 4 August, pp. 54–55. (illus.)
Barotte, René. "A Montréal: La France sera à l'avant-garde des arts plastiques". *Le Provençal,* Marseille, 19 March.
Barry, Edward. "When the historians get around to ...". *Chicago Tribune,* 20 November, section 2A, p. 4. (illus.)
Bloc, Cor. "Niki de Saint Phalle". *Groene Amsterdammer,* 16 September. (illus.)
Bloc, Cor. "Holland: Niki de Saint-Phalle". *Art International,* Vol. XI, No. 9, November, p. 47. (illus.)
Blume, Mary. "Tinguely's Machines Scare Niki's Nanas". *New York Herald Tribune – Washington Post,* Paris, 5 April, p. 12. (illus.)
Bourdon, David. "Expo '67". *Art International,* Vol. XI, No. 7, 20 September, pp. 19–24. (illus.)
Châtelain, Nicolas. "Montréal: Coups de canon, carillons sirènes et fanfares". *Le Figaro,* 28 April.
Cunningham, Bill. "Niki de Saint Phalle, in New York...". *Chicago Tribune,* 20 November, section 2A, p. 3. (illus.)
Descargues, Pierre. "Premières photos des Hybrides de Niki de Saint-Phalle dans lesquels vont se ruer les machines offensives de Tinguely". *Tribune de Lausanne,* 28 February. (illus.)
Fournier, Eva. "250 000 entrées pour le 1er jour l'Expo internationale de Montréal". *France-Soir,* 30 April.
Frater, Alexander. "The Lady In The Orang-Outang Skin Is Sitting On A Nana". *The Daily Telegraph,* 24 November, Magazine pp. 26–29, 31. (illus.)
Giaud, Claude. "L'exposition de la Galerie des Beaux-Arts...". *La France,* 15 November.
Glueck, Grace. "New York Gallery Notes". *Art in America,* Vol. 55, No. 2, March/April, pp. 102–108. (illus.)
Hahn, Otto. "Art: Les nanas demandent des sous". *L'Express,* No. 820, 6–12 March, pp. 98–99. (illus.)
Hénault, D. Todd. "Environmental Aspects of Expo 67" (with German and French texts). *Graphis,* Vol. XXIII, No. 132, p. 347.
Kaplan, Bernard. "Inside Niki's Nanas: The Life Urge In a Polyester Package". Montreal Star, 25 March.
"La perplexité canadienne devant les 'Nanas' de Niki de Saint-Phalle". *France-Soir,* 7 June, p. 18.
"La table de matières du sculpteur 1967". *Le Monde,* 15 December.
Lévêque, Jean-Jacques. "Créer à coups de fusil". *Arts,* No. 54, 5–11 October. (illus.)
Michel, Jacques. "Les 'nanas' et les 'machines' feront la foire a Montréal". *Le Monde,* 3 March.
"Montréal: le pop sur le toit". *Arts-Loisirs,* No. 84, 3–9 May, pp. 34–35. (illus.)
Müller, Gregoire. "Paris: Insanity Fair". Art & Artists, Vol. 2, June.
"Niki de Saint Phalle: les nanas au pouvoir". *Museumjournaal,* Series XII, No. 8, pp. 208–211. (illus.)
"Niki's Nanas". *Algemeen Handelsblad,* 9 September. (illus.)
"Nikis Puppen sind nicht von Pappe". Stern, No. 18, 13 April, pp. 71–72. (illus.)
"Paris en parle: Niki de Saint Phalle". *Vogue,* October, pp. 150–151. (illus.)
Pluchart, François. "Bravo le ministère des arts et lettres". *Combat,* 27 February. (illus.)
"Pour les fêtes des œuvres à grand tirage". *Les Lettres Françaises,* 4 January.
Restany, Pierre. "Montréal: un ballet ou une farce?". *Arts-Loisirs,* 10 January.
Robillard, Yves. "Les conceptions des arts visuels à l'Expo". *Vie des Arts,* Montréal, Automme, pp. 42–46, 67. (illus.)
Sheppard, Eugenia. "Niki's New Long Skirt". *World Journal Tribune,* 7 February, p. 9. (illus.)
Sorel, Frédéric. "'Nanas' obscènes, sculptures grotesques et hallucinations en musique...". *Minute,* 25 May, pp. 16–17. (illus.)
Sottsass, E., Jr. "Case de artiste a Parigi: dalla Francia con amore". *Domus,* No. 452, July, pp. 26–27. (illus.)
Sweetinburg, Thelma. "Decent Exposure... or My Fair Nana". *Women's Wear Daily,* Vol. 114, No. 70, 11 April, pp. 4–5. (illus.)
Van 'T Veer, Paul. "De Nana's aan de macht bij Niki de Saint Phalle". *Het Vrije Volk,* 2 September. (illus.)
Warnot, Jeanine. "La Fureur Poétique". *Le Figaro,* 21 March.
Welling, Dolf. "Heur eigen domein: Slanke Française propageert 'moeillijke figuren'". *Dordrechts Nieuwsblad,* 2 September. (illus.)
Weyer, Walter. "Wohin steuert die französische Kunst". *Holsteinischer Courier,* 23 November.

1968

Ammann, Jean-Christophe. "Schweizer Brief: Niki de Saint-Phalle in der Galerie Gimpel & Hanover, Zurich (18 Mai–16 July)." *Art International,* Vol. XII, No. 8, 20 October, p. 55.
Besson, George. "Les Arts: Le décor de la vie. Musée Galleria". *Les Lettres Françaises,* 17 April, p. 32.
Bonk, Siegfried. "In der kleinen Nana kann man sogar lieben". *Leverkusener Anzeiger,* 22 November. (illus.)
Colberg, Klaus. "Theater bei der 'documenta 4'". *Neue Zürcher Zeitung,* 9 July.
Cutler, Carol. "Art de Paris: Three Shows Out to Involve". *International Herald Tribune,* Paris, 23 April, p. 3.
Descargues, Pierre. "Niki de Saint-Phalle a écrit et décoré 'Ich' à Kassel". *Feuille d'Avis de Lausanne,* 2 July, p. 57. (illus.)
Descargues, Pierre. "'Ich': un 'Ubu' femelle". *Tribune de Lausanne,* 7 July, p. 3. (illus.)
Gerber, Dieter. "Im Hippieland der dickbäuchigen Nanas". *Generalanzeiger für Bonn,* 26 November. (illus.)
Glueck, Grace. "Tinguely's Machines Menace Niki's Nanas in the Park'. *The New York Times,* 2 May, p. 49. (illus.)
Hahn, Otto. "Expositions: Sept 'machines' cherchent leur voie". *L'Express,* 29 April. (illus.)
"Les Nanas au pouvoir". *The Times,* 1 October. (illus.)
"Les Nanas sur la plage". *Vogue,* Vol. 151, No. 8, 15 April, pp. 130–131. (illus.)
Lévêque, Jean-Jacques. "Les poètes de la cruauté". *Les Nouvelles Littéraires,* 14 November.

Lévêque, Jean-Jacques. "Musée Galleria: Une réflexion sur le mal industriel". *Le Nouveau Journal,* 20 April.
Melville, Robert. "The Obsessive Image: 1960–1968". *The Architectural Review,* Vol. CXLIII, June, pp. 463–465. (illus.)
Morschel, Jürgen. "Diana und ihre Puppen'. *Haller Tagblatt,* 17 December.
"New Beach Belle: A Girl Balloon'. *Life,* 3 May, pp. 66–67. (illus.)
"Niki de Saint Phalle: the romantic point of view". *Vogue,* Vol. 151, No. 1, January, pp. 82–85. (illus.)
"Nikis Debüt in Düsseldorf". *Aachener-Volkszeitung,* 16 November
"Peeled Nanas". *New York Daily News,* 2 May, pp. 44–45. (illus.)
Peppiatt, Michael. "Paris Letter". *Art International,* Vol. XII, No. 10, Christmas, pp. 60–61.
Pluchart, François. "Merveilleuse Niki de Saint Phalle". *Combat,* 11 October. (illus.)
Plnien, Eo. "Puppen für Erwachsene". *Die Welt,* 13 December. (illus.)
"Pour les beaux jours: une nana-pavillon de jardin". *L'illustre,* No. 47, 22 November. (illus.)
"Sculptures de joie et de bonheur – serigraphien (Gimpel & Hanover Galerie, Zurich)". *Das Werk,* Vol. 55, July, p. 490. (illus.)
Sello, Gottfried. "Kunstkalendar: Düsseldorf". *Die Zeit,* 29 November. (illus.)
Sheehy, Gail. "Nanas: In The Park". *New York,* Vol. 1, No. 9, 3 June, cover and pp. 18–22. (illus.)
Sheppard, Eugenia. "Giant Nanas, Iron Machines Inhabit the 'Fantastic Garden'". *The Washington Post,* 8 May, p. C10.
Strelow, Hans. "Alle Macht den Nanas". *Frankfurter Allgemeine Zeitung,* No. 136, 13–14 June. (illus.)
Strelow, Hans. "Pomp und Glanz der Kunst". *Rheinische Post,* No. 217, 19 November, p. 19. (illus.)
"U.S. Museums Go Mod". *Newsweek,* 1 April, pp. 32–36. (illus.)

1969

Armstrong, Lois. "Los Angeles". *Art News,* Vol. 68, No. 6, October, p. 74.
de Saint Phalle, Niki. "Letter to Diane". *The Paris Review,* No. 48, Fall, pp. 106–114. (illus.)
"Die Nanas an die Macht". *Belser Kunst Quartal,* Vol. 1, No. 4, 30 June, pp. 30–31. (illus.)
Goldman, J. "Prints by Painters". *Artist's Proof,* Vol. 9, p. 69. (illus.)
Honnef, Klaus. "Ausstellung: Kunstverein Düsseldorf". *Das Kunstwerk,* Vol. XXII, No. 5–6, February/March, pp. 59, 76. (illus.)
"Kunstmuseum: Luzern". *Das Werk,* Vol. 56, September, p. 652. (illus.)
"Kunst: Niki de Saint Phalle: Nanas an die Macht". *Der Spiegel,* No. 5, 27 January, pp. 104–107. (illus.)
Lange, Rudolf: "Die Frauen an die Macht". *Hannoversche Allgemeine Zeitung,* 7 March, p. 25. (illus.)
"Les 'Nanas' de Niki ou la danse de Saint-Phalle". *La Suisse,* 17 September. (illus.)
Phelan, Charlotte. "Leave It to the Nanas". *The Houston Post,* 25 March, section 1, p. 10. (illus.)
"Revolte mit naivem Esprit". *Die Kunst,* January.
Spencer, C. "London Exhibitions". *Sculpture International,* Vol. 2, No. 4, p. 22. (illus.)

1970

Borgeaud, B. "Exhibition in Paris". *Arts Magazine,* Vol. 44, April, p. 53.
Denvir, Bernard. "London". *Art International,* Vol. XIV, No. 2, February, p. 72.
"Diece anni dopo il 'nouveau réalisme' a Milano". *Domus,* No. 491, October, p. 45.
Gibson, Michael. "Around Paris Galleries". *International Herald Tribune,* Paris, 14–15 February.
"Gimpel & Hanover Galerie, Zurich: Ausstellung". *Das Werk,* Vol. 57, December, p. 827. (illus.)
Gräslund, Thu. "Konst för Miljoner: Ligger ock skräpar...". *Expressen,* 27 November. (illus.)
Hahn, Otto. "Les Nanas aux Halles". *L'Express,* 23 February. (illus.)
Kellberg, Christina. "Dyrbara skulpturer på Skeppsholmen stoppas au konstråd". *Dagens Nyheter,* 27 November. (illus.)
"Le rêve de Diane vu par Niki de St. Phalle". *Feuille d'Avis de Lausanne,* 2 March, p. 53. (illus.)
"Niki de Saint Phalle et les mecs". *Lui,* February. (illus.)
Piene, Nan R. "Art Under $500". *Art in America,* May/June, pp. 94–95.
Perruchot, Henri. "Les femmes artistes: Les Femmes sculptent aussi". *Jardin des Arts,* No. 191, October, pp. 2–13. (illus.)
Pluchart, François. "Le grand cirque de Niki". *Combat,* 16 February. (illus.)
Restany, Pierre. "E successo a Milano". *Domus,* No. 493, December, pp. 43–52.
Ricour, Monique. "Paris". *Art International,* Vol. XIV, No. 4, April, pp. 78–79. (illus.)
"Tania, Niki et Anne-Ella". *Les Lettres Françaises,* 18–24 February.

1971

"Bästa platen för 'Paradiset'". *Dagens Nyheter,* 8 May. (illus.)
"Des seins de 40 mètres carrés la 'folie' provençale de prince de Hesse". *France-Soir,* 7 August, pp. 1, 7. (illus.)
"Fest i Paradiset". *Svenska Dagbladet,* 21 May. (illus.)
Granath, Olle. "Ett jordiskt paradis". *Dagens Nyheter,* 12 May. (illus.)
Gräslund, Thu. "Klartecken för skära jättedamen på Skeppsholmen". *Expressen,* 23 March. (illus.)
Högardh, Lena. "Moderna museets Paradis invigt marinofficer protesterade förgäves". *Svenska Dagbladet,* 8 May. (illus.)
Kenedy, R. C. "Paris". *Art International,* Vol. XV, No. 2, February, p. 56.
"Man and wife and the museum". *Mobilia,* September.
"Moderna Museet under fire". *Design,* No. 272, August, p. 15. (illus.)
Olvång, Bengt. "Hanar & honor". *Aftonbladet,* 13 May, p. 4. (illus.)
Sagittarius. "apropo...". *Enska Dagbladet,* 13 June. (illus.)
"Sunflowers, Caviar, and pots of paint". *Vogue,* 15 November. (illus.)
Vaissière, Warwara de la. "Une autodidacte du rêve: Niki de Saint-Phalle". *Plaisir de France,* No. 394, November, pp. 46–51. (illus.)

1972

Braun, Werner. "Riding the Monster". *The Jerusalem Post,* 10 November, Magazine pp. 18–19. (illus.)
Brett, Guy. "Exclusively white". *The Times,* 12 December. (illus.)
Carlstedt, S. "Hur länge skall vi dras med Paradiset på Skeppsholmen?". *Svenska Dagbladet,* 5 February. (illus.)
"Entretien avec Niki de Saint-Phalle". *Pétroleprogrès,* No. 91, Spring, p. 20. (illus.)
Ford, Michael. "Niki de Saint Phalle: Gimpel Fils Devouring Mothers". *Arts Review,* 16 December.
"Galerie Iolas, Paris: Exposition". *L'œil,* No. 209, May, p. 35. (illus.)
"Giant Play Sculpture in Jerusalem". *Studio International,* Vol. 184, November, p. 162.
"Gimpel & Weitzenhoffer Gallery, New York: Exhibition". *Art News,* Vol. 70, January, p. 22.
Mullaly, Terence. "The Ghouls of Niki de Saint Phalle". *The Daily Telegraph,* December. (illus.)
Östlund, Bo. "Öarna öppna parker för kultur och fritid". *Svenska Dagbladet,* 26 April, p. 15. (illus.)
Pluchart, François. "Le risque de Niki-Phalle de Saint". *Combat,* 6 March. (illus.)

1973

Daval, Jean-Luc. "Lettre de Suisse-Genève". *Art International,* Vol. XVII, No. 1, January, pp. 47–48. (illus.)
Davis, Douglas. "Art: A Spring Sampler of Shows". *Newsweek,* 30 April, pp. 88–89. (illus.)
Denvir, Bernard. "London Letter". *Art International,* Vol. XVII, No. 2, Februar, pp. 30–31. (illus.)
Canaday, John. "Niki de Saint Phalle". *The New York Times,* 14 April.
Feaver, William. "London Letter". *Art International,* Vol. XVII, No. 3, March, p. 58.
"Gimpel Fils Gallery, London: Exhibition". *Apollo,* No. 97, January, p. 100. (illus.)
Haskell, Molly. "Film: Seasoned with Oedipal Sin". *The Village Voice,* 5 April, p. 75.
Henry, Gerrit. "Niki de St. Phalle". *Art News,* Vol. 72, No. 6, Summer, p. 92.
McColl, Patricia. "St. Phalle and the Dragon". *W.* 30 December, p. 10. (illus.)
Paris, Jeanne. "Women's roles: Sculptress has a sense of humor". *Long Island Press,* New York, 15 April, p. 24. (illus.)
Reichardt, J. "Arts: a cautionary tale". *Architectural Digest,* Vol. 43, No. 2, p. 121.
Roud, Richard. "Taboo or not taboo". *Arts Guardian,* 16 April.
"Saint-Phalle (Niki de)". *Les Muses Encyclopedie des Arts,* Vol. XII, No. 203, 3 October, cover and p. 4055. (illus.)
Schneider, Helmut. "Niki de Saint Phalles erster Film: Weg mit Daddy". *Die Zeit,* No. 44, 26 October, p. 24. (illus.)
Vaes, Guy. "Autopsie d'un cas Niki de Saint Phalle". *Spécial,* No. 437, 29 August, pp. 40–43. (illus.)

1974

"Architectural Projects and Realizations: Iolas Galerie, Paris". "*Arts Magazine,* Vol. 48, No. 8, May, p. 48.
"Aufstellung von drei Polyester 'Nanas'". *Das Kunstwerk,* Vol. XXVII, May, p. 79.
Demoriane, Helene. "Portrait: le fille à papa". *Le Point,* 18 February, pp. 17, 92.
"Der freundliche Golem". *Der Landbote,* 19 March. (illus.)
Doniol-Valcroze, Jacques. "Quoi de neuf... cinéma Daddy". *L'Express,* 18 February.
Figuérdo, Mariza. "Maïs: Informações". *Maïs,* No. 10, May. (illus.)
Grisolia, Michel. "Le papa et la putain". *Le Nouvel Observateur,* 18 Februar, p. 49.(illus.)
"Il n'y a que des 'chiottes' joyeuses en France". *Combat,* 19 February. (illus.)
Moutaigne, Pierre. "Niki de Saint Phalle: Je ne rêve pas d'être une star". *Film,* 15 February.
"Nanas aus Paris". *Hannoversche Allgemeine Zeitung,* No. 12, 15 January, p. 1. (illus.)
"Nouveaux Niki de Saint-Phalle: en manchettes". *Connaissance des Arts,* No. 265, March, p. 118.
Piper, Elizabeth. "Scandalous Art". *International Herald Tribune,* Paris, 25 January. (illus.)
"Projets et réalizations d'architecture de Niki de Saint Phalle". *L'Architecture d'aujourd'hui,* No. 172, March p. 11.
"Quand Niki de St. Phalle abandonne ses nanas par 'Daddy'". *L'Aurore,* 20 February.
Reif, Rita. "A Family Lives in a Group of Sculptures". *The New York Times,* 5 July. (illus.)
Seide, Adam. "Was kann Straßenkunst denn sein?". *Theater,* Hannover, No. 8, March, cover and pp. 14–15. (illus.)
"The Dragon House: A $ 40,000 Playhouse with Echoes". *The Miami Herald,* 3 March, pp. 1k, 10k.

1975

"Ausbruch in heitere Formen und Farben". *Der Bund,* No. 270, 18 November, p. 27. (illus.)

1976

Basoski, Corn. "Gekke Speelobjecten van Fantasierijke Vrouw Niki". *Hengelo Dagblad,* 31 July. (illus.)

Frenken, Ton. "Niki verdwaald in Rotterdam". *Brabants Dagblad,* 20 August. (illus.)

Glavimans, André. "De getatoeëerde wereld van Niki de Saint Phalle". *Spectator,* No. 34, 21 August, p. 57. (illus.)

Göthe, Kjell. "Ingen frid i 'Paradiset' nu måste det flytas". *Expressen,* 4 May, p. 10. (illus.)

Juffermans, Jan. "Niki de St. Phalle in Boymans". *Algemeen Dagblad,* 21 July. (illus.)

Kelk, Fanny. "Niki's Nana's blijven charmant". *Het Parool,* 4 August. (illus.)

"Niki de Saint Phalle". *Financieel Dagblad,* 30 August.(illus.)

"Niki, Nana's en speelmonsters". *De Waarheid,* 9 August. (illus.)

Nyström, Jimmy. "Moderate Trägårdh vid Paradisethan har vunnit efter fem år". *Aftonbladet,* 4 May. (illus.)

Peters, Philip. "Plezierige expositie van Niki de Saint-Phalle". *NRC Handelsblad,* 10 August. (illus.)

Schmidt, Bertus. "Niki is nietmeer tehouden". *Het Vrije Volk,* 27 July. (illus.)

Schwalb, Susan. "The Devouring Mothers (Book Review)". *Women Artists Newsletter.* Vol. 2, No. 5, November.

Tuitjer, Koos. "Nana's nog steeds niet uitgedanst". *De Limburger Maastricht,* 18 August. (illus.)

Welling, Dolf. "Kinderspel van Niki na het mannenvreten". *Haagsche Courant,* 6 August. (illus.)

1977

Anrep-Nordin, Monica. "Paradisskulpturerna: Vem betalor flyttningen?". *Svenska Dagbladet,* 8 May. (illus.)

Basson, Robert. "Un rêve plus long que la nuit". *Ecran,* No. 54, 15 January, pp. 53–54. (illus.)

Menck, Clara. "Das provokante Paradies". *Frankfurter Allgemeine Zeitung,* No. 212, 13 September, p. 19.

Romdahl, Margareta. "Paradisets skapare nej till flyttning". *På Stan Veckan,* 10–16 September, pp. 7–8. (illus.)

Sparten, Imer. "Sanslösa ganget och Paradiset". *Aftonbladet,* 13 September. (illus.)

Wall, Asa. "Vi tvirgas stänga Moderna museet". *Svenska Dagbladet,* 3 September, pp. 10–11. (illus.)

1978

Knecht, Susanne. "Kunstereignis statt Ochsnerkübel". *Brückenbauer,* No. 40, 6 October, pp. 12–13. (illus.)

Raynor, Vivien. "Niki de Saint-Phalle". *The New York Times,* 13 January, p. C-13.

1979

"Gimpel & Weitzenhoffer Gallery, New York: Exhibit". *Art News,* Vol. 78, Summer, p. 182. (illus.)

H.L.S. "Niki de Saint Phalle: Monumental Projects". *Art/World,* 20 April, p. 10.

"Objekte mit signalisierender Funktion". *Schwäbische Zeitung,* No. 181, 8 August. (illus.)

Rabinovich, Abraham. "Tale of a Dove". *The Jerusalem Post,* 5 October, p. 6. (illus.)

Russell, John. "Niki de Saint Phalle (Gimpel & Weitzenhoffer)". *The New York Times,* 13 April, p. C-21.

Tallmer, Jerry. "The rebel in a white leather suit". *The New York Post,* 21 April, p. 16. (illus.)

Wolff, Theodore F. "Joy of art: art of joy". *The Christian Science Monitor,* 23 October, p. 20. (illus.)

1980

Bordaz, Jean-Pierre. "Niki De Saint Phalle". *Cahiers,* May, pp. 497–498. (illus.)

Bouisset, M. "Centro Georges Pompidou, Paris: instalaciòn". *Goya,* No. 157, July/August, p. 37. (illus.)

Bushbaum. "Weihnachtliche Billig-Kunstmesse...". *Wiener Zeitung,* 13 December.

Cullinan, Helen. "Saint Phalle exhibit is a coup for Columbus". *The Plain Dealer,* Columbus, Ohio, 1 June. (illus.)

Fleisher, Pat. "Editorial: October in Paris". *Artmagazine,* November/December, p. 11. (illus.)

Gilson, Nancy. "Artist de Saint Phalle's solo exhibit at museum". *Columbus Citizen Journal,* Columbus, Ohio, 19 May, p. 10. (illus.)

Hahn, Otto. "Niki l'iconoclaste". *L'Express,* 23 July. (illus.)

Hall, Dieter. "Niki de Saint-Phalle und ihre 'Nanas'". *Schaffhauser Nachrichten,* No. 84, 11 April, p. 9. (illus.)

Hall, Jacqueline. "Works Challenge Columbus". *Columbus Dispatch,* Columbus, Ohio, 4 June, p. C-7, (illus.)

Hellgoth, Brigitte. "Ein Fest für die Plastik". *Art,* No. 9, September, pp. 94–105. (illus.)

Jaccard, Anne-Marie. "Niki dans le miroir". *Le Nouvel Illustré,* No. 29, 16 July, pp. 52–57. (illus.)

Jordan, James. "Niki de Saint Phalle: Remembrance of Things Past". *Dialogue/Ohio Arts Journal,* July/August. (illus.)

Kraft, Peter. "Ein Riesenarsenal erkämpfter Lebensfreude". *Salzburger Nachrichten,* 17 December.

K. S. "Die 'Nanas' in Linz". *Die Presse,* 12 December, p. 7. (illus.)

"Künstler Kochen". *DU,* No. 9, p. 6. (illus.)

Längsfeld, Wolfgang. "Ulms blumenbunte Kunst-Skulpturen in der Landesgartenschau". *Süddeutsche Zeitung,* No. 133, p. 10. (illus.)

Mayer, Gerhard. "Die Nanas an die Macht". *Wochenpresse,* No. 50, 10 December, pp. 26–27. (illus.)

Michel, Jacques. "Niki de Saint-Phalle en rétrospective". *Le Monde,* 16 July, p. 15.

Mock, Jean-Yves. "Les Années Niki de Saint Phalle". *Vogue,* No. 667, June/July, pp. 204–209. (illus.)

N. D. "Les pimpantes 'Nanas' de Niki au Centre Pompidou". *France-Soir,* 2 August, p. 3. (illus.)

"Niki de Saint Phalle". *Life Is Art Magazine,* Japan, April, pp. 89–98. (illus.)

"Nikis Kaktus für die Nanas". *Schweizer Illustrierte,* 24 March. (illus.)

"Ohne die Kunst wäre ich im Irrenhaus". *Tages-Anzeiger,* 2 April. (illus.)

Oliver, Richard. "Niki de Saint Phalle Meets 'The New Man'". *New York Herald Tribune,* Paris, 19–20 July, p. 8W. (illus.)

Paul et Guy. "Niki de Saint-Phalle, une rétrospective". *Libération,* 27 July, p. 16. (illus.)

p.k.w. "Galerien: Freudvolle Szenerien". *Weltwoche,* 26 March.

Schober, Herta. "Eine Welt der heiteren Monster". *Volksblatt,* Linz, No. 296, 20 December, p. 8. (illus.)

"Skulpturen-Ausstellung: Bisher 50 000 Besucher". *Basler Zeitung,* No. 191, 16 August, p. 3. (illus.)

1981

Andrechen, Jana. "Notes on Niki de Saint Phalle". *La Jolla Light,* California, 22 October. (illus.)

Chauvit, J. P. "Air Transat 81: L' Equipage de pilote privé". *Pilote Privé,* No. 88, 15 May, cover and pp. 20–22. (illus.)

"Expositions à Genève". *La Suisse,* 21 May.

Fredriksson, Inger. "Mot paradiset med fötterna på jorden". *Dy Nag,* 14 October. (illus.)

Hedberg, Gösta. "Moderna Museet". *Nerikes Allehanda,* 11 September. (illus.)

Larieux, Jean-Marie. "Une nouvelle aventure volante dans l' art". *Arts,* No. 18, 15 May, cover and pp. 10–11. (illus.)

Lind, Ingela. "Niki de Saint Phalle retrospecktivt: Balansakt mot banaliteten". *Dagens Nyheter,* 6 October. (illus.)

Lindgren, Sören G. "Niki de Saint Phalle på Moderna museet". *Smalandposten,* 30 September. (illus.)

Lippki, Erika. "Das vergessene Leben". *Der Tagesspiegel,* 8 May. (illus.)

"Neue Objekte von Niki de Saint Phalle". *Architektur & Wohnen,* No. 2, June, pp. 139–143. (illus.)

Nyblom, Birgitte. "Före och efter Paradiset". *Dagens Nyheter,* 12 September. (illus.)

Olvång, Bengt. "Man känner sig medryckt och glad". *Aftonbladet,* 23 September. (illus.)

Reilly, Richard. "Designer's maquettes: Artwork Exhibition With A Switch". *The San Diego Union,* 16 October. (illus.)

Sauré, W. "Pariser Kunstereignisse (Galerie Sammy Kinge: Ausstellung)". *Das Kunstwerk,* Vol. XXXIV; No. 4, pp. 66. (illus.)

Schnierle, Barbara. "Entwürfe für eine andere Welt". *Tip,* December, pp. 62–63. (illus.)

Stam, Cecilia. "Förlorade Paradis". *Stockholms-Tidningen,* 2 October. (illus.)

Sten, Aase. "Niki de Saint Phalle – viktig för kvinnliga konstnarers frigörelse". *Katrineholms-Kuriren,* 5 November.

Wallert, Evert. "Djärva Niki i Moderna museet". *Norrtelje Tidning,* 15 September.

Weibull, Nina. "I hjärtat an kvinnan finns en liten flicka". *Expressen,* 19 September, p. 5. (illus.)

Wretholm, Eugen. "Den desperata leken". *Svenska Dagbladet,* 19 September. (illus.)

1982

Blakeston, Oswell. "Niki de Saint Phalle: Gimpel Fils". *Arts Review,* Vol. XXXIV, No. 13, 18 June.

"Gimpel Fils Gallery, London: Exhibit". *Art & Artists,* No. 189, June p. 31. (illus.)

Nelson, David. "Sensory Art Forms Share Spotlight". *La Jolla Light,* California, 30 September, p. B-9. (illus.)

Restany, Pierre. "Le Nouveau Réalisme". *Flash Art International,* No. 100, February/March.

"Szene-Luftiges von Niki de St. Phalle". *Der Spiegel,* 17 May. (illus.)

Taylor, Angela. "An Artist With A Sense of Fashion". *The New york Times,* 5 September, Style section, p. 23. (illus.)

Vaizey, Marina. "Drawing up a revolution". *The Sunday Times,* 20 June, p. 39. (illus.)

Wolff, Theodore F. "Niki de Saint Phalle". *The Christian Science Monitor,* 24 May.

Zeindler, Peter. "Ein Garten der Wunder". *Annabelle,* 13 May, pp. 122–126. (illus.)

1983

Astruc, Philippe and Leglu, Dominique. "Niki de Saint Phalle: Soleil sur l' Ircam". *Libération,* 17 May. (illus.)

Berlin, Brigid; Bilotti, Carlo; Warhol, Andy. "Niki de Saint Phalle". *Interview,* October, pp. 66–67. (illus.)

B. K. "Chirac et Lang l'ont inaugurée Ensemble: Oh! la belle fontaine!". *Le Matin,* 17 march. (illus.)

Bouilhet, Daniele. "Niki de Saint Phalle ou la delire des femmes". *Harper's Bazaar,* No. 4, July/August. (illus.)

Byrne, Reneta. "Artist creates perfume, sculpture with a nose and eye for the unusual". *The San Antonio Light,* 28 October, p. 3G. (illus.)

Daigneault, Gilles. "Heurs et malheurs de la sculpture". *Le Devoir,* 16 April. (illus.)

Demonpion, Denis. "Niki de Saint-Phalle: Une fontaine de joie pour Paris". *Paris-Match,* 3 June. (illus.)

Doren, Phyllis van. "Museum Without

Walls". *Westways*, Vol. 75, No. 7, July, pp. 48–51. (illus.)
Failing, P. "Big Bird on Campus". *Art News*, Vol. 82, November, p. 135.
Hellman, Mary. "Storm Bars 'Sun God' Debut". *The San Diego Union*, 28 January.
Knight, Christopher. "Monumental art projet begins at UC San Diego". *Los Angeles Herald Tribune*, 2 March, pp. B1, B4. (illus.)
Leuba, E. "Paris: la fontaine Beaubourg". *Le Messager Suisse*, No. 5, May.
Michel, Jacques. "Entre l'église Saint-Merri et Beaubourg". *Le Monde*, 19 March.
"Niki de Saint Phalle a (peut-être) trouvé une solution au problème des prisons". *France-Soir*, 7 June, p. 2. (illus.)
Pacadis, Alain. "A la claire fontaine". *Libération*, 21 March. (illus.)
Renard, D. "Jean Tinguely, Niki de Saint Phalle". *Flash Art International*, No. 113, Summer.
"Vanity Fair Nominates: La Fontaine Stravinsky". *Vanity Fair*, July, p. 38. (illus.)
Varenne, Françoise. "Beaubourg: inauguration des fontaines Stravinski". *Le Figaro*, 17 March. (illus.)
"Women Artists". *Bijutsu Techno*, Japan, Vol. 35, No. 515, September, cover and p. 50. (illus.)

1984

Castany, Sara Maria. "Niki de Saint Phalle: La han llamado genio y bruja...". *Buenhogar*, Venezuela, No. 7, March, pp. 26–29, 74. (illus.)
G.P.E. "Niki de Saint Phalle, en vitrine...". *Nord Matin*, 21 November. (illus.)
Heinz, Liane. "Hannah Höch und Niki de Saint-Phalle". Dada-Zeitung, 18 March, cover and pp. 22–23. (illus.)
"Künstlerateliers als Kunstprogramm-Werkstatt heute". *Das Kunstwerk*, Vol. XXXVII, June, p. 43.
"Les 'Nanas' de Niki de Saint-Phalle sont entrées dans Lille". *La Voix du Nord*, 27 November. (illus.)
Martin, Bradley. "Théâtre à l'eau". *Décoration International*, No. 73, July/August, cover and pp. 124–129. (illus.)
Meyer, Eliane. Interview: Ich bin eine Besessene!". *Jardin des Modes*, November, pp. 17–20. (illus.)
"Niki de Saint Phalle". *Kateigaho*, Japan, July, p. 291. (illus.)
Saint Phalle, Niki de. "Hantée par le rêve d'un autre". *Le Nouvel Observateur*, 20 July, pp. 62–63.
Vincendon, Mireille. "Niki de Saint-Phalle des Nanas au parfum". *Marie-Claire*, July, p. 137. (illus.)

1985

Beaumont, Mary Rose. "Niki de Saint Phalle: Gimpel Fils". *Arts Review*, Vol. XXXVII, No. 14, 19 July, p. 369. (illus.)
Burr, J. "Gimpel Fils Gallery, London: Exhibit". *Apollo*, No. 122, July, p. 72. (illus.)
Colby, Joy Hakanson. "76 artists flock to produce a menagerie of a show". *The Detroit News*, 22 December, p. 48.
Miller, Sanda. "Rebel sculpture". *The Times*, 2 August, p. 16.
Mullaly, Terence. "Art: Fairytales". *The Daily Telegraph*, 29 July.
New Work (Gimpel Fils)". *Art & Artists*, No. 227, August, pp. 32–33. (illus.)
Raynor, Vivien. "Niki de Saint Phalle". *The New York Times*, 6 September.
Stephan, Peter. "Jean Tinguely und Niki de Saint Phalle: Hommage à Igor Strawinsky". *Die Kunst*, No. 10, October, pp. 822–826. (illus.)
Strathern, Oona. "If it's Tuesday it must be Belgium". *Arts Review*, 6 September, pp. 415–416. (illus.)
Wolff, Theodore F. "Playful sculptor de Saint Phalle". *The Christian Science Monitor*, 16 September.
Wyss, Barbara. "Niki de Saint Phalle". *Basler Zeitung*, 15 June. (illus.)
Zeindler, Peter. "Die Welt ist eine Brust". *Basler Magazine*, No. 23, 8 June, pp. 1–5. (illus.)

1986

Aspesi, Natalia. "La donna che arriva dal passato". *Grazia*, No. 2381, 12 October, pp. 50–55. (illus.)
Bouisset, Maïten. "Les Nouveaux Réalistes". *Beaux-Arts*, No. 36, June, pp. 38–46. (illus.)
Daure, Armand; Michalet, Bénédicte; Nahon, Pierre. "Les Nouveau Réalistes" (3 articles). *Canal*, No. 2, Summer, pp. 9–15. (illus.)
"Drömmar tar form". *Hufvudstadbladet*, Finland, 6 December, Kultur p. 5. (illus.)
Gaigneron, Axelle de. "Knokke-le-Dragon". *Connaissance des Arts*, No. 407, January, pp. 40–48. (illus.)
Kino, Hana. "Niki de Saint Phalle – I Wish to Come in Touch with the Spirit of This Great and Passionate Artist". *Hot Dog Press*, Japan, No. 49, 10 May, p. 4. (illus.)
Kivirinta, Marja-Terttu. "Tarot-kortit elävät villeissä veistoksissa". *Helsingin Sanomat*, December, p. 24. (illus.)
Lecombre, Sylvain. "Les Nouveaux Réalistes à Parigi venticinque anni dopo" (with English text). *Domus*, No. 676, October, pp. 12–13. (illus.)
Masuda, Yoko-Shizue. "Praise to Niki de Saint Phalle – Witch or Angel?" *Monthly Ueno*, Japan, No. 325, May, pp. 37–41. (illus.)
Michishita, Kyoko. "Prediction of New Matriarchalism: Charm of Mythical Artist Niki de Saint Phalle". *Sankei Newspaper*, Japan, 16. May. (illus.)
Miyasako, Chizuru. "Big Mother Under Cloudless Sky – Niki de Saint Phalle and Shizue Masuda". *So-En*, Japan, July, p. 210. (illus.)
Pirtola, Erikki. "Rohkeat vedot ratkaisevat". *Ilta: Sanomat*, Finland, December, p. 21. (illus.)
Saint Phalle, Niki de. "Major Arcana". *Tique*, No. 2, Summer, pp. 59–65. (illus.)
Schaake, Marlet. "Porträt: Niki de Saint Phalle. Sie trägt gern dick auf". *Cosmopolitan*, No. 11, November, pp. 116–123. (illus.)
Segi, Shinichi. "Portrait of Soul – Niki de Saint Phalle". *Weekly Post*, 25 April. (illus.)
Takeuchi, Nanae. "Niki de Saint Phalle Exhibition". *Mainichi Daily News*, Japan, 27 April. (illus.)
Thon, Carole. "Éros est au parfum". *Bat/ L'Aventure de la Communication*, No. 86, June/July, cover and pp. 34–36. (illus.)
Yoshida, Yoshie. "Imaginative Power of Niki de Saint Phalle – Attack to the Man-Ruled Culture and Creation of Matriarchal Myths of the Modern Age". *Mainichi Newspaper*, 2 April. p. 4. (illus.)

1987

"An Artist Throws the Book at Misinformation". *Newsweek*, 15 June, p. 61. (illus.)
Billard, Pierre. "Voyage en Nikiland". *Le Point*, No. 758, 30 March, pp. 134–136. (illus.)
Chayat, Sherry. "Contemporary artists rediscover the sacred". *Syracuse-Herald-Journal*, Syracuse, New York, 22 January, p. D8.
Colberg, Klaus. "Visionen des Widersprüchlichen". *Schwäbische Zeitung*, 28 March. (illus.)
Dattenberger, Simone. "Mit magischer Kraft". *Münchner Merkur*, No. 77, 26 March. (illus.)
Dengler, Christine. "Populäre Polyester-Plastiken". *Reichenhaller Tagblatt*, 6 July.
Desarzens, Corinne. "Niki de Saint Phalle au-delà du miroir". *Tribune de Genève*, 9 October, p. 13. (illus.)
Diehl, Fred. "Künstler privat: Niki de Saint Phalle". *Pan*, April, pp. 62–63. (illus.)
Dubuc, Madeleine. "De l'art dans les chaises; des chaises dans les arts". *La Presse*, Montreal, 14 April. (illus.)
Ehret, Gloria. "Frauen sind Fabelwesen". *Die Welt*, 3 April. (illus.)
"Elämän salaisuudet korteissa". *Kotilääkäri*, Finland, January, p. 26. (illus.)
Fanelli, Franco. "Mostre: Niki de Saint Phalle". *Vernissage*, July. (illus.)
Fenn, Walter. "Die fröhlichen Monster". *Nürnberger Nachrichten*, No. 72, 27 March. (illus.)
Goetz, Joachim. "Die Stunde der Nanas". *Madame*, June, pp. 24, 28. (illus.)
Graziani, Benno. "Les tarots fantastiques". *L'Express*, No. 8, 7 May, pp. 36–42. (illus.)
Gugg, Anton. "Niki de Saint Phalle". *Noema*, January. (illus.)
Gunasinghe, Zora. "Niki de Saint Phalle: Een toneeldecor in Kassel en een Tarottuin in Toscane". *Ruimte*, No. 4, February, pp. 2–3, 16–20, 38. (illus.)
Harrison, Helen. "From 'Targets' to Nanas to Tarot". *The New York Times*, Long Island Weekly pp. 1, 30. (illus.)
Hegewisch, Katharina. "Befreiung zur Phantasie". *Frankfurter Allgemeine Zeitung*, No. 106, 8 May, p. 29. (illus.)
Herz, Hans-Michael. "Niki de Saint Phalle". *Weltkunst*, May, p. 12. (illus.)
Hofmann, Isabelle. "Für sie war Kunst wichtige Therapie". *Hamburger Morgenpost*, 26 May. (illus.)
Jaumonet, Léopold. "Exposition: Niki de Saint-Phalle". *Ecoute*, 9 June, p. 6. (illus.)
Jones, Baird. "Catching Up With Niki de Saint Phalle In Nassau". *Downtown*, New York, 11 November, p. 12A. (illus.)
Karcher, Eva. "Hexen, Erdmütter und menschenfressende Riesenfrauen". *Münchner Theaterzeitung*, April. (illus.)
Kipphoff, Petra. "Gräfin Dracula schließt Frieden". *Die Zeit*, No. 16, 10 April, p. 61. (illus.)
Krauß, Annette. "Mütter und Hexen". *Donau Kurier Ingolstadt*, No. 85, 11–12 April. (illus.)
Kronthaler, Helmut. "Aggression und Harmonie". *Straubinger Tagblatt*, No. 85, 11 April. (illus.)
Lalanne, Dorothée. "L'enfrance de l'art". *Vogue*, No. 675, April, pp. 162–167, (illus.)
Längsfeld, Wolfgang. "Von der Provokation zur Spiritualität". *Süddeutsche Zeitung*, No. 74, March. (illus.)
Lehmann, H. "Die Bildwelt des Phantastischen". *Trierscher Volksfreund*, 3 April.
Lettau, Annette. "Die fröhliche Anarchie". *Hannoverscher Allgemeine Zeitung*, 18 April. (illus.)
Lipson, Karin. "A Sculptor By Many Other Fames". *Newsday*, 13 September, Part II, pp. 39, 47. (illus.)
Miracco, Franco. "L'imperatrice dei tarocchi". *Epoca*, No. 1895, January, pp. 102–107. (illus.)
Morché, Pascal. "Kunst voll Gefühl". *Harper's Bazaar*, June, p. 96. (illus.)
Müller, Elizabeth. "Skurrile Monster-Damen". *Abendzeitung*, No. 71, 26 March. (illus.)
Müller-Mehlis, Reinhard. "Alle Macht den Nanas!". *Die Kunst*, April, pp. 285–288. (illus.)
Pfeifer, Hartmut. "Der Sieg der Nanas über King-Kong". *Hypo-Press*, No. 2, 17 January. (illus.)
Prince Michael of Greece. "House of Cards". *Architectural Digest*, Vol. 44, No. 9, September, cover and pp. 124–131. (illus.)
Rainer, Wolfgang. "Böse, bunte Träume". *Stuttgarter Zeitung*, 30 April. (illus.)
Robinson, Yvonne. "Munich: Niki de Saint Phalle". *Arts Review*, Vol. XXXIX, No. 8, 24 April, pp. 258–259. (illus.)
Rose, Barbara. "A garden of earthly delights". *Vogue*, Vol. 177, No. 12, Decem-

ber, pp. 266–272, 365–367. (illus.)
Rötzer, Florian. "Im Disneyland der Mythen". *Die Tageszeitung,* 22 April. (illus.)
Schwartz, D. "Les Nouveaux Réalistes (Kunstmuseum, Winterthur, Switzerland)". *Die Kunst,* No. 2, February, p. 111.
Selz, Peter. "Alternate Aesthetics. Quests For Spiritual Quintessence". *Arts Magazine,* October, pp. 46–47.
Stachelhaus, Heiner. "Nanas wie am Fließband". *Neue Rhein Zeitung,* 3 April. (illus.)
Stephan, Peter. "Der neue Symbolismus bei Niki de Saint Phalle". *Artis,* No. 4, April, pp. 10–13. (illus.)
Valentini, Ruth. "L'évangile selon Niki de Saint-Phalle". *Le Nouvel Observateur,* No. 1177, 29 May, p. 9. (illus.)
"Venus Ade". *Stern,* No. 18, 23 April, pp. 44–67. (illus.)
V. H. "Le Sida. C'est Facile a éviter". *Madame Figaro,* 13 June, p. 37. (illus.)
Wavrin, Isabelle de. "Nouveaux Réalistes: L'ascension ne fait que commencer". *La Vie Française,* 26 January, p. 95.
Weiss, Christina. "Von der Aggression zur Versöhnung". *Art,* March, pp. 16–17. (illus.)

1988

Berger, Françoise and Bresson, Gilles. "Mitterrand cerné, n'a pas lâché le morceau". *Libération,* 11 March, p. 10. (illus.)
Berthoud, Roger. "Sculptor whose mad dreams come true". *The Independent,* 22 June, Living Section p. 13. (illus.)
Boudier, Laurent. "Histoire d'eau". *Télérama,* No. 2002, 25 May, pp. 72–73.
Bowe, Nicola Gordon. "The Bird in the Work of Niki de Saint Phalle". *The GPA Irish Arts Review,* 1988 Yearbook, pp. 31–36. (illus.)
Brizard, Caroline. "Les particules qui competent". *Le Nouvel Observateur,* 15–21 July. (illus.)
Couret, Jean-Paul. "Mitterrand dampens journalistic speculation". *The Independent,* 11 March. (illus.)
Darimont, Petra. "Hommage à Niki de Saint Phalle". *Beispiele,* No. 2, June, pp. 42–45. (illus.)
"Exhibition: Art Kite". *Bijutsu Techo: Monthly Arts Magazine,* Japan, Vol. 40, No. 598, August, cover and pp. 194–199. (illus.)
Fohanno, Danielle. "Château-Chinon: 400 Journalistes pour inaugrer une fontaine!". *Le Parisien,* 11 March, p. 2. (illus.)
Freudenheim, S. "Under the Singing Eucalyptus Tree". *Artforum,* Vol. 26, April, pp. 126–127. (illus.)
Herzfeld, John. "Looking at Life: AIDS Is Here". *Art News,* January. (illus.)
Hulten, Pontus. "Niki de Saint Phalle". *Manads Journalen,* Finland, 4 April, pp. 54–61. (illus.)
Lalanne, Dorothée. "I monumenti de Niki". *Vogue Décoration,* No. 15, September. (illus.)
Liu, Catherine. "Nouveaux Réalistes (Zabriskie Gallery, New York)", *Artforum,* Vol. 27, November, pp. 144–145.
Loon, Flip van. "Niki de Saint Phalle". *Ritz,* August. (illus.)
Mahler, Annemarie. "Parfum-Kunst". *Schweizer Illustrierte,* 3 October, pp. 70–71, 73.
Meyer Rubinstein, Raphael. "Europa Resurgent: Objects and Activities of the Nouveaux Réalistes". *Arts Magazine,* Vol. 63, No. 1, September, cover and pp. 68–75.
Picard, Denis. "Sur la colline embelliée". *Connaissance des Arts,* No. 431, January, pp. 78–81. (illus.)
Reed, Susan. "Artist Niki de Saint Phalle Sketches Lifesaving Truths for Teenagers Unwary of Aids". *People Magazine,* 11 January, pp. 51–52. (illus.)
Robinson, Yvonne. "Niki de Saint Phalle and Jean Tinguely: A Collaboration That Has Lasted Over 30 Years". *Arts Review,* Vol. XL, 3 June, back cover and p. 389. (illus.)
Schlag, Beatrice. "Wo Götter sich erheben". *Sonntagszeitung,* 27 November, p. 42–43. (illus.)
Urquhart, Rachel. "The Allure of Eau de Glamour Gal". *San Francisco Chronicle,* 15 August, p. B4. (illus.)
Vincent, Claude. "Au Château-Chinon: Mitterrand décide... de ne rien dire". *France-Soir,* 11 March, p. 6. (illus.)

1989

"Au Palais Bénédictine: Niki de Saint-Phalle expose ses 'œuvres des années 80'". *Le Progrés,* 1–2 July. (illus.)
Bouisset, Maïten. "Niki de Saint-Phalle: Le monde coloré des Nanas". *Beaux-Arts,* May, pp. 44–46. (illus.)
Bouzerand, Jacques and Pierrand, Jean. "Ya-t-il une esthétique Mitterrand". *Le Point,* No. 885, 4 September, pp. 10–14.
Brunhammer, Yvonne. "Furniture mobilier". *Connaissance des Arts, Special Issue for exhibition: "L'art de vivre: Decorative arts and design in France* 1789–1989, pp. 14–21. (illus.)
Couturier, Elizabeth. "Le match de Paris". *L'Express,* 2 June, pp. 4–5. (illus.)
Couturier, Elizabeth. "Niki de Saint Phalle". *Paris Match,* 25 May, pp. 3–5. (illus.)
Dunlop, Fiona. "Design: Niki in Wonderland". *The Sunday Times,* 28 May, Magazine pp. 68–71. (illus.)
Dussard, Thierry. "Saint-Phalle: L'armée, la banque, les arts et les lettres". *Le Point,* No. 855, 6 February, p. 96. (illus.)
Ernold-Gandouet, Marielle. "Paris: Niki de Saint Phalle". *L'Œil,* No. 407, June, p. 88. (illus.)
"Exposition d'Eté au Palais Bénédictine: Niki de Saint Phalle, sculpteur". *Le Progrès,* 24–25 June. (illus.)
"Fécamp". *Marie-Claire,* September. (illus.)
Fohr, Robert. "Niki et les Tarots". *Le Quotidien de Paris,* 7 June. (illus.)
Foldes, Lilly. "The Fantastic Garden of Niki de Saint Phalle". *Readers Digest,* England, February, (illus.)
Gandee, Charles. "My dinner with André". *House & Garden,* July.
Gunasinghe, Zora. "Giardino dei Tarocchi". *Tableau,* Vol. 12, No. 1, September, pp. 110–112. (illus.)
Hahn, Otto. "Coup de Cœur: Niki de Saint Phalle". *L'Express,* 2 June. (illus.)
Hulten, Pontus. "Niki de Saint Phalle: le jardin des Tarots". *Galeries Magazine,* No. 31, June/July, pp. 16–17. (illus.)
Monnin, Françoise. "Niki de Saint Phalle: Un gros ballon d'oxygène. *Artension,* 12 May. (illus.)
"Niki de Saint Phalle". *Arthemes,* April/May. (illus.)
"Niki + Jean (JGM, Galerie Paris)". *Connaissance des Arts,* No. 447, May, p. 138. (illus.)
Prince Michael of Greece. "Niki, dame des Tarots". *Maisons et Jardins,* September, pp. 174–185. (illus.)
Sager, Peter. "Wenn Nippons heiße Drachen steigen". *Zeit Magazin,* No. 19, 5 May, cover and pp. 12–20, 25. (illus.)
Schwarzacher, Lukas. "Das Fest der Fliegenden Bilder". *Art,* No. 6, June, pp. 68–74. (illus.)
"Six dames au parfum". *Madame Figaro,* 10 November, pp. 78–83.
Spector, Buzz. "A Profusion of Substance". *Artforum,* October, pp. 120–128. (illus.)
Vernon, Alexandre. "Au Palais Bénédictine: Le monde merveilleux de Niki de St. Phalle". *Le Progrès,* 8–9 July, pp. 1, 10. (illus.)
Wallach, Amei. "The Golem Legend in Many Guises". *Newsday,* 6 January. Weekend Section p. 15.
Weisenfeld, Gennifer. "Art takes to the sky in Hara kite exhibit". *The Japan Times,* 14 May, Lifestyle p. 10. (illus.)
White, Edmund. "Surreal Note in Belgium: Artist Roger Nellens Collection at Knokke". *Architectural Digest,* Vol. 46, No. 12, December, pp. 142–149. (illus.)

1990

Baker Sandback, Amy. "Virginia Dwan l'aventure d'un marchand d'art". *Art Press,* No. 15, October, pp. 41–46. (illus.)
Danto, Ginger. "Paris: Virginia Dwan and The Nouveaux Realistes". *Art News,* October, p. 156.
"Les grosses nanas de Niki". *Air International,* No. 37, July/August. (illus.)
"Niki de Saint Phalle". *Geijutso Shincho,* Japan, June, p. 48. (illus.)
"Port Chair Taste Tests Public Art". The San Diego Union, 6 March, pp. E1–E3. (illus.)

1991

Bass, Ruth. "Reviews: Niki de Saint Phalle (Gimpel/Weitzenhoffer)". *Art News,* Vol. 90, No. 1, January, p. 146. (illus.)
Henry, Gerrit. "Niki de Saint Phalle at Gimpel & Weitzenhoffer". *Art In America,* Vol. 79, No. 2, February, pp. 149–150. (illus.)
Turner, Jonathan. "Vasari Diary: A Park of Cards". *Art News,* Vol. 90, No. 7, September, p. 18. (illus.)
"Une semaine avec elle: "Expositions – Niki de Saint-Phalle dans le Haute Médoc". *Elle,* No. 2381, 26 August, p. 18. (illus.)
Welling, Wouter. "Niki de Saint Phalle: 'in mijn atelier ben ik god'". *Beelding,* No. 1, February, cover and pp. 18–21. (illus.)

Films by the artist

1971

Nana Island

Niki de Saint Phalle's first film. Unfinished.

1973

Daddy

The French version was subtitled *Journal d'une femme psychotique*
With Rainer von Diez, Mia Martin, Clarice Rivers, Niki de Saint Phalle, Marcel Lefranc and Jean-Pierre Raynaud
35 mm, sound, colour and b/w, 90 min, English soundtrack
Directed by Peter Whitehead
Script by Niki de Saint Phalle
Cameraman: Peter Whitehead
Edited by Peter Whitehead
Produced by Peter Schamoni and Tom G. Neuman
Distributors: Argos Films
Passed for audiences over 18
First showing: 20 February 1973.

1975

Camélia et le dragon / Un rêve plus long que la nuit

With Laura and Laurent Condominas, Marina Karella, Imbert Balzan, Rico Weber, Jean Tinguely, Bernhard Luginbühl, Henri Holstein, Daniel Spoerri, Samuel Mulholland, Silvio Barandun, Niki de Saint Phalle, Andrée Putman, Ursi Luginbühl, Régine de Forges, Françoise de Perche, Maris Beltrani, Dominique Maréchal, Roger Nellens, Sepp Imhof, Dominique Bondeau, Rudolf Tanner, Paul Wiedemer, Jean-Yves Mock and Bernard Pons
16 mm, sound, colour, 90 min
Script by Niki de Saint Phalle
Directed by Frédéric Rossif and Niki de Saint Phalle
Designed by Niki de Saint Phalle, with machines specially conceived by Jean Tinguely
Produced by Télé Hachette
Broadcast by Télé Hachette.

1977

A Travelling Companion / Le Compagnon de voyage

Collaborative work with Constantin Mulgrave after Hans Christian Andersen's fairy story *The Traveller* (unfinished)

Since 1990 Niki de Saint Phalle has been working with cameraman Bernard Zizerman on a film about her life's work.

Films about Niki de Saint Phalle

1961

'Niki de Saint Phalle', one of a series of documentary films by Louis Pauwels devoted to the avant-garde
Pierre Restany presents Arman, Gérard Dufrêne, Raymond Hains, Yves Klein, Niki de Saint Phalle and Jean Tinguely
sound, b/w, 10 min, French soundtrack
Directed by Yvan Jouhannot
Produced by ORTF (Office de la Radiodiffusion et Télévision Française)
Broadcast by INA (Institut National de l'Audiovisuel)
First shown on 25 April 1961

Atelier de l'Impasse Ronsin
16 mm, sound, b/w, 4 min
Conceived and produced by Gaumont Actualités
Broadcast by Gaumont

Two-part film about avant-garde artists in the series *David Brinkley's Journal*
16 mm, sound, colour, 30 min, English soundtrack
Produced by Ted Yates and Stuart Schulberg
First shown by NBC News on 13 December 1961.

1962

'The End of the World', in the series *David Brinkley's Journal*
A documentary film about the 'happening', *Study for the End of the World Number 2*, organised in the Nevada Desert on 21 March 1962 by Jean Tinguely and Niki de Saint Phalle
16 mm, sound, colour, 30 min, English soundtrack
Produced by Ted Yates and Stuart Schulberg
Broadcast by NBC News on 4 April 1962.

1963

'Het Nieuwe Realisme in München', in the series *Medium Plastische Kunsten*
A documentary study of the 'action-spectacles' organised as part of the exhibition *Les Nouveaux Réalistes* which was held in the Neue Galerie im Künstlerhaus in Munich during the Second Festival of the Nouveaux Réalistes. The recordings were made on 9 February 1963
16 mm, b/w, 30 min
Archive N° AE 1515
Produced by Ludo Bekkers
Directed by Filip Tas
Broadcast by BRNT (Belgian Television).

1964

'L'aventure de l'objet', in the series *Les Métamorphoses*
With Pierre Restany, Malaval and Niki de Saint-Pierre
16 mm, sound, colour, 30 min
Directed by Jean Antoine
Produced and broadcast by RTB (Radio-Télévision Belge).

1965

'Les Nanas de Niki de Saint Phalle', in the series *Dim Dam Dom*
Interview with Niki de Saint Phalle and her daughter Laura at the Galerie Alexandre Iolas on the occasion of the first showing of the Nanas in Paris. The artist provides a commentary on the works exhibited
16 mm, sound, b/w, 7 min
Directed by Jean-Christophe Averty and René Bernard
Produced by Daisy de Galard with the assistance of Michel Polac
Broadcast by ORTF on 28 or 29 October 1965.

1966

Hon
Documentary film about the building of *Hon* at Stockholm's Moderna Museet
Directed by Magnus Wibom and Lüfti Özbök.

Hon
Documentary film about the building and dismantling of *Hon* at Stockholm's Moderna Museet, with visitors to the exhibition
Directed by François de Menil
16 mm, sound, colour

Éloge de la folie
A documentary film by Roland Petit about his ballet of the same name
Scenario by by Jean Cau
Sets and costumes designed by Martial Raysse, Niki de Saint Phalle and Jean Tinguely
Broadcast by Télévision Internationale
Distributed by Comacico.

1968

ICH
Film made after the stage performances of *ICH (All about ME)*. Based on *MOI*, a story by Niki de Saint Phalle which was turned into a stage play by her and Rainer von Diez in 1968
16 mm, sound, colour
Produced and broadcast by ARD (Arbeitsgemeinschaft der Öffentlich-Rechtlichen Rundfunkanstalten der Bundesrepublik-Deutschland) within the framework of its third programme
Distributed by documenta GmbH, Kassel.

1972

'Autrefois la femme', in the series *Ombre et lumière*
With Dominique Rollin, Xavière Gauthier, Niki de Saint Phalle and André Masson
16 mm, sound, b/w, 60 min
Conceived by Daniel Le Comte
Produced by Daniel Le Comte to a commission from ORTF
Broadcast by INA.

1976

Les Nouveaux Réalistes
Interviews with artists from the Nouveaux Réalistes, including Arman, César, Christo, Martial Raysse and Jean Tinguely
The film included an excerpt from Niki de Saint Phalle's film, *Daddy*, a number of scenes from a shooting session on 26 February 1961 and shots of *Le paradis fantastique* in Stockholm
Commentary and interviews by Otto Hahn
16 mm, sound, colour, 70 min, French soundtrack
Directed by Adrian Maben
Produced by R.M. Productions, London
Production managers: Michèle Arnaud and Rainer Moritz.

1982

Niki
Highlights from films made by François de Menil over a period of fifteen years from 1967 to 1982
16 mm, sound, colour, 30 min, English soundtrack
Voice-over: Pontus Hulten
Produced by FDM (François de Menil) Foundation for the Arts Production
Coproduced by Monique Alexandre
Directed by François de Menil and Monique Alexandre
Photography by François de Menil
Additional photography by Hanno Fuchs, Michael Murphy, Bernard Auroux, Eric Breitbart and Tom McDonough
Published by Monique Alexandre
Assisted by Murphy Birdsall
Sound: Guillaume Sciama, Philippe Lemenuel and Yvonne Hanneman
Sound-mixer: Rick Dior
Music published by Variety Moszynski
Stills by Hans Namuth and Yoram Lehman
Also in 1972 Niki de Saint Phalle helped in the making of a similar film about Jean Tinguely, *Tinguely: A Kinetic Cosmos*, another FDM Foundation for the Arts Production.

1983

'Niki de Saint Phalle', in the series *Portraits d'artistes*
16 mm, sound, colour, 26 min, French soundtrack
Directed by Liliane Thorn-Petit
Produced by Liliane Thorn-Petit to a commission from RTL (Radio-Télévision Luxembourg)
Technical director: Jacques Navadic
Broadcast by RTL in December 1983

'Paris: La fontaine Stravinsky', in the series *Aujourd'hui en France*
The *Fontaine Stravinsky* after its completion
Directed by Christophe Loizillon
16 mm, sound, colour, 3'22"
Produced by the French Ministry of Foreign Affairs for foreign transmission.

1987

Niki de Saint Phalle: Ein Portrait
16 mm, sound, colour, 60 min, German soundtrack
Directed by Jürgen Müller and Philip Mathews
Produced by NDR (Norddeutscher Rundfunk), Hamburg
Camera: Volker Mach, Ardo Schmidt and Degio Tolla
Sound: Frank Anders
Film editor: Karen Klamtoth
Production manager: Norbert Klohn
Voice-over: Britta Subklew
Research: Gerd Kairat
Transmitted by NDR

1990

Le sida: Tu ne l'attraperas pas
A film by Philips Mathews based on drawings by Niki de Saint Phalle
16 mm, sound, colour, 8 min, French soundtrack
Animation by Steve Dovas and Barbara Nislick
With Marc Littlejohn, Cecilia Laureys, Josefina Larrain, Bloum Condominas, Elisabeth Tiso, Kathleen D'Aloia and Sarah Edwards
Camera: Daniel Esterman
Music by David Byrne
Film Editor: Jocelyne Melin
Voice-over: Mireille Darc
Produced by Agence française de lutte contre le sida

Photo credits

Photo credits (documentary section)

Allied-News-Photo
P. 20/21, ill. 1
Claes Annerstedt
P. 80/81, ill. 1
Sepp Bär
P. 72/73, ill. 6, 7; p. 86/87, ill. 1, 2, 3, 4
Benjamin
P. 20/21, ill. 3
Leonardo Bezzola
P. 54/55, ill. 2; p. 90/91, ill. 3, 5; p. 96/97, ill. 1, 2, 3, 4, 9, 10; p. 103/104, ill. 3, 5; p. 106/107, ill. 2; p. 108/109, ill. 2, 5; p. 110/111, ill. 1, 2, 3, 4; p. 112/113, ill. 1, 2, 3, 4, 6, 8; p. 126/127, ill. 6, 7, 8; p. 128/129, ill. 1, 2, 4; p. 132/133, ill. 5, 6; p. 134/135, ill. 2; p. 138/139, ill. 7
William Cheney
P. 56/57, ill. 4
Max F. Chiffelle
P. 50/51, ill. 3, 4
Henry Clarke
P. 20/21, ill. 5
William Claxton
P. 44/45, ill. 1, 2, 3, 4, 5, 6; p. 46/47, ill. 1, 2, 3, 4, 5, 6
Laurent Condominas
P. 22/23, ill. 1, 2; p. 24/25, ill. 1, 2, 3, 4, 5; p. 26/27, ill. 4, 5; p. 44/45, ill. 7; p. 54/55, ill. 3; p. 94/95, ill. 3; p. 98/99, ill. 6; p. 100/101, ill. 2, 4; p. 106/107, ill. 3, 4; p. 114/115, ill. 5; p. 116/117, ill. 5, 6, 7, 8; p. 118/119, ill. 1, 2, 3, 4, 5, 6; p. 120/121, ill. 1, 2, 3, 4, 5; p. 122/123; p. 130/131, ill. 1; p. 132/133, ill. 2, 3, 7; p. 134/135, ill. 1, 3, 5; p. 136/137, ill. 4, 8; p. 138/139, ill. 1, 2, 3, 4, 5, 6, 8, 9, 10
Conway Studios
P. 20/21, ill. 2
Ed van der Elsken
P. 48/49, ill. 3, 4, 5; p. 62/63, ill. 8
Jacques Faujour
P. 140/141, ill. 5
Gimpel & Weitzenhoffer Gallery
P. 98/99, ill. 2
Sherwin Greenberg, McGranahan & May
P. 78/79, ill. 1
Hans Hammarskiöld
P. 62/63, ill. 4, 9; p. 64/65, ill. 2, 7, 8; p. 66/67, ill. 4, 5; p. 68/69, ill. 3, 4, 5; p. 70/71, ill. 1, 2, 3, 4, 5, 6; p. 80/81, ill. 1, 2
F. Hatte
P. 128/129, ill. 3
Brigitte Hellgoth
P. 84/85, ill. 3, 4, 5, 6; p. 90/91, ill. 4
Hirshhorn Museum and Sculpture Garden
P. 54/55, ill. 4
Pontus Hulten
P. 62/63, ill. 5
Monique Jacot
P. 52/53, ill. 1, 2, 3, 4, 5; p. 124/125, ill. 1, 2, 3
Claude Magelhaes
P. 50/51, ill. 2
Heidi Meister
P. 42/43, ill. 7
Moderna Museet
P. 60/61, ill. 2, 8, 9, 10; p. 62/63, ill. 1, 2, 3, 7; p. 64/65, ill. 3, 4, 5, 6; p. 66/67, ill. 1, 2, 3; p. 68/69, ill. 1, 2; p. 70/71, ill. 7, 8
André Morain
P. 38/39, ill. 6; p. 86/87, ill. 5
Richard P. Meyer
P. 136/137, ill. 1, 2
Hans Namuth
P. 48/49, ill. 1, 2, 6, 7
Arnold Newman
P. 20/21, ill. 6
Lüfti Özbök
P. 60/61, ill. 1, 3, 4, 5, 6, 7; p. 62/63, ill. 6; p. 64/65, ill. 1
Lennart Olson/Tio
P. 34/35, ill. 1
Ad Petersen
P. 82/83, ill. 1, 2, 4, 5, 6; p. 84/85, ill. 2; p. 92/93, ill. 1, 8
Daniel Pype
P. 94/95, ill. 5, 6, 8, 9, 10
Larry Rivers
P. 54/55, ill. 5
Petter Runnqvist
P. 114/115, ill. 4
Harry Shunk
P. 28/29, ill. 1, 2, 3, 4, 5; p. 30/31, ill. 1, 2, 3, 4, 5, 6, 7, 8, 9, 10; p. 32/33, ill. 1, 3, 4, 5, 6, 7, 8, 9; p. 34/35, ill. 2, 3, 4, 5, 6; p. 36/37, ill. 1, 2, 3, 4; p. 38/39, ill. 1, 2, 3, 4, 5; p. 40, 41, ill. 1, 2, 3, 4, 5, 6, 7; p. 42/43, ill. 1, 2, 3, 4, 5, 6, 8; p. 58/59, ill. 2, 3; p. 72/73, ill. 1, 2, 3, 4, 5; p. 74/75, ill. 1, 2, 3, 4, 5, 6, 7, 8; p. 76/77, ill. 1, 2; p. 78/79, ill. 2, 3, 4, 5, 6, 7; p. 80/81, ill. 3; p. 88/89, ill. 1, 2, 3, 4, 5, 6, 7; p. 92/93, ill. 2, 3, 4, 5, 6, 7, 9
Vera Spoerri
P. 22/23, ill. 3, 4
Stuart Collection
P. 126/127, ill. 4
Stedelijk Museum
P. 32/33, ill. 2
Vogue Magazin
P. 20/21, ill. 4
Gilles Walusinski
P. 124/125, ill. 4
Rico Weber
P. 94/95, ill. 2, 7; p. 96/97, ill. 5, 6

Photo credits (photographic section)

Christies, London
P. 232
Laurent Condominas
P. 189, 190, 191, 192, 194, 195, 196, 197, 198, 199, 200, 201, 202, 203, 204, 205, 206, 207, 208, 209, 211, 212, 213, 214, 215, 216, 217, 218, 219, 223, 224, 225, 227, 229, 230, 233, 235, 237, 238, 239, 240, 242, 244, 245, 247, 248, 249, 250, 251, 254, 255, 257, 258, 259, 260, 261, 262, 263, 264, 265, 266, 267, 268, 269, 270, 271, 272, 273, 274, 275, 276, 277, 278, 279, 280, 281, 282
Jacques Faujour
P. 226, 228, 243
Hans Hammarskiöld
P. 188, 222
Pontus Hulten
P. 236
Galerie Alexandre Iolas, Paris
P. 231
Yoram Lehman
P. 246
Galerie Hans Mayer, Düsseldorf
P. 256
Musée d'Art Moderne, Centre Georges Pompidou, Paris
P. 220
Museum moderner Kunst, Stiftung Ludwig, Wien
P. 241
Statens Konstmuseer, Stockholm
P. 193, 212
Harry Shunk
P. 210, 234, 252
Petter Runnqvist
P. 253